GOOD
OR
GOD?

What Leaders Are Saying about *Good or God?*

"*Good or God?* is a powerful journey through Scripture that will challenge and transform your perspective on what it means to live the good life."
  —MARK BATTERSON, *New York Times* best-selling author of *The Circle Maker*

"*Good or God?* is an amazing lesson in discernment that will challenge you to truly seek the Lord for His perfect will in your life."
  —JOYCE MEYER, Bible teacher and best-selling author

"John Bevere is a respected teacher, leader, and author, and beyond all of that he is a good friend and fellow kingdom builder. His desire to see each person live not just a good life but a God life will increase your faith and challenge you to walk boldly into all that Jesus has for you. John's teaching and personal revelations will give you new insight into the will of God and His very best plans for your future."
  —BRIAN HOUSTON, senior pastor of Hillsong Church

"When I read the stories of people who did unprecedented things out of love for God, I find myself longing to be among them. *Good or God?* speaks to what happens in the minds and hearts of those who truly embrace God's best—rather than settling for easier counterfeits. If you share this desire to know and serve God in a radical way, I urge you to read this book."
  —JOHN C. MAXWELL, best-selling author and speaker

"John Bevere's book *Good or God?* will challenge you to never settle for less than God's best. John does a brilliant job of reminding us that we will find God when we look for Him."
  —JENTEZEN FRANKLIN, senior pastor of Free Chapel and *New York Times* best-selling author of *Fasting*

"*Good or God?* will shake you to your core. If you want to stick to business as usual, this isn't the book for you. But if you want your perspective to be forever altered, devour this message. It will transform your life!"
  —CHRISTINE CAINE, founder of The A21 Campaign and best-selling author of *Unstoppable*

"Challenging. Clear. Needed. *Good or God?* is an essential reminder that being good is not the goal. This book highlights the potential for people to move from the mundane life of moral obedience into an exhilarating life that comes from Jesus alone."

> —Louie Giglio, pastor of Passion City Church, Atlanta, Georgia,
> and founder of Passion Conferences

"Like a struck match shattering the utter darkness, John Bevere illumines the path toward the manifest presence of God while kindling an insatiable desire on the part of the reader that is satisfied only in intimate relationship with Him."

> —Bishop T. D. Jakes, CEO of TDJ Enterprises and *New York Times*
> best-selling author

"The goodness of God is all around us, but do we truly understand it? In *Good or God?*, John Bevere examines what it means to be good and what God has to do with it. As you read through this important book, you will be intrigued, challenged, and motivated to seek God's best for yourself and to share it with others."

> —Craig Groeschel, senior pastor of LifeChurch.tv and author of *From
> This Day Forward* and *Five Commitments to Fail-Proof Your Marriage*

"Once again, John Bevere has delivered an incredible, life-changing call to action for the body of Christ. In his new book *Good or God?*, he shows the reader how they can get the most out of their relationship with God and set a higher standard for all areas of their life."

> —Matthew Barnett, senior pastor of Angelus Temple, Los Angeles,
> California, and cofounder of the Dream Center

"In *Good or God?*, John Bevere challenges us to rethink our understanding of God's goodness and to recognize areas where we've settled for our own standards instead of His. With keen biblical insight and vulnerable moments from his own experience, John inspires readers to refuse the counterfeit goodness the world offers and to re-surrender their hearts to the perfect holiness of our heavenly Father. *Good or God?* is a must-read for every follower of Jesus who refuses to settle for less than God's best."

> —Chris Hodges, senior pastor of Church of the Highlands and
> author of *Fresh Air* and *Four Cups*

JOHN BEVERE

GOOD

OR

GOD?

WHY GOOD WITHOUT GOD ISN'T ENOUGH

GOOD OR GOD?
PUBLISHED BY MESSENGER INTERNATIONAL, INC.
PO Box 888
Palmer Lake, CO 80133
MessengerInternational.org

Any italicization or words in brackets added to scripture quotations are the author's additions for emphasis or clarity.

ISBN 978-1-933185-94-1
ISBN 978-1-933185-96-5 (electronic)

Cover design by Allan Nygren

Printed in the United States of America

SPECIAL MARKET SALES
Organizations, churches, pastors, and small group leaders can receive special discounts when purchasing this book and other Messenger International resources. For information, please call 1-800-648-1477 or write to orders@messengerinternational.org.

I dedicate this book to our son…
Arden Christopher Bevere

You are diligent, strong, tender, and wise. I am amazed
by your sensitivity to those who are hurting.
Son, I'm so proud of you and love you forever.

CONTENTS

ACKNOWLEDGMENTS

To my wife, children, and grandchildren: You are each a gift from God and have brought such richness to my life. I love you forever and ever.

To the team, board members, and partners of Messenger International: Thank you for standing with Lisa and me. We couldn't have asked God for more loyal and true friends to journey with us in reaching out to the nations of the world with the glorious gospel of Jesus Christ.

To Bruce, Jaylynn, Vincent, Allison, Addison, and Loran: Thank you for your diligence to polish up this message with your editing skills. I'm in awe of your God-given gifts.

To Allan: Thank you for a spectacular cover design for this message. It's clean and classy.

To Addison, Colleen, Esther, Tom, Matt, Arden, Allan, Jaylynn, and David: Thank you for reading this message in its formative stages and giving wise and sound input on difficult sections.

To Tom, Esther, Addison, Austin, and John: Thank you for your contributions of sound wisdom in publishing and marketing this book.

To Rob and Vanessa: Thank you for your tireless labor to get this message out to the nations of the world.

To our Father, our Lord Jesus Christ, and the Holy Spirit: Thank You for saving us completely from our sins, for adopting us as Your children, and for giving this message for Your beloved people. To You be all the glory.

ABOUT THIS BOOK

Good or God? may be read cover to cover just like any other book. I've included additional content at the end of the book for those who wish to use *Good or God?* as an interactive study. You can complete this study individually or in a group setting. It has been designed to be used over the course of six weeks, but feel free to adapt it to your needs.

Each week includes:

- Questions for group discussion or individual reflection
- A weekly devotion to incorporate into your personal time with God
- *Reflect*: A verse to meditate on throughout the week
- *Apply*: A simple way to apply what you've learned in your daily life

The book chapters that correspond to each week are listed above that week's discussion questions.

If you're reading this book as part of a *Good or God?* curriculum study, we recommend that you watch or listen to each week's teaching session and answer the discussion questions in the back of the book as a group. Then have each group member read the corresponding book chapters and devotion before your next meeting. There is one curriculum session for each week of the study.

Enjoy!

INTRODUCTION

Recently I was on the phone with a well-respected national leader. We were saying our goodbyes when he unexpectedly said, "John, wait just a minute. I need to say something to you. You've written numerous books in the past twenty years, but there is now one you *have* to write. It is a timely and prophetic message to the church; it's heaven's mandate for you."

By the time he was finished speaking, I was on my knees in awe of the presence of God. Within weeks of the phone call, an overwhelming passion to write this book emerged within me.

This message centers on one simple question: is good enough?

In these times the terms *good* and *God* are seemingly synonymous. We believe that what is generally accepted as good must be aligned with God's will. Generosity, humility, and justice are good. Selfishness, arrogance, and cruelty are evil. The distinction seems pretty straightforward. But is that all there is to it? If *good* is so obvious, why does Hebrews 5:14 teach that we must have discernment to recognize it?

The apostle Paul writes, "Do not be conformed to this world, but be transformed by the renewing of your mind, that you may prove what is that *good* and acceptable and perfect will of God" (Romans 12:2). We cannot discern what is truly good for our lives without first having our minds renewed. Without the transformation that comes through the renewing of our minds, we miss out on the amazing, God-infused life available to us in Christ.

Before the foundation of the world, God designed a plan for your life, one that is overflowing with fulfilled purpose, immense joy, and great satisfaction. His will and plan for you are perfectly and completely good. But there is a counterfeit good that can keep you from embracing God's best.

Sadly, many of us have settled for the knockoff. We've unknowingly (and at times knowingly) rejected *God* in pursuit of what's apparently *good*.

The early church leaders repeatedly warned us about this deception (to be deceived is to believe we're aligned with truth, when in actuality we're not). Jesus Himself warned that deception would be so cleverly concealed in our time even the elect could fall prey to it. Can we treat these warnings lightly? Can we brush them off, assuming we are above deception and can instinctively discern good from evil?

The good news is that God is not trying to hide His best from us. He's not in the business of pulling the shades over our eyes. He promises that those who seek will find. If we commit to the journey of seeking truth, we will not be duped by its counterfeit. The question is, will we look to the Source of truth, or will we settle for a superficial knowledge of God and His good will? My hope is that in reading this book, you will solidify your resolve never to settle for less than God's best.

Let's pray before we begin:

Father, in Jesus's name, open my eyes, ears, and heart to see, hear, and perceive Your will for my life. Holy Spirit, teach me, deeply and profoundly, the ways of Jesus Christ as I read this message. I look to You as my Teacher. May You speak to me from every sentence of this book. May my life be forever changed. Amen.

WHAT IS GOOD?

"No one is good but One, that is, God."
—MARK 10:18

Everything in the universe is good to the
degree it conforms to the nature of God
and evil as it fails to do so.
—A.W. TOZER

Good and evil. We all know the difference, right? Aren't we born into this world with an inherent knowledge of what is right and wrong?

I've often heard people say that human beings are inherently good. Is that true? We know that the movies, documentaries, and other programs that warm our hearts are those highlighting the goodness of humankind. I don't know of any story, novel, or movie that's gained massive popularity in which evil triumphs over good.

We all grew up watching the good guys go through tough challenges. The odds were stacked against them and they faced inevitable defeat, often right up to the very end, but suddenly our heroes broke through to victory or justice. We anticipated and applauded these finales. We expected good to always win out because, after all, God is on the side of good, right?

In recent years producers and networks initiated a trend when they introduced reality television shows featuring makeovers. It began with shows about fixing up a struggling family's home. We sat glued to our televisions, admiring the excitement and generosity of philanthropists in their outreach to the poor and needy. We anticipated the shock of those who benefitted, then teared up in that climactic moment when the poor souls beheld their refurbished house. Then came another show that helped "losers" struggling with obesity lose large amounts of weight, while still other programs helped with dress, hair, make-up, and more.

Soon afterward celebrities joined the trend. Recognized artists made a way for those who otherwise would have had no opportunity to showcase their voices or dancing skills. We cheered as we witnessed the unknown candidate given the chance to become a sensational star overnight. What kindness, what generosity, what goodwill!

Any program about highlighting benevolence, protecting the innocent, or sacrificing time to help the underdog grew in popularity. Included in our list of reality viewing were shows about police or bounty hunters apprehending evil criminals. These too became some of the most-watched programs.

To sum it all up, our entertainment is often centered on the good of humanity.

Sales and Marketing 101 teaches us that a product must feel, look, sound, taste, or smell good in order to succeed in the marketplace. It must elevate the consumer's senses or emotions to a better and happier state. We know that good items will sell. After all, who would want to purchase something bad? And only twisted people would desire to procure evil.

We hear comments such as "he's a good man" or "she's a good woman," and we normally accept this evaluation at face value. The vulnerable quickly let down their guard and embrace every statement or action from those proclaimed to be *good* as safe and trustworthy. But are these assessments always accurate?

Could we ever fall into the delusional state of calling what's right *wrong* or what's wrong *right*? Doesn't everybody know the difference? And we certainly could never fall into the deceived state of calling good *evil* or evil *good*. Correct?

Consider this. Many centuries ago, a wealthy young leader approached

Jesus Christ. He was an honest and morally pure man. He'd never committed adultery, murdered, lied, stolen, or cheated someone in a business deal. He had always respected his parents. He was a model citizen and was most likely admired by many. He honored Jesus with the greeting of "Good Teacher."

This was a leader speaking to another leader; one good man appealing to another good man. He sought common ground with the notable Teacher he'd never personally met. Perhaps he reasoned within himself, *If I cajole the heart of this Prophet by appealing to His goodness, I'll convince Him to give a favorable response to my inquiry.* However, before Jesus acknowledged his question, He first countered, "Why do you call Me good? No one is good but One, that is, God" (Mark 10:18).

Why would Jesus correct a man who called Him good? Was Jesus not good? Of course He was! So why did He say this? Could it have been that "good" was the wrong standard of judgment? In other words, is it possible that man's standard of what is good is different from God's standard?

If you or I were to put ourselves in this man's shoes, how would we have fared if we had greeted Jesus as "good Teacher"? I can answer for myself. After being a child of God for years, reading through my Bible more than once, studying Scripture for hours, praying daily, and even being in full-time ministry and authoring a few best-selling Christian books, I would have received the same response as the wealthy young leader. Jesus would have said, "John, why do you call Me good?" in exactly the same manner. How do I know this? The Spirit of God has dealt with me similarly to the way Jesus did with this ruler.

Shocking News

Let me explain. In the late 1990s, I flew to Sweden for a conference. It was an overnight flight that landed in Stockholm early in the morning. After landing, grabbing my bags, and clearing customs, I was met and warmly greeted by my Swedish host. Before we exited the terminal, he informed me of what would become the news story of the year and quite possibly the decade.

He said, "John, a very tragic thing happened last night while you were flying here, so you probably don't know. Let me update you."

"What happened?" I asked, both alarmed and curious.

My host told me about a fatal automobile accident that had occurred just a few hours earlier. One of the victims was possibly the most recognized and beloved person on the planet. Everything she did made the news. My wife, Lisa, and I admired her charitable work and enjoyed reading articles about her in magazines and newspapers. I'm being a bit vulnerable here, but not only did I like the articles, I also loved the pictures that portrayed her life. Simply put, I was a big fan. Any time a story involving her came on the news, I would stop what I was doing and pay attention.

The news of this woman's death shocked me beyond words. She was a young mother with small children, in addition to being a vibrant stateswoman who was both smart and beautiful. She was using her worldwide influence to do a great amount of good for orphans and landmine victims in war-torn countries. That was enough to win my heart, but her attractive qualities went further. She loved and was always aware of her fans, greeting them with either a genuine smile or some other warm, personal acknowledgment.

I was in shock and disbelief at the news of her passing. How could she be dead? How could this have happened?

My host drove me to my hotel. The first thing I did when I walked into my room was turn on the television. News reports about the accident were on every channel. I couldn't understand most of them because they were in Swedish, so I surfed the channels until I found CNN and BBC Sky News. I sat on the edge of my bed, bags still unpacked, in utter disbelief.

The news reports showed thousands of mourners outside the woman's residence. People of all ages had gathered, and the cameras showed them putting flowers on the gates while tears streamed down their faces. Many were embracing or huddled in groups praying. The world was in shock.

For the next four days this tragedy was featured on the front page of every newspaper in the free world. The reports of the accident, the investigation, her family's response, and the funeral dominated all media. Heads of state, world leaders, and hundreds of celebrities attended her memorial service, which was one of the most watched events in television history.

That first day in Stockholm I grieved hour after hour in my hotel room, struggling even to prepare for my upcoming evening service. My mind kept wandering to questions I had, and I struggled with anger over the senseless events that had led to her death. Yet alongside the grief, I sensed a competing thought trying to come to the surface.

I attempted to shake it off, but I couldn't. Finally, after several hours of sensing a discord between my emotions and my spirit, I got down on my knees at the end of my bed and prayed. "Father, I'm grieving over this woman's death. However, in my heart I feel as if something is wrong. What's going on?"

Almost immediately, I heard deep in my heart, "Read Revelation chapter eighteen." I had no idea what was in Revelation 18 because at the time, I'm sad to say, it was a book I had not studied in much depth. I opened my Bible and began to read. My heart started racing when I got to the seventh verse:

> "In the measure that she glorified herself and lived luxuriously, in the
> same measure give her torment and sorrow; for she says in her heart,
> 'I sit as queen, and am no widow, and will not see sorrow.' Therefore
> her plagues will come in one day—death and mourning and famine.
> And she will be utterly burned with fire, for strong is the Lord God
> who judges her. The kings of the earth who committed fornication
> and lived luxuriously with her will weep and lament for her…"
> (Revelation 18:7–9)

I felt a flurry of emotion as soon as I read these verses. There were clear parallels between the woman described in the passage and the woman whose death was dominating the airwaves. It was as if a bucket of ice water had been thrown in my face. I felt shocked, bewildered, and confused. How could these scriptures in any way apply to this benevolent celebrity?

It's important to point out that the apostle John was not referring to any individual in these verses. This passage highlights a spirit that is pervasive in our fallen world. However, there was enough resemblance to the current situation that the Spirit of God used these scriptures to bring about a shift in my understanding. Have you ever had God use an account in Scripture to speak to a personal experience? That is what was happening here.

The Spirit of God was challenging how I measured *good* in a way similar to what Jesus had done with the wealthy young leader. Aware of what I sensed God was revealing to me, I protested out loud in my hotel room, "Lord, how could this scripture have anything to do with her? She did all kinds of humanitarian work with landmine victims and orphans and—"

"She flaunted her defiance to authority and her adultery to the world," the Lord countered. "She was not submitted to Me."

Still in disbelief, I again protested, "But what about all the good she did for humanity?"

Then I heard the Spirit of God say, "Son, it wasn't the *evil* side of the tree of the knowledge of good and evil that Eve was drawn to. It was the *good* side."

I was paralyzed by these words spoken so clearly to my heart. After a few moments I opened my Bible to Genesis 3 to confirm what I'd just heard. Sure enough, I read:

> When the woman saw that the tree was *good* for food, that it was *pleas-ant* to the eyes, and a tree *desirable* to make one wise, she took of its fruit and ate. (Genesis 3:6)

I saw the words *good, pleasant,* and *desirable* and my jaw dropped. Then I heard the Spirit of God say, "There is a good that is not of Me. It is not submitted to Me."

I sat there and contemplated what I had heard and read. The Word of God had exposed and corrected me. My standard of good was apparently different from the divine standard of good.

God proceeded to speak to my heart. He showed me how most "good" people, and especially Christian people, are not drawn to lewd sexual orgies, dark music with blatantly rebellious lyrics, rock stars who flaunt Satanism in their concerts, mass murder, grand larceny, or any such blatantly evil behavior. Most are deceived by and drawn to behavior and things that seem right, good, and wise but are contrary to His wisdom. We are told:

There is a way that *seems right* to a man, but its end is the way of death. (Proverbs 14:12)

Let's first discuss the latter part of this verse: "but its end is the *way of death.*" Many Christians don't pay close attention to these words because they think, *I'm saved, headed for heaven, and will not see death.* In their minds, the statement only applies to nonbelievers. However, let's rethink what God's Word is saying here.

Look at the words "the way of death." Scripture speaks with some frequency of the way of life and the way of death. God declares to His own (not to those who don't belong to Him), "Thus says the Lord: 'Behold, I set before you the *way of life* and the *way of death*'" (Jeremiah 21:8).

Way here means the wisdom we live by. You'll see this word often throughout Scripture. Jesus frames it as follows: "The *way* is broad that leads to destruction [death], and there are many who enter through it. For the gate is small and the *way* is narrow that leads to life…" (Matthew 7:13–14 NASB). But is Jesus only addressing eternity here?

God placed the tree of life in the center of the Garden of Eden. It represented God's way of life, His wisdom. The other central tree in the garden was called the tree of the knowledge of good and evil. This tree represented the way of death; it stood for man's wisdom apart from God. Partaking of its fruit didn't just impact Adam and Eve in the afterlife; it affected them immediately. Before their foolish act, they had been unrestrained, productive, healthy, and successful at whatever they set their hearts to do. But once they partook of the forbidden tree, life became hard. They were plagued with sickness, lack, stressful toil, and difficulties they'd never known. They had entered into the way of death.

However, God is a Redeemer. He'd already planned to recover what man had lost. He made a covenant in order to restore the *way of life*. His wisdom would once again produce true happiness, pleasant living, peace, abundance, and other great benefits:

> Happy is the man who finds wisdom…all the things you desire cannot compare with her. Length of days is in her right hand, in her left hand riches and honor. Her ways are ways of pleasantness, and all her paths are peace. She is a *tree of life* to those who take hold of her, and happy are those who retain her. (Proverbs 3:13–18)

Scripture shows that God's wisdom applied to our lives results in fruitful living, productivity, success, a long life, peace of mind, and honor. A tree is something others partake of. According to this scripture, if we follow the way of life (wisdom), we become a tree of life—a source of nourishment to those who partake of what we produce. The converse is also true. If we live by the wisdom of man, we become a detrimental tree, and those who partake of what we produce will gravitate toward toil, stress, unproductivity, sickness, selfishness, and the other byproducts of spiritual death.

Returning to Proverbs 14:12, we read, "There is a way that *seems right* to a man, but its end is the way of death." When we examine the first part of this verse, we know it can easily apply to anyone, Christian and nonbeliever alike. There is a way that seems right—it seems good, wise, beneficial, strategic, acceptable, profitable, and so forth. Yet the warning is clear: what seems good may actually be detrimental, harmful, and nonproductive—the way of death.

The author of Hebrews writes this sobering exhortation to believers:

> …We have much to say…since you have become dull of hearing. For though by this time you ought to be teachers, you need someone to

teach you again the first principles of the oracles of God; and you have come to need milk and not solid food. …But solid food belongs to those who are of full age, that is, those who by reason of use have their *senses exercised to discern both good and evil.* (Hebrews 5:11–12, 14)

It's clear that discernment is a key factor in determining what is truly good and what is truly evil. In other words, what's truly good is not always clear to our natural thinking, reasoning, or senses.

You may ask, "Didn't the author of Hebrews say that our senses can be trained to tell the difference?" He did, but what senses was he referring to? You'll notice that at the beginning of these verses, the author said he was writing to these Christians whose hearing had grown dull. What hearing was he referring to? Did all of these Hebrew believers need hearing aids? Hardly. He was referencing the ability to hear in our hearts. Jesus constantly taught, "He who has ears to hear, let him hear!" (Matthew 11:15). Virtually all those who received this teaching had physical ears, yet not all of them had a discerning heart to hear the Word of God, which was best for their lives.

We will delve deeper into spiritual discernment a bit later in this book; however, the important point at this juncture is that good and evil cannot always be differentiated on the surface level. Before my encounter with truth in that hotel room in Stockholm, I believed good and bad were right before us, plain and evident. Yet consider another example: One of Jesus's main team members, Peter, spoke of protection and long life to Jesus. It seemed certain that he was giving his Boss good counsel. Yet Jesus reprimanded him sharply by stating his interests were clearly not God's (see Matthew 16:21–23). This is only one of many scriptural examples I could give illustrating how good and evil are not openly evident.

Solomon prayed, "Give me an understanding heart so that I can…know the difference between right and wrong" (1 Kings 3:9 NLT). It takes an enlightened heart, one that is trained, to identify what God calls *good* and *evil.* Eve was perfect in every way, and in the garden where she resided the presence of God was powerful and strong. However, what she discerned to be good, pleasant, and profitable was actually evil and detrimental for her life. She was deceived and suffered because of it.

This brings us to the purpose of this book: to illuminate, through the Scriptures and the help of the Holy Spirit, the difference between what is good for your life and what will ultimately be detrimental. If Eve, who was perfect and living in a flawless environment, could still be deceived, how much easier is it for those of us with imperfect minds and living in a corrupted world—a skewed society—to be deceived into judging what is damaging to be good?

2

HOW'D IT HAPPEN?

So don't be misled, my dear
brothers and sisters. Whatever is
good and perfect is a gift coming
down to us from God our Father...
—JAMES 1:16-17 NLT

[The Christian] does not think God will
love us because we are good, but that God
will make us good because He loves us...
—C.S. LEWIS

That day in Sweden, I sat in my hotel room stunned, my emotions raging. I was in awe of the divine response to my grief over the celebrity's death, yet I was troubled. I was perplexed and full of questions. I had been in ministry for years, had written books, and had taught believers on every continent (except Antarctica), yet my ignorance regarding what is truly good had just been exposed.

The predominant questions surging through my mind were, *What else have I viewed as good that's not good in God's eyes?* and, equally important, *What have been the consequences?*

Before I begin addressing these questions, it would be beneficial to go back again to where it all began: the Garden of Eden. This is a logical step, for this is the reference the Spirit of God had used to grab my attention in that hotel room. There is a nagging question about the garden story that I—and many others—have wrestled with for years: just how did the serpent get Eve to turn on God?

Let's think this through. Eve lived in a perfect environment. No father, husband, relative, boss, or teacher had ever abused her. She lived in total peace and tranquility and was abundantly provided for with no sickness or lack of resources. Best of all, she lived in harmony with her Creator. God's presence permeated the atmosphere of the earth, and He frequently walked in the garden with Adam and Eve. So how did the serpent get this woman, as well as the man, to turn on God?

If we can find answers to this mystery, we will gain beneficial insight into how the enemy can do the same to us today. If we know his tactics, we won't so easily fall prey to deception and disobedience to our Creator.

A Magnificent Garden

In the beginning God created a perfect world, one that was beautiful, flawless, and loaded with resources and other delights to the soul. God didn't create only a few varieties of animals, trees, and landscapes. He designed and created over one million living creatures, over two hundred fifty thousand plants, over one hundred thousand species of trees, and myriad different rocks, soils, and natural resources. The earth was a masterpiece. Thousands of years later, scientists still study it and marvel at its complexity. They've not yet mastered the understanding of our world and probably never will.

God designed and created all this just for the object of His affection: humankind. And as astonishing as the planet turned out to be, the Creator was compelled to go even further. He personally planted—not created—a wondrous garden on the earth.

I love landscapes and gardens. Well, let me be truthful. I don't love working in either—you can ask Lisa about that. She'll frown as she tells you about my disdain for gardening. What I love, however, is simply sitting in or strolling through manicured gardens, orchards, vineyards, or forests. I admire the colors, the scents, the soil, and the varieties of trees and plants.

Recently I was speaking in Konstanz, Germany, a city named after the lake it sits beside. Lake Konstanz is the largest lake in Germany, for it receives melting ice and snow waters from the Alps. Lisa and I were there together visiting close friends who are also pastors, Freimut (a good German name) and his wife, Joanna.

We had a couple of free days during our trip, and our hosts graciously offered a variety of fun activities to fill our time. We discovered there is no lack of things to do in Konstanz; however, the one thing I wanted to do most was not proposed.

Located within Lake Konstanz is a place called Flower Island. Its proper name is Mainau, but Flower Island is more descriptive because the entire island is a garden. I wanted to go walk through it, but it would take a full day to see it all.

Lisa, Joanna, and Freimut initially thought I was joking when I asked to visit the island. After all, who would have thought a guy who loves sports and competitive activities would want to do something as boring as walking through a big garden? After I brought it up a couple times, though, our friends remarked, "We didn't think you were serious. Do you really want to go?"

"Yes!" I said. So we planned the outing—in spite of little enthusiasm from the others.

It was a spectacular day. We drove across a bridge to the island, paid admission at the front gate, and began our tour. It didn't take long before I was captivated. I was amazed by the beauty and complexity of this vast garden. The good news was that I wasn't alone. The joking and jeering of the other three ceased once we all beheld this masterpiece.

Every section of this enormous garden was a feast to the eyes. The beautiful flowerbeds were all perfectly aligned, with walking paths contouring through their midst so that every plant was visible. There were maps made out of flowers and huge statues of animals, children, and even houses all made out of different trees, plants, and flowers. Stunning water features were also scattered throughout.

We all enjoyed the beauty and creativity of a place that would take more than half a day to fully tour—we only saw half of it! Many times that afternoon I pondered, *If men and women could come up with this magnificent island, a feast of beauty for the eyes with an abundance of fragrances to delight the sense of smell, what must the garden of God have looked like?* For it wasn't a skilled horticulturist or landscape architect who designed Eden. It was the Master Creator Himself.

God planted the rich, luscious Garden of Eden, placed Adam in it, and brought every animal to him. The Master wanted to see what Adam would name each of the over 1.25 million species of animals on the earth. What intelligence this man must have possessed! But Adam had not only the ability to name all these different animals but also the capacity to remember the name of each one—and with no iPad with Google capabilities to help! Adam was brilliant.

However, God didn't bring the animals to Adam just to name them; He also wanted to see which animal would be Adam's choice for a suitable companion.

The man named all the birds and all the animals, but not one of them was a suitable companion to help him. Then the Lord God made the man fall into a deep sleep, and while he was sleeping, He took out one of the man's ribs and closed up the flesh. He formed a woman out of the rib and brought her to the man. Then Adam said:

> "At last, here is one of my own kind—Bone taken from my bone, and flesh from my flesh. 'Woman' is her name because she was taken out of man." (Genesis 2:23 TEV)

The perfect companion for the man was woman. They would complement and complete each other. Together they were given the assignment to guard and keep the planet and, more specifically, the garden.

Before Eve was taken from Adam, God had given a clear directive: "You may eat the fruit of any tree in the garden, except the tree that gives knowledge of what is good and what is bad. You must not eat the fruit of that tree; if you do, you will die the same day" (Genesis 2:16–17 TEV).

We don't know the timing of the next recorded event. It could have been after a few weeks, years, decades, or even longer. But the day came when the most cunning beast, the serpent, targeted Eve and questioned God's command.

(How could a snake talk? I personally believe animals could communicate to humans before the Fall. This is why we don't see Eve alarmed or taken aback when the snake approached her. This knowledge about animals speaking must have been passed down through the generations, because when Balaam's donkey spoke, it didn't shock Balaam either; see Numbers 22:21–35. He just carried on a conversation with his beast of burden, not showing any surprise or that he was caught off-guard.)

How Did He Do It?

Let me restate the purpose of our investigation into what happened in Eden. We are seeking to know how this devil-possessed serpent could get Eve to turn on God in a perfect environment. Let's examine his approach:

> He said to the woman, "Has God indeed said, 'You shall not eat of every tree of the garden'?" (Genesis 3:1)

With this inquiry the serpent initiated the first step of his strategy. His objective was to sway Eve from godly wisdom. His cleverly crafted question enticed the woman to momentarily lose sight of the myriad available fruit trees and redirect her focus to the single one withheld.

God's exact words to Adam and Eve had been, "You may eat the fruit of any tree in the garden, except…" His generosity emphasized, "You may eat from any tree." There are thousands of known fruit trees in the world, and my guess is that every one was represented in the garden. How clever was this serpent? Eve could have eaten from thousands of trees, but after Satan's twisted question, she could not get her eyes off the only one that was forbidden.

It's no different today. God has freely given each of us so many gifts—every blessing heaven offers (see Ephesians 1:3). It would take another book just to list them! We are also told that all things are ours in Christ Jesus (see 1 Corinthians 3:21–23). However, what's our enemy's strategy? It's no different than it was in the garden. He seeks to cover up God's generosity so we only see what is "withheld." Why does God restrain us from anything? We'll look into this important question in a few pages, but to put it simply, it's for our own good. He knows better than we do what's best for us.

Siding with the truth that she knew, Eve quickly responded to this talking snake:

> "We may eat the fruit of the trees of the garden; but of the fruit of the tree which is in the midst of the garden, God has said, 'You shall not eat it, *nor shall you touch it*, lest you die.'" (Genesis 3:2–3)

It is interesting to note the inaccuracy of Eve's reply. God never said anything about not touching the fruit of the tree. This may seem insignificant, but it gives us a clue as to why the serpent targeted her and not Adam.

Eve was not yet on the scene when the original command was given, so she hadn't heard it from the mouth of God as Adam had. I personally believe there was a previous day when she and Adam had been walking through this vast garden and came upon the tree of the knowledge of good and evil. Adam pointed it out and told Eve what God had said about this particular tree. I refer to this kind of interaction as *communicated* knowledge. On the other hand, for Adam the command had been *revealed* knowledge. What's the difference? Revealed knowledge is when God shows us something directly.

Revealed versus Communicated Knowledge

One day Jesus asked His disciples, "Who do men say that I, the Son of Man, am?" (Matthew 16:13). One by one, the disciples listed all they had heard from others: a resurrected John the Baptist, Elijah, Jeremiah, or one of the other prophets—those were some of the reports these men had heard through their day's version of Twitter, Facebook, Instagram, and blogs.

Once Jesus got past what they'd discovered through communicated knowledge, He then questioned, "But who do you say that I am?" (verse 15)

The disciples stood paralyzed with no response. Had Jesus not asked the first question, they likely would have been influenced by others' comments, and their responses would have reflected communicated knowledge. But with His two questions, Jesus's motive was to strip away this secondhand knowledge in order to find out what God had revealed to them. Peter was the only one with an answer. He blurted out, "You are the Christ, the Son of the living God" (verse 16).

I can imagine that Jesus smiled, put His hand on Peter's back to affirm him, and announced, "Flesh and blood has not revealed this to you, but My Father who is in heaven" (verse 17). Peter wasn't mimicking information from what he'd read online or seen randomly in someone's magazine article! He was sharing truth God had imparted directly to him.

Jesus then declared that this type of *revelation knowledge* is what the church would be built on and that hell's forces could not stop those who possessed it. On the contrary, hell's forces can more easily deceive those who only possess *communicated knowledge.*

We attain revealed knowledge in many ways. It can occur as we are reading Scripture or an inspired book, quieting ourselves in prayer, listening to our pastor speak, receiving a vision as Peter did on a rooftop (see Acts 10:9–16), or simply encountering the Word of God revealed to our hearts by the Holy Spirit. It's hard to generalize how it occurs. Sometimes you may hear a still, small voice deep in your heart. Other times you simply *know* because the revelation was dropped into your spirit. Other times your heart begins to race and you sense the presence of God as you read Scripture. However it comes, the bottom line is that you know you've heard from God, and this *revealed* knowledge cannot be taken from you.

On the other hand, *communicated* knowledge comes by merely hearing or reading someone else's statements about what they've heard from God. The knowledge may be accurate, but if the Spirit doesn't reveal it to your heart, it can be easily distorted.

For example, I've heard some people boldly flaunt their knowledge of the Bible: "You know, John, money is the root of all evil." What these misguided friends have read—or have heard a minister quote—is 1 Timothy 6:10, which says, "For the *love* of money is the root of all kinds of evil" (NLT).

Money is merely a tool. That's it. You can misuse a tool, or you can use it correctly. A gun is a tool. In a thief's hand a gun will be misused in a robbery. However, a gun in a policeman's hand can be used to stop someone from raping or murdering a woman. It's the same gun, and there's nothing inherently evil or good about it. In the same way, money is a tool, and it is not the root of all evil. The *love of money* is the root of every kind of evil.

Individuals who make erroneous comments like this possess communicated knowledge rather than revealed knowledge. In my experience this communicated knowledge is sometimes more dangerous than the absence of knowledge.

The words Eve used to describe the command to not touch the fruit of the tree indicate that she possessed merely communicated knowledge. God's presence was in the garden. He walked with Adam and Eve, most likely on a daily basis (see Genesis 3:8). It's perfectly fine that Adam shared with his wife what God had commanded, but what she likely didn't do was seek her Creator directly about what was spoken.

It should be a characteristic of those who seek God to dig more deeply into knowing and understanding Him. Hear what the people of Berea did when Paul brought them his message from heaven:

And the people of Berea were more open-minded than those in Thessalonica, and they listened eagerly to Paul's message. They searched the Scriptures day after day to see if Paul and Silas were teaching the truth. (Acts 17:11 NLT)

The Bereans were in the game! They listened to Paul intently, then searched the Scriptures themselves. I love the word *open-minded*. Their minds were open to the voice of the Spirit. The channels between their spirits and minds were clear, open to receive revelation knowledge.

Unlike too many believers today, these Bereans didn't get all their content simply off podcasts, blog posts, or discussions on Twitter or Facebook. Likewise, when Jesus discussed His identity with the disciples, He wasn't interested in what people were saying on the social media of His day. He wanted to know, "Guys, what has God revealed to you?"

It might have been on one of their journeys as a group that Peter heard someone say, "Jesus must be the Christ." At that moment, awareness exploded in his mind and heart, spurred by the presence of the Holy Spirit. *That's it! He is the Son of God. He is the Christ. Wow! Until now I just couldn't put my finger on it, but now I know He's the Christ!* This is often how we experience God revealing His truth to our hearts.

Or maybe it happened differently with Peter. The revelation may have come to his heart one night as he was drifting off to sleep, or in the daytime while he was walking between towns, or in a moment when he was watching Jesus speak to other team members at a campsite. Perhaps in one of those moments, without Peter realizing it, God reminded him of one of the Old Testament scriptures, like Isaiah 9:6–7, that foretold the Christ's coming.

Or maybe Peter's spiritual "aha moment" came as Jesus was healing someone. Suddenly the disciple remembered one of his childhood rabbis reading an Old Testament prophecy about the coming Messiah: "He Himself took our infirmities and bore our sicknesses" (Matthew 8:17, confirming Isaiah 53:4).

There are so many ways the revelation of Jesus's true identity could have happened to Peter; the important point is that *God Himself revealed it.*

I think it is safe to say this is not what happened with Eve. She didn't have *revealed* knowledge; instead she settled for *communicated* knowledge. Perhaps Adam sent her a direct message on Twitter: "Hey, sweetheart, I saw you looking at the tree of the knowledge of good and evil. Don't touch it! God says we'll die if we eat that fruit!"

Phase Two

Now that the serpent had Eve's attention solely focused on the one and only forbidden tree, he could initiate step two of his persuasive ploy. This step would be to negate God's Word. However, it would be cleverly wrapped in what seemed to be sound reasoning, along with the promise of a benefit. Satan countered:

> Then the serpent said to the woman, "You will not surely die. *For God knows* that in the day you eat of it your eyes will be opened, and you will be like God, knowing good and evil." (Genesis 3:4–5)

Consider the serpent's words: "for God knows." They imply something is being withheld—and not just anything, but something that would make Adam and Eve's life better. This something would take them to a higher level! Since there was *good* in this tree, the serpent carefully calculated his logic to appear sound. It worked.

> So when the woman saw that the tree was *good* for food, that it was *pleasant* to the eyes, and a tree *desirable to make one wise*, she took of its fruit and ate. (Genesis 3:6)

Eve saw that the tree was good, it was pleasant, and it would make her wise. These all are desirable, beneficial traits.

As Eve was staring at the tree, her thoughts began to go down a new road: *Wait a minute. There's something good and beneficial in that tree, and God's forbidden it. My husband and I could have a better life. We could be wiser and happier, but it's being withheld. I thought our Creator was loving and gracious, but in reality, He's deceptive. He's hiding something good from us.*

With every second that these thoughts permeated her mind, Eve's desire to eat the fruit grew. Her desire was justified the longer she believed there was something good for her in that tree.

The serpent's ultimate tactic was to pervert the character of God in Eve's eyes. If he was successful, he could get her to turn on God. Why? Because God's rule is established and upheld by His character.

King David wrote, "Righteousness and justice are the foundation of Your throne" (Psalm 89:14). As a king, David knew these traits are the foundation of a lasting leader. If a king is truthful, just, and wise, his reign will not end. If instead a ruler is deceitful and unjust, his reign will not last.

God's character is perfect, but the snake was out to convince Eve otherwise. He sought to skew the evidence. The appearance of the forbidden tree was good and pleasant. It seemed that it would make one wise, but appearances can be deceiving. This is why we are told, "We fix our attention, not on things that are seen, but on things that are unseen" (2 Corinthians 4:18 TEV). That which is unseen is the Word of God. His Word is just and accurate.

Don't Be Deceived

The enemy was able to get Eve to turn on her Creator by undermining her perspective of God's character. Often I've had to fight off similar thoughts in the heat of a battle when I'm not seeing a prayer answered as quickly as I'd hoped. In those situations I remind myself of the faithfulness of God. I coach myself through the reality: *God is not the problem, He's not withholding, and He's a good and gracious Father.*

The serpent got Eve to believe there was something good for her that

God was withholding. If this was successfully accomplished in a perfect environment, with a woman who had never before been abused, offended, or taken advantage of, how much easier is the enemy's task today in a fallen world filled with offense, corruption, perversion, and deceit? For this reason we are strongly warned by the apostle James:

> Do not be deceived, my beloved brethren. (James 1:16)

As I like to say, there is only one problem with deception: it's deceiving! The one who is deceived believes wholeheartedly that he or she is correct, accurate, and on the side of truth. But in reality, he or she is wrong, inaccurate, and not on the side of truth. How scary!

Eve was deceived and consequently fell into transgression. James doesn't want us to fall into the same trap. So let's examine his entire statement:

> Do not be deceived, my beloved brethren. Every good gift and
> every perfect gift is from above, and comes down from the Father
> of lights, with whom there is no variation or shadow of turning.
> (James 1:16–17)

James doesn't say that *most* good gifts come from God. That's the opinion of many. No, we are explicitly told that *every* good and perfect gift comes from God. We could just as easily write, "There is nothing good for you outside of God's will." Don't take this next statement lightly or superficially, because there's great depth to it. *It doesn't matter how good something looks, how happy it makes you, how much fun it is, how rich and successful you'll become, how deeply spiritual it appears, how sensible it seems, how popular or accepted it is—and the list goes on and on. If something is contrary to the wisdom (or Word) of God, it will ultimately be detrimental and bring sorrow to your life.*

Eve fully believed she was making a wise choice—a good choice, one that would improve her and her husband's life. It didn't. And if you think thousands of years later your wisdom about what seems good is more beneficial than God's, you are just as deceived as Eve was, and you will fall into great sorrow.

I know you may think I'm being a bit negative or narrow-minded here, but that's not my intent. I'm simply warning you. This book is filled with instruction about how to recognize what is truly good for your life, ministry, business, relationships, and more. However, to completely present the message of Jesus Christ, I have to both *warn* and *teach*. Paul confirms this when he writes:

> Him we preach, *warning* every man and *teaching* every man in all
> wisdom, that we may present every man perfect in Christ Jesus.
> (Colossians 1:28)

You and I cannot be brought to maturity without both warnings and instructions. I look at it like this. Anytime you purchase a new electronic device or tool or appliance, on the first or second page of the instruction manual you will see the words "Warning: Read Before Using." The manufacturer then lists several warnings about what to do—or more frequently, not to do—with the product. These warnings are given to inform you how not to bring severe damage to yourself or the item you purchased. You will have years of great service from the item if you don't violate the warnings. But if the manufacturer did not give the warnings, you might inadvertently do what would bring harm or cause the loss of the product. You would then write a nasty email to the company and chew them out for not properly warning you.

Paul tells us we are to pay attention to the warnings of the New Testament. If we heed them, we will have years of successful living in harmony with our Creator. However, if we ignore or violate the warnings, we too will suffer in a manner similar to Adam and Eve. Then we will write blog posts, letters, and emails about how unfair life is due to the hardships and sorrows we've encountered. Yet God clearly states:

Study this Book of Instruction continually. Meditate on it day and night so you will be sure to obey everything written in it. Only then will you *prosper* and *succeed* in all you do. (Joshua 1:8 NLT)

God guarantees a successful and prosperous life if we carefully obey what is written in His book of instructions. However, this book does not just contain motivating, comforting teachings. It also holds warnings.

Unfortunately, in our day ministers and teachers often avoid these important warnings. These parts of Scripture may be perceived as negative, and we don't want discouraging messages coming from the pulpit because such an approach would be unattractive and thwart church or conference attendance. Consequently, there are many train wrecks among believers that could have been avoided if the individuals had been both taught and warned.

I urge you to settle it now: There is nothing good for you outside of God's wisdom or Word, nothing at all. If you believe this, let's go further in our search for the difference between good and God.

3

THE UNIVERSAL
STANDARD OF GOOD

Every word of God proves true.
—Proverbs 30:5 NLT

We best oppose error by promoting a solid
knowledge of the word of truth...
—Matthew Henry

In this book I will address three aspects of the concept of *good*. The first targets our core relationship with God; the second, our character and behavior; and the third, our plans and strategies. They are closely connected, as the first is our foundation, the second is what holds our lives together, and the third represents the building of our lives. If the first two are strong, our labor will be maximized and lasting. But if either of those is faulty, our life's work will be hindered and fleeting.

I remember building our first house like it happened yesterday. The whole process from start to finish captivated both Lisa and me. Once construction began, we'd drive to the job site daily to check out the progress.

The foundation wasn't that interesting, so consequently we spent the least amount of time examining it. But around the same time, some friends of ours built a much nicer first home. A few years after moving in, their walls developed huge gaping cracks running from the floor to the ceiling. One evening we were there for dinner and, noticing the glaring problem, we asked what was wrong. With obvious disgust they shared that the home's foundation was faulty. Their builder had cut corners, and their attempts to get restitution had turned ugly. Correcting the problem ended up being an extremely expensive and time-consuming process. Their experience highlighted to me the importance of a good foundation. Even though the laying of the foundation wasn't the most exciting part of our building process to observe, it was most essential to constructing a home that would last.

Once the foundation of our home was laid, framing was the next step. This construction stage made our trips to the job site more interesting. Our visits were longer as we were now able to walk through the house. We were thrilled to see the rooms coming into shape, and we were getting a more realistic picture of what the finished house would look like.

The final stage was just pure excitement, and we spent more time inspecting our house during this phase than any other. Once the framing and drywall were completed, we observed the installation of trim, crown molding, cabinets, flooring, countertops, and eventually the lights. This was our first house, and we could arrange and decorate it however we wished. Every day seemed like Christmas morning to us. It was all coming together.

Here's my point: if the first two phases of our home's construction—the foundation and framing—had not been sound, the rest would have suffered, either immediately or, as in our friends' case, over the course of time.

In the same way, the final aspect of this book's message—which is about our life plans and strategies—will be the most delightful to discuss. It deals with the decisions we make in business, ministry, or our life quests.

There are choices we face in these areas that appear good; however, quite often they are not God's best. If selected, these paths will rob us of our maximum potential. It is an unchangeable truth: "No good thing will He withhold from those who walk uprightly" (Psalm 84:11). He wants good for you, and His good is always magnificent.

We'll get to this discussion a little later, but just as our builder carefully concentrated on the first steps of construction, in this book we must first lay the foundation and set up the framing.

Good Defined

Let's look at the word *good*. The Hebrew word for good is *tob*. A few of the definitions found in *The Complete Word Study Dictionary* are: "to be happy, acceptable, to do well, right." The *New International Encyclopedia of Bible Words* takes it deeper by stating:

> This simple word means "good" in the broadest possible sense. It includes the beautiful, the attractive, the useful, the profitable, the desirable, the morally right.
>
> The concept that links all these uses of "good" is evaluation. To determine the good, one must compare things, qualities, and actions with other things, qualities, and actions....
>
> The account of the Creation introduces *tob* biblically, as God views each day's work and pronounces it good. God too evaluates. It is in fact because God shared His image and likeness with mankind that human beings have the capacity to make value judgments. But sin has distorted humanity's perceptions. Because of this, only God is able to evaluate perfectly. The writers of the OT were convinced that not only was God the giver and the measure of good but also that He alone knows what is truly beneficial for us and what is morally right. Only because God has shared His evaluation of good in His Word are we who rely on Him able to affirm with confidence that a certain thing, quality, or course of action is beneficial.[1]

The key word is *evaluation*. Adam and Eve chose to evaluate *good* and *acceptable* apart from God's counsel. They made an assessment according to a different set of standards: their own. This has been the root of man's hostility with the Creator ever since. It has taken various shapes and forms, but it always comes down to this one underlying motive: "I know what *is right* for my life and don't need anyone to tell me otherwise." Yet God declares: "There is a way that *seems right* to a man, but its end is the way of death" (Proverbs 16:25).

In the first chapter I quoted these exact words, but the scripture reference was Proverbs 14:12. It's not by chance that this statement is repeated. Whenever a statement is repeated in Scripture, it's for emphasis. We must always remember, some matters are weightier than others to God (see Matthew 23:23). When repetition of a statement occurs, we need to pay even closer attention. In this case, this is a stronger warning.

God knows how easily the line between good and evil can be distorted. If it happened in the garden, how much more easily can it occur today? God warns there will be *ways*—behavioral patterns, thought processes, beliefs, customs, or even traditions—that seem acceptable by our evaluation but will eventually prove faulty in the building of our lives, and will in time take a toll. The result may take months or years to appear or sometimes not even show up until the Day of Judgment. Paul says, "Remember, the sins of some people are obvious, leading them to certain judgment. But there are others whose sins will not be revealed until later" (1 Timothy 5:24 NLT). I don't know about you, but the second part of that verse causes me to tremble. Not that it makes me scared of God, but rather it makes me terrified to be away from Him.

The bottom line is, do I truly believe God's wisdom is perfect and trust Him for what's best for my life? Every human being must solidify the answer to this question in his or her heart. And this core conviction cannot vary from one matter to another. Either God's wisdom is perfect in all cases, or it's flawed and we are better off making our own decisions independent of Him.

So what is the standard of good we are to trust in? What leads to the way of life? The apostle Paul tells us:

All Scripture is inspired by God and is useful to teach us what is true and to make us realize what is wrong in our lives. It corrects us when we are wrong and teaches us to do what is right. (2 Timothy 3:16 NLT)

Let's examine some key elements of Paul's statement.

All Scripture. Not some. Not just the ones we like or agree with. Not just the scriptures that fit in with our way of thinking or believing. It's all Scripture. Be honest with yourself: do you view God's wisdom as right in some areas but out of date or irrelevant in other cases?

Eve knew God was the Creator, and she enjoyed the riches of His goodness along with the wonder of His presence. She was granted beautiful surroundings, peace, harmony, well-being, and an abundance of delicious food from a host of trees. Yet once convinced an area of God's wisdom wasn't right, she fell into the way of death. If Eve could be swayed in a flawless environment, what is our protection in the midst of corruption? It's none other than Scripture.

Scripture is useful to teach us what is true and what is right. Something can have the appearance of good yet be just the opposite. There are concepts, assumptions, opinions, qualities, ways of reasoning, and thought patterns that seem good and right yet aren't. Due to these hidden dangers, God has given us a life instruction manual so that we don't *unknowingly* veer away from truth and fall into the ways of death. It's the Bible.

You and I must ask ourselves (and answer honestly), do I consistently read my Bible? Do I study it? Do I spend time searching out God's wisdom for my life? Or do I, like Eve, presume I'm fluent in His Word? Am I—while living on a corrupted planet and also battling the tempter—better than Eve at understanding the truth and staying on track?

All Scripture is inspired by God. There are no exceptions or hidden clauses within this statement; it's an all or not-at-all prospect. If all Scripture is not inspired, then we have a flawed manual.

The Certainty of Scripture

Let's review some of the details concerning the Bible. It's composed of six-ty-six books, written in various languages over a period of roughly 1,500 years by over forty men on three continents (Africa, Asia, and Europe). These human writers came from vastly different backgrounds, occupations, and perspectives. They were fishermen, shepherds, military men, kings, a royal cupbearer, a medical doctor, a tax collector, a tentmaker, and others. Some wrote from prison while others penned their words in a palace.

Although the writings of these men cover numerous topics, the unity found throughout the different books is remarkable—but definitely not co-incidental. Their central theme is this: humankind's sin predicament, the resulting separation from their Creator, their inability to restore relationship with Him, and the divine answer of a Messiah, the Lord Jesus Christ. This content is interwoven consistently from Genesis to Revelation.

The fact that the writers of the Bible did not (and could not) come together to plan what they would write is awe-inspiring! No one person or committee oversaw and set the direction for the process. God Himself did. Since the Scriptures were written over such a lengthy period of time, most writers did not personally know one another or live in the same era. Books were added to the existing collection as they were written throughout the 1,500 years. (Stop a moment and think back 1,500 years from today. That's so far back it predates the British Empire. Staggering!)

Now, generations later, it's overwhelming to think the Bible we read came forth as one book written by men who had no explicit knowledge of the overall structure. Their individual roles could be compared to that of different people from different generations and cultures writing chapters of a novel, none of them having had an overall outline or even a storyline to go by. The amazing coherence of this book proves its divine origin. Like a sym-phony, each individual part of the Bible contributes to the overall harmony that is orchestrated by one God.

This knowledge alone is overwhelming evidence of the divine inspiration of Scripture. But let's take it one step further by discussing the accuracy of these different writers.

Prophecies predicting the arrival of the Messiah were written in various Old Testament books over hundreds of years, in some instances over a thousand years before Jesus's birth. Most Bible scholars agree there are over three hundred of these prophecies in the Old Testament. Once Jesus Christ came into the world He declared to His Father, "Look, I have come to do your will, O God—as is written about me in the Scriptures" (Hebrews 10:7 NLT). And to the people Jesus declared, "Scriptures speak about me!" (John 5:39 TEV)

Jesus's fulfillment of all these prophetic writings is overwhelming evidence of the divine inspiration of Scripture. A common rebuttal to this conclusion is that you can find other historical figures that would fit the prophecies of Messiah. This is true; certain individuals could fulfill one, two, or even a few prophecies. However, to find one person to fulfill them all is virtually impossible.

Let me illustrate. The next few pages will be more technical and scientific in nature, but I assure you this information is important and delightful to ponder.

The Accuracy of Scripture

In the mid-1900s, a science professor named Peter Stoner published a book entitled *Science Speaks*. In this work he discussed the prophecies of Christ in the light of the science of probability. Concerning his findings, H. Harold Hartzler, PhD, wrote in the foreword to *Science Speaks*:

> The manuscript for Science Speaks has been carefully reviewed by
> a committee of the American Scientific Affiliation members and
> by the Executive Council of the same group and has been found,

in general, to be dependable and accurate in regard to the scientific material presented. The mathematical analysis included is based upon principles of probability which are thoroughly sound and Professor Stoner has applied these principles in a proper and convincing way.[2]

Stoner didn't perform this study alone but drew conclusions from over six hundred science students from twelve different classes. He carefully weighed their findings and then edited portions to make their data more conservative. Their initial assessment included the following eight prophecies about Jesus Christ:

1. Christ is to be born in Bethlehem (prophesied in Micah 5:2; fulfilled in Matthew 2:1–7; John 7:42; Luke 2:4–7)
2. Christ is to be preceded by a messenger (prophesied in Isaiah 40:3 and Malachi 3:1; fulfilled in Matthew 3:1–3; 11:10; John 1:23; Luke 1:13–17)
3. Christ is to enter Jerusalem on a donkey (prophesied in Zechariah 9:9; fulfilled in Luke 19:28–37; Matthew 21:1–11)
4. Christ is to be betrayed by a friend (prophesied in Psalm 41:9 and 55:12–14; fulfilled in Matthew 10:4; 26:47–50; John 13:21–27)
5. Christ is to be sold for thirty pieces of silver (prophesied in Zechariah 11:12; fulfilled in Matthew 26:15; 27:3)
6. The money for which Christ is sold is to be thrown "to the potter" in God's house (prophesied in Zechariah 11:13; fulfilled in Matthew 27:5–7)
7. Christ is to be silent before His accusers (prophesied in Isaiah 53:7; fulfilled in Matthew 27:12; Mark 14:60–61; 15:3–5)
8. Christ is to be executed by crucifixion as a thief (prophesied in Psalm 22:16; Zechariah 12:10 and Isaiah 53:5, 12; fulfilled in Luke 23:33; John 20:25; Matthew 27:38; Mark 15:24–27)

Before continuing, let me give a simple illustration of the science of probability. Imagine that we take nine yellow tennis balls and one white tennis ball, put them into a five-gallon bucket, and shake them all up. Then we blindfold a man and ask him to pick one ball out of the bucket. The chances of him picking the white ball would be one in ten. This is simple probability.

Along this line, Peter Stoner stated the following in regard to the eight prophecies listed on the previous page:

> ...We find that the chance that any man might have lived down to the present time and fulfilled all eight prophecies is 1 in [100,000,000,000,000,000].[3]

This statistic is staggering, but unless you're a mathematician or scientist, it's difficult to comprehend. Stoner illustrates with a clever example, which I'll paraphrase. If it were possible for us to obtain 100,000,000,000,000,000 silver dollars, we would have a problem: how to store them. There is no warehouse or building large enough in the entire world. The volume would be so enormous the coins would cover the entire state of Texas two feet deep. That's a massive amount of coins.

Suppose we did manage to obtain these coins. Let's now mark one of these silver dollars, then shuffle the entire load and redistribute them over the state of Texas. Now blindfold a man, put him in a helicopter, and fly him over the state, waiting for him to give the order to set down. Once on the ground, he can get out of the helicopter, still blindfolded, and pick out one coin. The chance of him picking the one marked coin in the entire state of Texas is the same chance that any one man, from the time of the prophets to modern times, would fulfill the eight Messianic prophecies.

Stoner wrote:

> This means that the fulfillment of these eight prophecies alone proves that God inspired the writing of those prophecies to a definiteness which lacks only one chance in [100,000,000,000,000,000] of being absolute.[4]

It's staggering to ponder these odds. However, Stoner doesn't stop with the initial eight prophecies. He branches out to consider eight more Old Testament prophecies (sixteen total) foretelling Jesus's life. He states:

The chance that one man would fulfill all sixteen is…1 in 10^{45}.[5]

What is this number? It would be a 1 with 45 zeroes following it. Or:

1,000,000,000,000,000,000,000,000,000,000,000,000,000,000,000

Stoner illustrates this probability, and again I'll paraphrase. If we were to take this number of silver dollars, the earth would be too small to store them. We would have to combine them into a solid ball. This ball or sphere would have a diameter sixty times greater than the distance from the earth to the sun—that's 5.5 billion miles!

Allow me to help you understand how big this sphere would be. I frequently fly to other countries to teach the Word of God. Amazingly, we can now fly nonstop to the other side of our planet in just twenty-four hours. The apostles would have loved our day! However, if we wanted to fly around our sphere of silver dollars in a jet airplane, we couldn't do it, because no known person in our era has lived long enough. It would take over four hundred years to fly non-stop around this globe of silver dollars! If we began our flight the day the Pilgrims landed in Plymouth, Massachusetts, in 1620 AD, we would still not be finished circling this globe of silver dollars.

We must also keep in mind that this is not like the previous example— silver dollars covering the state of Texas two feet deep. No, this entire globe is composed of the silver dollars.

Imagine marking one of these silver dollars and thoroughly stirring it into this massive globe, then blindfolding a man and telling him to pick out any one dollar. Would you expect it to be the marked one? Now you have an idea of the chance of one person fulfilling just sixteen of the prophecies written about Jesus hundreds of years before His birth.

But there's more! Once again, Stoner did not stop at sixteen fulfilled prophecies but branched out to forty-eight prophecies. It's really beyond staggering, but try to comprehend what he wrote next:

> In order to extend this consideration beyond all bounds of human comprehension, let us consider forty-eight prophecies, similar in their human chance of fulfillment to the eight which we originally considered, using a much more conservative number… Applying the same principle of probability used so far, we find the chance that any one man fulfilled all forty-eight prophecies to be 1 in 10^{157}.[6]

That's the number 1 with 157 zeroes behind it. It would be a waste of space for me to write that number out. Stoner once again helped us to comprehend such a number with another illustration. This time the silver dollar is entirely too large. We have to turn to a smaller object.

The electron is about as small an object as we know of. Electrons are so small that if we laid them side by side on a one inch line, it would take over nineteen million years to count them at the rate of 250 per minute. That's very tiny. Don't forget, this is a single line just one inch long. I don't want to overwhelm you with the time it would take to count one square inch, and certainly not one cubic inch, of electrons. It's inconceivably longer.

With this in mind, let's ask how big a ball containing 10^{157} electrons would be. To keep it simple, it would be a ball with a radius bigger than the distance to the farthest point humankind has seen in outer space, which is thirteen billion light-years away. (A light-year is how far light travels in one year at a speed of 186,282 miles per second—not per hour.) If we had a ball of electrons whose radius was thirteen billion light years, we still wouldn't have 10^{157} electrons. In fact, we would be far from it.

The probability of a man being blindfolded, then released into that globe of electrons, and picking out the correct, marked electron is the same chance that any one man in history could have fulfilled just forty-eight of the prophecies about the Christ written by the various writers of the Old Testament.

Would you like me to expand our discussion to the over three hundred total prophecies? You're probably thinking, *Please, no!* I hope you're thinking this, because it's virtually impossible to illustrate in a way that our finite minds can grasp.

So let me summarize. We have over three hundred prophecies penned by different men, in different languages, from various countries, written over hundreds of years, and all fulfilled in one Man! How could anyone deny that the true Author of Scripture is God Himself? Do these words from His lips take on greater meaning?

Every word of God proves true. (Proverbs 30:5 NLT)

He is the One who declares, "I am alert and active, watching over My word to perform it" (Jeremiah 1:12 AMP). For this very reason, "there has not failed one word of all His good promise" (1 Kings 8:56).

God's Word is more reliable than the sun that rises each morning, which Jesus affirms by stating, "Heaven and earth will pass away, but My words will by no means pass away" (Matthew 24:35). Our Creator has left His undeniable fingerprints for us to know that He is God and His will is revealed in Scripture.

Carefully Heed

To reiterate the apostle Paul's words in 2 Timothy 3:16, "All Scripture is inspired by God…and teaches us to do what is right [good]." This isn't a complex idea; in fact it's quite simple. Scripture is God's Word and can be trusted as the universal standard for evaluating and determining what is truly good. If you think your own wisdom, or a friend's, an expert's, or society's, is more beneficial than God's wisdom, please reconsider. For Scripture declares:

God looks down from heaven on the entire human race; he looks to
see if anyone is truly wise, if anyone seeks God. But no, all have turned
away; all have become corrupt. No one does *good*, not a single one!
(Psalm 53:2–3 NLT)

As we've discussed in this chapter, God has provided undeniable evidence of the validity of Scripture. In these verses the psalmist emphasizes
how any wisdom contrary to God's Word, even if it appears good, is actually
corrupt and detrimental to our well-being.

Let's examine the words surrounding Paul's declaration to Timothy:

You must remain faithful to the things you have been taught. You know
they are *true*… You have been taught the holy Scriptures from childhood… All Scripture is inspired by God and is useful to teach us what
is *true* and to make us realize what is wrong in our lives. It corrects us
when we are wrong and teaches us to do what is right. God uses it to
prepare and equip his people… (2 Timothy 3:14–17 NLT)

We must remain faithful to the things we've been taught. Paul is not
referring to men's opinions, psychology, sociology, or any other wisdom con-
trived by this world's system; he's referring to the Scriptures. The apostle
urges his spiritual son to remain faithful to them. He stresses the importance
of keeping them in the forefront of his heart. What a different world we
would live in if Adam and Eve had done just this.

Consider this hypothetical scenario. You're facing a journey that requires
you to hike across a massive landmine field. Not only are there hidden explo-
sive devices, but there are also quicksand pits, deadly traps, poisonous plants,
and sinkholes.

Before you begin, you're handed a map that reveals the location of every
landmine and sinkhole, as well as clues to look for in avoiding traps, quicksand, and poisonous plants. How would you handle this map? Would you

stuff it in your backpack with your energy bars and water bottle, but due to the challenges of your trip neglect reading it? Would you consult it only when the opportunity presented itself? Would you view it as casual reading? Would you look it over at the start and then pack it away, confident you could remember all the information? Would any of these actions describe your behavior? If so, you would probably leave the field severely wounded or in a body bag.

Permit me to state the obvious. A wise person would carefully read the map, study it, ponder the information, and then pack it in such a way as to easily access it. He'd frequently refer to it on his journey, cautiously choosing his route according to what he learned. If you were faced with such a journey, wouldn't you do the same?

The fact is, we all face such a journey every day, and our map is the Bible. With this truth in mind, listen to God's counsel in Scripture. I will list a few key verses. Please don't skim them but vigilantly read each word. They are meant to both encourage and warn us about how to handle the "Scripture map" during our journey across the deadly landmine field of this world. As you read, notice in particular the words *careful* or *carefully*.

"You must be *careful* to obey all the commands of the LORD your God, following his instructions in every detail." (Deuteronomy 5:32 NLT)

Not *some*, but *all* of God's commands. We are to heed and follow every detail of His instructions. He deeply loves us and doesn't want us seriously injured or killed on our journey. Again:

Listen closely…and be *careful* to obey. Then all will go well with you… (Deuteronomy 6:3 NLT)

When we both listen and carefully obey, then all goes well for us. God Himself guarantees this promise! We see the same instructions in Deuteronomy 8:1; 12:28, 32; and 28:13. If you look them up, you'll discover that if we heed God's commands, we will enjoy full lives, our labor will multiply in effectiveness, and in society we will always be on top, never beneath or behind. Are you grasping how important it is to carefully read, listen to, and obey His words?

You may counter, "But John, these instructions were given under the law; these are Old Testament requirements. We are under the new covenant of grace. Didn't Jesus free us from this tedious bondage?" Jesus did liberate us from the law, but not from the continuing admonition to carefully heed God's Word; it remains crucial for us. Listen to these New Testament instructions:

> Moses said, "The LORD your God will raise up for you a Prophet [Jesus] like me from among your own people. Listen *carefully* to everything he tells you." (Acts 3:22 NLT)

Once again we are instructed to listen *carefully* to everything—not most things—Jesus tells us. Listen to the apostle James:

> But if you look *carefully* into the perfect law that sets you free, and if you do what it says and don't forget what you heard, then God will bless you for doing it. (James 1:25 NLT)

Additionally, we are instructed:

> Through the power of the Holy Spirit who lives within us, *carefully* guard the precious truth that has been entrusted to you. (2 Timothy 1:14 NLT)

> So we must listen very *carefully* to the truth we have heard, or we may drift away from it. (Hebrews 2:1 NLT)

Drifting in life normally doesn't happen by a conscious choice, but rather it happens unknowingly. When I was a boy fishing on the lake, sometimes my eagerness to get started caused me to not anchor the boat before I began. I'd get busy fishing and look up thirty minutes later and not recognize the shoreline. I had drifted inadvertently.

We drift from truth when we don't pay it careful attention. It occurs when we've not read, listened to, pondered, and obeyed Scripture. What we don't keep in focus before us eventually fades. We then easily drift, and God's will is replaced by the influence of people around us and the voices of society. We then embrace what seems good according to our own swayed evaluation.

In the previous chapter we established an important truth: there is nothing good for us outside the will of God. Do you agree God's will is revealed in Scripture? If so, it's time to construct our foundation.

4

THE FOUNDATION

The godly have a lasting foundation.
—PROVERBS 10:25 NLT

If you believe in the Gospel what you like,
and reject what you don't like, it is not
the Gospel you believe, but yourself.
—ST. AUGUSTINE OF HIPPO

et me restate the three facets of this book's message: the first speaks to our foundation, the second addresses what holds our lives together, and the third represents the building of our lives. These aspects will be the focus of our discussions for the remainder of this book.

The foundation is critically important to a correct relationship with God. If you're a longtime believer, I strongly suggest not skipping over the concise discussion that follows. It'll be beneficial not only to shore up your groundwork, but also to help those you lead or influence into a relationship with our Creator.

We are told:

The Scriptures say, "No one is righteous—not even one. No one is truly wise...all have turned away; all have become useless. *No one does good, not a single one.*" (Romans 3:10–12 NLT)

No one does good, not a single one. Other than Jesus Christ, there is not one human being who has ever lived or ever will live who consistently did or does good according to God's evaluation. The reason for this: every human being was born a slave. Yes, you were born a slave, and so was I. "A slave of what?" you may ask. Sin. Paul writes to those who've been freed, "Once you were slaves of sin" (Romans 6:17 NLT).

Adam and Eve died the moment they disobeyed God. God warned of this fate before they ate the forbidden fruit. However, it was years before either experienced physical death.

This brings up the question, how did Adam and Eve die the day they ate the fruit? Death occurred in their core nature—their spirit. They were separated from God, the Giver of life, and now had inherent attributes contrary to His. Consequently, their descendants would be born with these same innate qualities, which would be passed on from generation to generation to this day. Genesis 5:3 confirms this reality: "When Adam was 130 years old, he had a son who was just like him, his very spirit and image" (The Message).

Humankind was now incapable of truly knowing or practicing good; their internal moral compass had been compromised. Consequently, only the influence of God on the earth would steer human beings toward what is truly good and right, for man was now governed by sin. Without divine guidance, good and evil were distorted. The new lord and chief influencer of humanity was now he who had possessed the serpent—Satan, the king of disobedience.

The earth had been given to humankind by God. He had put them in charge of it, but they had delivered their authority to Satan. Thousands of years later, the devil took Jesus to a high mountain, pointed out the world, and boldly stated, "All this authority I will give You, and their glory; for *this* has been delivered to me, and I give it to whomever I wish" (Luke 4:6). Satan was able to say such a thing because this rulership had been delivered to him in the garden.

God couldn't come to the earth in the form of deity to rescue us because the earth had been given to humans. Humankind had relinquished authority; only a human being could take it back. God came up with a plan long before Adam's transgression, as He foresaw Adam's choice before time began. He strategized to come as a Man and purchase back humanity's freedom from slavery. God sent His Son, Jesus Christ—born of a woman, which made Him 100 percent man, but conceived by the Holy Spirit of God, making Him 100 percent God. Therefore, Jesus was free from the curse of slavery you and I were born under.

Jesus lived a perfect life on earth. He never committed one disobedient act. As the only innocent human being who has ever lived, He gave His life for the freedom of humankind. On the cross He took the judgment of every man and woman who'd already lived, was living, or would live in the future. He shed His royal blood as the payment to liberate us from slavery.

He died and was buried. Since He had lived a perfect life before God, the Spirit of God raised Him from the dead three days later. He is now seated at the right hand of God Almighty, who has made this decree:

> If you confess with your mouth the Lord Jesus and believe in your
> heart that God has raised Him from the dead, you will be saved. For
> with the heart one believes unto righteousness, and with the mouth
> confession is made unto salvation. (Romans 10:9–10)

The moment we receive Jesus Christ as our Lord, an amazing miracle occurs. Our nature of sin and death instantly passes away, and a brand-new person is born, created in the very image of Jesus. This fresh birth pertains to our spirit (our real being), not our physical body. Our physical body is still corrupt and will one day pass away. New life comes entirely through the gift of God's grace and is in no way attached to any good behavior or merited by any works we've done. Period.

It's important to point out that the scripture from Romans quoted above states you must confess the *Lord* Jesus, not the *Savior* Jesus. Herein lies a fundamental flaw prevalent in the Western church. The word *lord* is the Greek word *kurios*, which means "master, owner, supreme in authority."

To confess Jesus as merely Savior doesn't bring freedom or new life. I realize this is a strong statement that cuts against the grain of our accepted appeals to the lost, but it is true to Scripture.

The word *savior* is found 36 times in the Bible. The word *lord* occurs over 7,800 times. Where do you think God places the emphasis? *Lord* declares the *position* He holds in our life, whereas *Savior* describes the *work* He's done for us. We cannot partake of the benefit of His *work* unless we come under His *position* as Lord and King.

We were born slaves. Simply put, sin owned us. However, we have been created with a free will; therefore we must make a firm decision and declaration that we're changing masters. Salvation has been provided for every human being, but as individuals, we have to choose to accept it under God's terms.

The Island Prison Camp

I'll use a fictional story to explain this truth.

On a certain island, your entire family is in the prison camp of an evil lord. This land had originally been given to your grandfather by a very good king from a distant country. However, your grandfather made a huge mistake; he didn't guard it. This evil lord and his gang of rebels came by stealth and took over the island, making your grandfather and all his descendants slaves. The evil lord and his cohorts then built prison camps and put your entire family behind bars.

The way of life on the island, which progressively took on the nature of the evil lord and his cronies, decayed to total corruption and debauchery. Consequently, the good king condemned the island. However, due to the love the king has for your family, before annihilating the island, he came and fought against the evil lord's army and defeated them.

The king then threw open every prison door and declared, "All prisoners are now free. Any of you can walk out of the prison camps *if* you renounce the evil lord's rule and give your allegiance to me."

Due to the king's kindness, your family's longed-for liberty has come.

However, the good king will not force you to follow him. Each prisoner has to make the move. (If the king required it, rather than giving each person a choice, it would simply be another form of tyranny.) If you decide to embrace liberty, that choice requires that you walk out of your cell, follow the king to his ship, sail back to his country, become one of his subjects, and live by the laws of his great country. The opportunity is put before you, but you must agree to his terms.

The good king is viewed as the *savior* of your family. However, to benefit from his saving work, each family member has to agree to submit wholeheartedly to him, which includes submitting to the laws of his reign. *Not one of the prisoners in your family can merely accept the king's salvation from the island yet not submit to his lordship.*

If you choose not to follow the good monarch, you'll simply stay where you are. However, the king's battleships are stationed just off the shore, ready to bomb and annihilate the condemned island once he leaves. Those in your family who choose not to come under the *lordship* of the good king will suffer the same fate as the evil lord and his gang, even though the king battled to free all of you and threw open the prison doors.

Hear me, dear reader. God never created hell for you or any other human being. He created it for Satan and his angelic troops. Jesus will say on Judgment Day to those who did not give themselves to His sovereignty:

"Depart from Me, you cursed, into the everlasting fire *prepared for the devil and his angels.*" (Matthew 25:41)

Hell is a very real place. Jesus spoke more frequently of it than of heaven. He didn't see mentioning its description—the torment involved, as well as the fact that it was never-ending—as a lack of compassion. It's the eternal home of the dead who reject His loving rule.

According to Jesus this place of punishment and excruciating anguish wasn't prepared for human beings, but sadly, by his disobedience, our father Adam included us in condemning judgment. Now Satan's fate is our fate unless we change lords. Even though Jesus rescued all humankind from God's wrath, many will be judged with Satan, for they will still possess his nature. In essence they chose to stay on the island.

You may ask, "Why couldn't God just be merciful and allow people into His kingdom just as they are?" Those who don't give themselves to the ownership of Jesus still possess a spiritual nature that is corrupt and evil. Once they leave this earth, that nature is theirs forever. If permitted into the everlasting kingdom of God, they would pollute and bring harm to many innocent people

It was for this very reason God sent Adam and Eve away from the tree of life in the garden:

> Then the LORD God said, "Look, the human beings have become like us, knowing both good and evil. What if they reach out, take fruit from the tree of life, and eat it? Then they will live forever!" So the LORD God banished them from the Garden of Eden... (Genesis 3:22–23 NLT)

God's love protected us from maintaining a dead nature permanently.

Lordship

Because the Western church has emphasized the work Jesus did for us as Savior rather than His position as Lord, lack of submission to His position of authority creates a significant fault in our foundation. Hear Paul's words:

> As you accepted Christ Jesus *as your Lord*, you must continue to follow him. Let your roots grow down into him, and *let your lives be built on him.* (Colossians 2:6–7 NLT)

Paul doesn't state, "As you accepted Christ Jesus as your *Savior.*" Our lives must be submitted to and built upon His position of lordship, not upon His work as Savior. Another way of saying this is that we submit to Him as our supreme and only King, and then we benefit from His salvation. This plays out practically by our firm adherence to His Word, wisdom, counsel, directives, correction, and instruction whether we see the reason for it or not. We no longer feed from the tree of our own evaluation of what is right or wrong. We live in Him; His life becomes ours.

Consider this. Over the three decades of my marriage to Lisa, I've received the benefit of living with a great chef. Lisa is magnificent at creating gourmet meals. I've had friends who have asked Lisa if she'd teach their wives how to make pesto sauces, salad dressings, and other savory delights.

I have sometimes referred to Lisa as my "little gourmet chef." I may have called her this a dozen or so times throughout our marriage, but more properly, in the past thirty years I've referred to her thousands of times as my wife. Why? Because that declares the *position* she holds in my life. The other title conveys a *benefit* I've received from her being my wife.

Just because Lisa cooks for me doesn't mean I belong to her. When I was single, on one of my birthdays, she made me an amazing meal. That didn't give us a lasting relationship. It was the covenant I made to forsake all other girls and give my heart solely to her as husband that solidified our marriage relationship.

Our relationship with Jesus is similar to this. In order to receive His work of salvation, we must submit to His lordship, ownership, and reign. We give our lives completely because we are confident of His perfect leadership, character, and love and that He knows what's best. Though He intensely desires our freedom and loves us perfectly, He is the King of all kings and Lord of all lords and will not come into our lives as second to anything or anyone else.

Countless times in churches in America and other Western countries, I've witnessed ministers offer salvation to seekers without mentioning lordship. "All you have to do is confess Jesus as Savior and you'll be a child of God," the ministers have said. Or, "Why don't you make Jesus your Savior today?" Or, "Let's just all pray this prayer: Jesus, come into my heart and save me today. Thank You for making me a child of God. Amen." All their calls to join the family of God are offered without a single word about forsaking the world's system and one's own independent ways in order to follow Him.

This message seems good and correlates with isolated scriptures in the New Testament. However, does it line up with the overall instruction of the New Testament? Is it God's wisdom? Or have we abbreviated and edited the true salvation message to come up with one that sounds good and appeals to the desires of seekers? Are we feeding from the tree of our own evaluation?

Deny Yourself

Let's look at the Master's message. Jesus made it clear to the multitudes:

> "Whoever desires to come after Me, let him deny himself, and take up his cross, and follow Me. For whoever *desires* to save his life will lose it, but whoever loses his life for My sake and the gospel's will save it." (Mark 8:34–35)

We must deny ourselves if we are to follow Him. Period. What does this mean? Simply put, you cannot serve two masters, for you can only be loyal to one if each calls for a different action or response. When our flesh, which is still unredeemed, desires one thing and the Word of God directs us a different way, if we have not already chosen to follow Jesus as our supreme Master, then we can easily choose our independent way while still looking to and confessing Him as our Savior. Is it possible we are misled and embracing this belief?

Perhaps this is why Jesus said, "So why do you keep calling me 'Lord, Lord!' when you don't do what I say?" (Luke 6:46 NLT). In other words, *Lord* becomes an empty, meaningless title. If we really don't mean it when we say "Lord," Jesus would rather us call Him "great Teacher." At least then we can benefit from His teachings and not be deceived in thinking we belong to Him when in fact we may not.

According to Mark 8:34–35 and many other scriptures in the New Testament, the denying of our self is not optional in regard to following Him "off the island" of this condemned world. It's mandatory in order to be saved from the wrath to come. I've discovered this is a difficult concept for westerners to grasp. I believe the reason for this is that we are a people trying to understand *kingdom principles* with a *democratic mindset*. Democracy has worked in America and other Western countries, but if we try to relate to God with a democratic mindset, we will not connect. He's a king—a real King, not a figurehead monarch like the one in England.

Democracy is defined as "government by the people; a form of government in which the supreme power is vested in the people and exercised directly by them or by their elected agents." This is the mentality we are raised with in America and other Western countries. It's programmed into our core thinking and reasoning. Subsequently, if we don't like something, we believe we can challenge or change it because we have "inalienable" personal rights and freedom of speech to express our views.

Let me reemphasize. This form of government has been successful for the United States because it's a system designed for mortal people living in a pluralistic society. But these ideas don't carry over to the kingdom of God. It may make us westerners wince, but God is a dictator—thankfully, He's a benevolent One, but He has the final say in all aspects of life. If we carry our democratic mindset into our walk with God, we'll have nothing more than a make-believe relationship.

Life is different under a true Monarch. *Lord* and *king* are synonymous in the aspect of carrying the meaning of *supreme in authority*. If we are going to truly follow God, we simply cannot use democratic reasoning in the way we respond to His leadership. It's no different than when Eve and Adam chose the tree of the knowledge of good and evil. We human beings are still in the driver's seat and decide what we think is best for our lives.

Take Up Your Cross

Next Jesus declared that we should take up our cross. What does this imply? It can't mean to *deny our self,* for why would Jesus repeat Himself unnecessarily? We find the key in Paul's letter to the Galatians, where he states:

> I have been *crucified* with Christ; it is no longer I who live, but Christ lives in me; and the life which I now live in the flesh I live by faith in the Son of God, who loved me and gave Himself for me. (Galatians 2:20)

Paul was not speaking of a physical crucifixion, for he wouldn't have been alive to write this letter. He's referring to his decision to follow the Master years earlier. Paul had taken up his cross. The secret of what this had entailed is found in his words "it is no longer I who live, but Christ lives in me." This should be the declaration of every true child of God. No longer are we independent, feeding from the tree of our evaluation of what is good and evil. No, we now live in Him, our very life drawn from Him. We depend on the provision of the cross: freedom from slavery so we can now live an obedient life empowered by God.

The cross offers a completely new way of life. As Paul declares in a different letter, "As Christ was raised from the dead by the glory of the Father, even so we also should walk in *newness of life*" (Romans 6:4). This newness of life gives us the ability to walk away from what we previously couldn't. Sin's tyranny over us is broken, but we must choose to live it out. We elect to give ourselves completely to His will.

Paul continues to spell this out practically: "Those *who are* Christ's have *crucified* the flesh with its passions and desires" (Galatians 5:24). And again, "God forbid that I should boast except in the cross of our Lord Jesus Christ, by whom the world has been *crucified* to me, and I to the world" (Galatians 6:14). The cross empowers us to walk free from sinful flesh and the strong influences of the world's system.

As a young man, before I met Jesus, there were behavioral patterns in my life I couldn't put aside. I regretted my recurring hurtful, prideful, and lustful behavior, but the more I tried to free myself, the more frustrated I became. I was hopelessly bound and subject to sin's domination. However, once I was crucified with Christ I could begin to live free.

> We know that our old sinful selves were crucified with Christ so that sin might lose its power in our lives. We are no longer slaves to sin. For when we died with Christ we were set free from the power of sin. (Romans 6:6–7 NLT)

I hope you are not skimming over this! Drink the words in deeply, for they're very real and hold the power to your freedom. The truth gets even more exciting. Embracing the cross does more than just free us from sin; it enables us to live obedient to Him. We are told, "The message of the cross is foolish to those who are headed for destruction! But we who are being saved know it is the very power of God" (1 Corinthians 1:18 NLT). What was previously impossible to do in our own ability, we can now do: walk in His ways. We can now imitate God. We can now follow Jesus.

To sum it up, it's impossible to follow Jesus without denying our self (forsaking our own ways and embracing His supreme authority) and taking up the cross (incorporating its empowerment to walk away from sin and the world's system). The life we now live is by faith in His ability working in and through us. We draw from Him. What a glorious package of salvation God has provided for us!

A Solemn Warning

Jesus warned that after His departure a gospel would be proclaimed and widely accepted that would offer salvation apart from lordship. The apostles were more specific and stated it would take place closer to the time of Jesus's return—that is, in our day. This widespread and heretical message would reduce *Lord* to merely a title rather than a position Jesus holds in people's lives. People will call Him Lord but not deny themselves, take up their cross, and follow Him. Read carefully Jesus's words:

> "Not everyone who says to Me, 'Lord, Lord,' shall enter the king-
> dom of heaven, but he who does the will of My Father in heaven."
> (Matthew 7:21)

Jesus identified people who would declare *Him* Lord—not Mohammad, Joseph Smith, Buddha, Krishna, Confucius, or any other false prophet of our era. No, these people would call Jesus Christ their Lord and say it with passion.

Why did Jesus use the word *Lord* twice in this verse? We understand that when a word or phrase is repeated in Scripture it is not accidental. The writer is communicating emphasis. However, in cases such as this, the duplication is not just for emphasis but to show intensity of emotion. For example, in the Old Testament, when news reached King David about his son's execution by Joab's army, his response was intensely emotional: "But the king covered his face, and the king *cried out with a loud voice*, 'O my son Absalom! O Absalom, my son, my son!'" (2 Samuel 19:4) I don't think David actually said "my son" twice. Rather the writer repeated the words twice so that the reader would understand just how highly charged David's cry of grief was.

The same pattern appears in the book of Revelation: "I heard an angel flying through the midst of heaven, saying with a loud voice, 'Woe, woe, woe to the inhabitants of the earth'" (Revelation 8:13). Other translations state the angel was "crying with a loud voice." Again, the writer repeats the word *woe* to emphasize a great intensity of emotion.

In the same way, the Master is communicating these people's strong sentiments for Him. They are not merely in agreement with the teaching that Jesus Christ is the Son of God; they are emotionally invested and passionate in their belief. We are talking about people who are excited to be Christians, most likely those who are emotional when speaking of their faith and weep during a worship service.

Not only do they feel deeply for the cause of Christ, but they are also involved in His service:

> "I can see it now—at the Final Judgment thousands strutting up to me
> and saying, 'Master, we preached the Message, we bashed the demons,
> our God-sponsored projects had everyone talking.'" (Matthew 7:22
> The Message)

I use *The Message* Bible here because it best conveys the fact that these people weren't sideliners. They were directly involved in or supported the work of their churches. They were also outspoken in their belief of the gospel: "We preached the Message." They were a part of changing people's lives for the better.

This paraphrased Bible version uses the word *thousands*. However, most translations use the word *many*. The Greek word is *polus*, defined as "much of number, quantity, amount."[7] Often the word is used in the sense of "mostly." In any case, Jesus is not referring to a small group of people but a vast group—in fact, quite possibly a majority of the overall number.

So let's summarize: Jesus is speaking of people who believe in the teachings of the Gospels. They call Him Lord, are emotionally invested, give voice to the message, and are active in Christian service. We would easily identify them as true Christians. So what's the separating factor? How do they differ from authentic believers? Jesus tells us:

> "And then I will declare to them, 'I never knew you; depart from Me,
> you who practice lawlessness!'" (Matthew 7:23).

The key statement is "practice lawlessness," which is the Greek word *anomia*. Thayer's *Greek-English Lexicon of the New Testament* defines it as the condition of being without law, because of ignorance of it or because of violating it. The *Encyclopedia of Bible Words* adds insight by stating that *anomia* can reflect "actions that are…in active violation of either divine or innate moral principles." Simply put, one who is lawless doesn't adhere to the authority of God's Word.

These men and women don't *periodically* stumble; rather, they habitually ignore, neglect, or disobey God's Word. If truly saved by grace, they'd not only despise the thought of sinning but also choose to walk away from repetitive sin. They'd crucify their flesh with its passions and desires and pursue godly character and fruitfulness.

It is interesting to note that Jesus will someday declare to them, "I never knew you." The word *knew* is the Greek word *ginosko*, which means "to intimately know." These people never had a true relationship with Jesus. Even though they call Him Master and Lord, it's only a title, for they didn't do what He said. The evidence that someone truly has a relationship with Him is that they keep His Word:

> When we obey God, we are sure that we know him. But if we claim to know him and don't obey him, we are lying and the truth isn't in our hearts. (1 John 2:3–4 CEV)

This is also James's implication when he writes, "Show me how anyone can have faith without actions. I will show you my faith by my actions" (James 2:18 TEV). And these statements also perfectly line up with the way Jesus began this entire discourse: "You can identify people by their actions" (Matthew 7:20 NLT). The actions Jesus speaks of are not Christian service, speaking the message, or attending church, for those who are turned away from heaven will have these qualities.

Tim Keller addressed these words of Jesus when he said:

> Now this is saying something very incisive. These people have an intellectually stimulating faith and they have an emotionally gratifying faith and they have a socially redemptive faith. We all want that.

We want to be intellectually stimulated, we want to be emotionally involved, and we want to be socially useful. It's possible to want intellectual stimulation, to want emotional gratification, and to want social usefulness and not want God...because if you really have God in your life, you have to give up your own will, and that shows us the difference between someone who is actually trying to use God and trying to serve God.[8]

To use God is to seek Him for what we can get out of Him, even if it's only to make it to heaven. To serve God is to be motivated entirely by our love for Him, and if we love Him, we will keep His words.

Today, most would consider a person who calls Jesus Lord, believes in His teachings, is emotionally involved, and is active in Christian service to be a child of God. Yet we've clearly seen from the words of Jesus that these qualities are not the deciding factors in identifying a true believer.

Let me say it like this. You will certainly find these qualities in a true believer; in fact, a person cannot be a true believer without them. However, possessing these qualities doesn't mean someone is a genuine child of God. The deciding factor is this: have they denied themselves and taken up their cross, and are they following Him? In essence, *are they obedient to His words?*

This discussion was Jesus's closing subject in His famous Sermon on the Mount. To put a cap on His startling words, He concluded with:

"Therefore whoever hears these sayings of Mine, and does them, I will liken him to a wise man who built his house on the rock: and the rain descended, the floods came, and the winds blew and beat on that house; and it did not fall, for it was founded on the rock. But everyone who hears these sayings of Mine, and does not do them, will be like a foolish man who built his house on the sand: and the rain descended, the floods came, and the winds blew and beat on that house; and it fell. And great was its fall." (Matthew 7:24–27)

This parable relates to His warning about the many who will be denied entrance into heaven, for He connects them by saying "therefore."

If you examine the two groups of people identified in this parable, it all comes down to one slight difference. Both hear His words, but the first group "does them." The second group "does not do them." Both houses are made of the same material—the same teachings. They both look identical in worship and service. The critical difference is the foundation. One house was founded on the lordship of Jesus Christ. The other remained attached to an evaluation of what was determined to be *good* and *evil*—the same "tree" of philosophy Adam and Eve turned to.

It's sobering to think that the same folly still repeats itself, from the garden to the present day. It takes on a different form, but it's the same root. Again, it comes down to this: *do we think we know best about how to live, or do we believe that God knows what's best?*

5

IS DESIRE ENOUGH?

So now finish doing it, that your
[enthusiastic] readiness in desiring it may
be equaled by your completion of it...
—2 Corinthians 8:11 AMP

The golden rule for understanding spiritually
is not intellect, but obedience.
—Oswald Chambers

Consider this: A young man is dating a young woman. She's attractive, healthy, organized, a gourmet cook, great with children, and—best of all—has a delightful personality. He's in love and decides she's the one he'd like to spend the rest of his life with. He creates a special moment, kneels down on one knee, opens a small box to reveal a sparkling diamond ring, and proposes to her.

Much to the man's delight, the young woman breaks out in a huge smile, lets out a shriek of joy, bursts into tears, and after gaining a little composure excitedly responds, "Yes! Yes! Yes! I can't believe this! I'm shocked and overwhelmed. This is the happiest day of my life! I love you so much! Yes, I'll marry you!"

They embrace each other in sheer bliss. With emotions still running high, she looks into his eyes and passionately promises, "We will have such a great life. I'll be the best wife, create a beautiful home, keep it spotless, make delicious meals for you and the kids, stay healthy, dress fashionably, and make beautiful love to you anytime you desire."

The young man thinks, *Wow! Amazing! I have to be the most fortunate guy alive.*

She then makes one more attention-grabbing statement, "Of course there are other boys I still like, so I may date them periodically."

Stunned, the young man stammers, "That's not going to work!"

"Why not, honey?"

He's dumbfounded. The special moment is ruined. The ecstasy is gone. His mind is racing. *Could she be joking? But why joke about something like this, especially after I've just proposed?*

After an awkward silence, which seems like an eternity, she tries to re-capture the mood by enthusiastically offering a compromise. "Okay, how about if I just spend one day a year with my other boyfriends? I'll give myself exclusively to you for 364 days a year. Just give me one day with them."

The young man can't believe what he's hearing. It's now obvious she's not pulling his leg; she's serious. So he again replies, "No, that doesn't work either."

She's puzzled, but because she loves him so much, she offers an even bet-ter deal. "Okay, what about four hours a year? Just give me four hours every calendar year to spend with my other boyfriends."

"No!" the young man says, even more firmly this time.

Again, she counters, "How about twenty minutes a year? Just one good fling in bed with another boyfriend!"

"No!"

In hopes of bringing resolution, she pleads, "Honey, I do love you; in fact, I'm crazy about you. I love you more than any other man. But I have this need. I just have to be with other guys. I simply can't be a one-man woman. I sincerely *desire* to be loyal to you, and I know it's the proper thing to walk away from all other relationships, but let's be real. There are so many great guys, and I love their attention. Why should I have to give this up? Why can't I have both?"

The young man is so disappointed that this time he doesn't answer; he just hangs his head. After a few more awkward moments, she softly states, "I just have to be honest; I think you're asking too much. I want to enjoy a full life."

The young man's heard enough. "This is preposterous. We're not getting married. In fact, I'm through dating you."

They go their separate ways.

Let's think this through. This young man's getting a gorgeous woman with a great personality. She's superb in all aspects of domestic life, loves him, is willing to serve, and wants to give her best to him. She's ecstatic to marry him. All of this adds up nicely. All he needs to do is give her twenty minutes a year with another guy! Why isn't he agreeing to her terms?

Of course the answer is obvious: she isn't giving him her entire heart and life. She knows it would be the right thing to do, and on some level desires it; but the reality is that she's too attached to other guys. It's one thing to *desire*; it's another thing to actually *do*.

No healthy man would ever marry a girl like this, so why would we believe Jesus is coming for a bride who acts the same way? Let's again look at His words:

> "Whoever desires to come after Me, let him deny himself, and take up
> his cross, and follow Me. For whoever *desires* to save his life will lose
> it, but whoever loses his life for My sake and the gospel's will save it."
> (Mark 8:34–35)

Notice that just *desiring* to save our lives will cost us everything. Jesus didn't say, "Whoever *desires* to lose his life for My sake will save it." Just *desiring* to lose your life isn't enough. It's no different than the girl in the proposal story.

To enter a covenant relationship with the most wonderful Person in the universe, you have to give yourself fully to Him, which certainly includes all aspects of His leadership. Interestingly, the Bible compares our relationship with God to a woman's relationship with her husband. Paul writes:

As the Scriptures say, "A man leaves his father and mother to get married, and he becomes like one person with his wife." This is a great mystery, but I understand it to mean Christ and his church. (Ephesians 5:31–32 CEV)

Even though Paul used this to instruct a husband and wife in their marriage relationship, he also made clear it's truly written to illustrate our relationship with Jesus. No man would marry a woman who merely has a *desire* to give herself entirely to him but in actuality won't do it. Do you think we can do the same with Jesus? Perhaps this is why James writes:

You adulterers! Don't you realize that friendship with the world makes you an enemy of God? I say it again: If you want to be a friend of the world, you make yourself an enemy of God. (James 4:4 NLT)

Again, he was strongly emphasizing this point, for he stated it twice. This is not a trivial matter; it's a core part of a true relationship with God.

An adulterer is one who has a covenant with one person, yet in violation of the covenant seeks out a relationship with another. This person is not devoted to the binding agreement of the relationship.

The covenant we make to follow Jesus is to deny our self and walk away from the world system that surrounds us. We can do nothing less than give Him our complete allegiance and obedience. This means we embrace His will and desires over our own. In exchange for giving Him our lives, we in turn get His life. This is like a healthy marriage between a man and woman.

I Still Want My Life

There are many who would gladly receive the benefits of salvation if only they could keep their own lives too. Interestingly, most realize there is a forsaking that must be done to follow God, and they're not ready to pay the price. They are being honest with God and themselves.

I once had a neighbor (I'll give him the name Kevin) who was one of these people. He was a WWF wrestler, one of their superstars. He and his family lived three doors down from us. When they first moved into the neighborhood, his wife warned him to stay clear of us. "They're Jesus Freaks," she said.

A couple months later, while suffering an intense panic attack, the lady collapsed, weeping, into Lisa's arms. This incident opened the door for Lisa to share Jesus with her, and the wrestler's wife was gloriously saved. Shortly afterward the couple's two boys gave their lives to Jesus as well.

Our families continued to grow close, and Kevin and I became good friends. We spent a lot of time together. We hung out frequently and often played basketball, street hockey, and golf with our boys.

One evening God showed me some events that would soon occur in Kevin's life. It was late, about 10 p.m., but I felt compelled to talk to him. When he answered the door, I shared the three things that would happen in his life within nine months.

Sure enough, all three came to pass. I thought, *Certainly now Kevin will give his life to Jesus Christ.* But still there was no change.

A few months later God showed me another event that would take place in Kevin's life. I again spoke to him about it. This time I probed further. "Kevin, you've witnessed God foretell three things that have now taken place in your life. You can see He is reaching out to you. Why aren't you giving your life to Jesus?"

Kevin was 6 feet 4 inches tall, weighed 240 pounds, and had only 4 percent body fat. Visually, he was intimidating. He looked down at me and said, "Because I know there is a price to pay. I know that you have to give Jesus your life and submit to Him, and I'm not willing to give up my lifestyle."

He then said, "John, there is a well-known wrestler in our organization. He says he is a born-again Christian, and he's talked about God on the same TV program that you've been interviewed on. Yet I know he's using drugs and is sexually loose. Come on, man, how is he any different than me? I just refuse to be a hypocrite like him. I'd rather enjoy my life in the spotlight of fame and the accompanying perks than put on a facade."

I was devastated by Kevin's report, yet his story is not isolated. There are countless people who attend church, call Jesus their Savior, and declare they are children of God but have not given their lives to His lordship. Are they truly saved?

Is it possible to birth converts in our Christian circles who aren't children of God? Jesus stated to the leaders of His day, "You cross land and sea to make one convert, and then you turn that person into twice the child of hell you yourselves are!" (Matthew 23:15 NLT) I'm not saying our leaders in the Western church are children of hell. However, what I'm asking is, what kind of converts are we spawning?

The consequence of not calling for seekers to lose their lives is converts who have found an improved lifestyle and the promise of an afterlife. Once the familiar "sinner's prayer" is recited, a new convert's conscience is appeased. In theory, he or she is no longer distant from God. Such converts belong to a community of fellow believers and share a common bond. Now on the side of apparent *good*, they are concerned for—and even sometimes participate in caring for—victims of social injustice, the poor, and the needy. Add this to the perks of hearing motivating teachings and the promise of heaven, and you have an attractive package most would want to be a part of.

But are these converts truly saved or are they deceived, thus making it more difficult for them to hear the actual truth? Could this message be what produces the misled followers mentioned in Matthew 7 who will hear Jesus declare, "Depart from Me, I never knew you"?

Is Our Message the Same as His?

Is this the way Jesus reaches out to the lost? Let's return to the story of the wealthy young leader who is commonly referred to as the rich young ruler.

A few years back I was addressing a conference of a couple hundred pastors who oversee some of the largest churches in the United States. I asked this group, "Let's imagine the rich young ruler's approach to Jesus. Can you see him getting out of his Rolls-Royce chariot, wearing an Armani cloak, sporting a Rolex wrist sundial? Several personal assistants follow him as he saunters up to Jesus. With a cool, reserved, slightly arrogant tone, he asks, 'Good Teacher, what must I do to be saved?'

"Do you think that's how the scene might look today?" I asked the pastors. Sadly, the majority of them raised their hands in agreement.

"That's not the way Scripture reports it happening!" I said. Then I read how it's actually recorded:

> Now as He was going out on the road, one came *running, knelt before Him*, and asked Him, "Good Teacher, what shall I do that I may inherit eternal life?" (Mark 10:17)

In front of the crowds of people, this man came *running* after Jesus and *knelt before Him* and pleaded to know what he must do to be saved. No arrogance with this guy.

I thought it best to illustrate how this went down. I asked one of the leaders in the audience to stand on the opposite side of the large platform from me. I then ran at him full speed, and when I was only a few feet away, I slid to my knees, grabbed his shirttail, and loudly and passionately pleaded, "What must I do to be saved? What must I do to inherit eternal life?"

To this day, either in my personal life or in ministry, I've never had any person, rich or poor, chase me down, fall to his knees, and cry out, "What must I do to get born again?" Without a doubt, the young ruler was both passionate and sincere!

So Jesus said to him, "Why do you call Me good? No one is good but One, that is, God" (Mark 10:18).

As I stated earlier, the man hoped to invoke a favorable response by honoring Jesus with the title, "Good Teacher." Yet Jesus would not allow this flattery to blind His discernment. Salvation was not to be "dumbed down" to the rich man's evaluation of good and bad.

On the other hand, this man did have a good measure of integrity. He did not call Jesus Lord or King. He knew that to call Jesus Lord, he would need to do exactly what Jesus asked him to do! How many today possess this much character? They may call Jesus Lord and confess their belief in the Bible. Yet they'll evaluate life choices through their own knowledge of what's good and evil rather than carefully following what the Lord asks of them in Scripture. They smile and say *amen* to biblical teaching, but if it doesn't suit their purposes, they conveniently block it out as if it doesn't apply to their life. They hear but don't apply to themselves what the Spirit says. Many times they feel the message is appropriate for others they deem "worse off" than they are.

Hear how Jesus addressed this man who passionately desired eternal life:

> "You know the commandments: 'Do not commit adultery,' 'Do not murder,' 'Do not steal,' 'Do not bear false witness,' 'Do not defraud,' 'Honor your father and your mother.'"
>
> And he answered and said to Him, "Teacher, all these things I have kept from my youth." (Mark 10:19–20)

Jesus quoted the last six of the Ten Commandments, all of which deal with human relationships. The wealthy man eagerly replied that he had kept all of them his entire life. I believe he had. By these standards we can see he was a good, honest, and upright man. He was leaning on these good character traits, hoping they would be enough to earn him favor with God.

However, Jesus purposely omitted the first four commandments. These deal with a man's relationship with God, the first of them being to have no other gods or idols before Almighty God. In other words, nothing in our lives should come before our affection and love for, and commitment and submission to, Him. This young man had not fulfilled these commandments, nor at that moment was he willing to. Jesus was about to expose something in his life that would eventually keep him from finishing well.

Then Jesus, looking at him, *loved him*, and said to him, "One thing you lack: Go your way, sell whatever you have and give to the poor, and you will have treasure in heaven; and come, take up the cross, and follow Me." (Mark 10:21)

Notice, Jesus loved him! But how did He show His love for the rich young man? He warned this seeker. Jesus knew that inevitably there would come a day when this man's money would sway him from obedience to Jesus's authority (lordship). Jesus was more concerned for him to stay the course, not merely to start well.

For this man the hurdle was his money. For others it could be a girlfriend or boyfriend, sports, shopping, business, philosophy, education, food addiction, or sexual preference. In fact, the stumbling block can be anything we give our affections and strength to more than we do to Jesus.

Did Jesus love the young man by broadening the message to accommodate his other love? Did He ease up the truth in order to not offend him? Why didn't He just have him pray the sinner's prayer, hoping he would forsake his love for money at a later time? After all, he was a prime candidate showing great interest in being saved. All Jesus had to do was draw in the net and He would have had a wealthy, hard-serving, prominent Christian!

But Jesus truly loved this man. He gave him truth—a very strong word—and ran the risk of losing this excited, powerful man. Jesus looked into his eyes and told him he lacked something, and it wasn't passion but the readiness of heart and mind to obey the King of Kings no matter the cost.

I believe this man merely regarded Jesus as Savior, in which case obedience was optional. If by his estimation Jesus's counsel was *good*, he'd heed it. However, if he concluded that Jesus's council was *not good*, he could walk away.

Can you imagine telling an eager seeker they lack something and it will keep them from eternal life? However, if you truly love someone, you must be truthful, even if you know it means rejection.

Many Christians and ministers flatter for fear of being rejected by their listeners. They crave acceptance. Honestly, I used to be like this. Everybody I met liked me because I always told them what they wanted to hear. I hated confrontation and rejection and wanted everyone happy. Then God exposed my insecure, selfish motives. He revealed the focus of my love. It was myself, not the people I spoke to.

It is much better to tell the truth than to compromise truth and have someone believe a lie. It is far better they hear the truth now than that they believe they can keep other idols in their life—and then one day, when it's too late, shockingly hear the Master say, "Depart; I never knew you, you who were deceived!"

Now observe the passionate seeker's response to Jesus's message to him:

> But [the rich young ruler] was *sad* at this word, and went away *sorrow-ful*, for he had great possessions. Then Jesus looked around and said to His disciples, "How hard it is for those who have riches to enter the kingdom of God!" (Mark 10:22–23)

This man who was so eager walked away full of sorrow!

"Oh, Jesus, how could You do that? The man came excited, and after hearing Your talk, he left sad! Don't You know You're supposed to bring a positive message to seekers? Your conversations or speeches should lift people up and make them feel good, not sadden them. Pastor Jesus, Your church's attendance will drop if You keep treating eager men and women like this, especially wealthy and influential ones. Go after him and soften the message; surely he will embrace the whole truth after a while!"

That is what Jesus might hear today from His leadership team or board members in the Western church! Jesus would be called on the carpet and His resignation requested.

How dare He offend this potentially huge giver who with one stroke of the pen could sign a check that would underwrite all the church's outreaches for the year! He could be the one to pay off the several million dollars of building debt. Pastor Jesus just doesn't understand the dynamics of building a big, effective ministry. Maybe He's even forgotten how to positively influence people. He should tone down His talks and teach motivational messages—give uplifting speeches that build self-esteem.

Does this sound like what could happen in the Western church? We've fallen into the trap of doing almost anything to get a convert and create a following. We employ accommodation techniques to build church attendance, gain followers on Twitter, increase our fan base on Facebook, or get people to read our blogs. This is nothing less than communicating to God that our wisdom is sounder than His. Again, it's choosing the *good* over *God*.

It's true: invitations for people to choose Christ are needed—but they must be based on truth. We must realize God never called us to broaden the message of the New Testament, making it easier for people who still want to live independently of His ways to get saved. Salvation is not found in the tree of the knowledge of what we evaluate as good and evil. It is only found in the tree of life, according to His Word. Other lovers and idols must be forsaken, just as the girl who says yes to a marriage proposal must say goodbye to relationships with any other men. Jesus must be received as Lord, not just as Savior. This is the tree of life!

Now observe what Jesus did after this wealthy man walked away:

> Then Jesus looked around and said to His disciples, "How hard it is for those who have riches to enter the kingdom of God!" And the disciples were astonished at His words. But Jesus answered again and said to them, "Children, how hard it is for those who trust in riches to enter the kingdom of God!" (Mark 10:23–24)

One day I was contemplating this event, and the Holy Spirit directed my attention to a significant point. I visualized this wealthy man, respected in his community, slowly walking away from Jesus in sorrow, his head down and a dejected look on his face. I realized that the Master didn't run after him, grab him by the shoulders and say, "Wait a minute, My friend. Let Me remind you of the wisdom of Solomon. He wrote in Proverbs 19:17, 'If you help the poor, you are lending to the Lord—and he will repay you!' (NLT) I told you to sell what you have and give it to the poor; but remember, according to Proverbs, whatever you give to the poor, the Lord will repay you. Not only repay, He'll give you one hundred times as much as you gave away!"

This rich young man was most likely a good businessman. So if Jesus had approached winning him in this way, he might have perked up and responded, "Really?"

Jesus then could have said, "Yes! Can you now see I'm just trying to position you for a huge blessing, a harvest of finances? You will be the wealthiest man in the nation, not just this community." At that point the man would have been more than likely to sign up to follow Jesus.

It is true that the Word of God tells us that when we give it will be given back to us, just as a seed returns back much more to the farmer than what he started with. This truth was confirmed immediately after the man walked away, for Peter—half protesting, half questioning—blurted out:

> "We've given up everything to follow you," he said.
>
> "Yes," Jesus replied, "and I assure you that everyone who has given up house or brothers or sisters or mother or father or children or property, for my sake and for the Good News, will receive now in return a hundred times as many houses, brothers, sisters, mothers, children, and property—along with persecution. And in the world to come that person will have eternal life." (Mark 10:28–30 NLT)

At this point Jesus looked at these who had already forsaken all to follow Him and said, "You will receive a hundred times as much of what you have given up now in this life—houses and lands, with persecutions—and in the age to come, eternal life."

Why didn't Jesus say these words, or Solomon's words from Proverbs, to the rich young man who eagerly wanted eternal life? Why did it appear He was withholding this information? The answer is simple: Jesus never used the blessings, perks, rewards, or benefits of the kingdom to entice people to follow Him. When He called Peter, James, John, and the others, it was simply, "Follow Me." It wasn't, "Follow Me and I'll give you blessings, peace, prosperity, a better life, and more." It wasn't, "Follow Me for what I can do for you." It was, "Follow Me for who I am. I'm Jesus Christ, Your Creator, the Master, and King of the universe."

If money had been the motive for Peter, James, John, and Andrew to follow Jesus, they would never have left their business. The day they left their business had been one of the most profitable days of their fishing career. Thanks to Jesus, they'd brought in two overflowing boatloads of fish! They were not aware of the "hundred times as much" promise. This was the first they'd heard of it. What they did know was that Jesus had the words of life, so they left all. Money was not the deciding factor.

God has never demanded a person be perfect in order to follow Jesus. He only asks for the willingness and commitment to obey Him! This young ruler probably possessed characteristics much more polished than Peter's. However, Peter was willing to do anything the Lord asked of him. This is still what Jesus means when He calls us to forsake all to follow Him.

My Plan versus His

When I received Jesus Christ as Lord in 1979, God immediately began dealing with me about the ministry. I was majoring in mechanical engineering at Purdue University where I was on the dean's list, started on the varsity tennis team, and had plans to attend Harvard for an MBA. My personal plans were to marry a great girl and eventually move into corporate sales or management. I wanted nothing to do with the ministry. All the ministers I had met were men who I thought couldn't do much else in life. They lived in smelly houses and their kids were weird. I had grown up in a town of 3,000 people, and this was the limited model I had of ministry. I had never met and spent time with a good minister, of which I've since learned there are many.

But then the Spirit of God came on me during a church service and said, "John, I have called you to My ministry. What are you going to do about it?"

I thought, *My family will disown me; they're all Catholic. I'll end up like all the other ministers living in poverty and filth.* But obeying God was paramount for me, so I bowed my head and prayed, "Yes, Lord. I will obey You and preach no matter what the cost! I will go wherever You tell me to go and say what You tell me to say."

The reality of that decision has been nothing like what I presumed, but God didn't show me that up front. He just wanted to know if I would forsake all to follow Him.

If you study the ministries of Peter, Paul, and the other disciples in the book of Acts and the epistles, you will see that their messages lined up exactly with what Jesus preached to the wealthy young man! Today we have deviated from this path. It is the root reason for America's failing spiritual condition. It's the reason so many think they belong to Jesus when in reality they don't. We have to return to the lordship of Jesus so we will have a healthy foundation. We are still eating from the wrong tree. What passes as *good* is robbing us of what is best for our lives.

We miss many of the great blessings God wants for us because we've substituted a marketable message for the accurate scriptural message. Let's be honest, if this rich young man came to many of our cutting-edge churches today, he would have been "saved," and before long he would be considered a prized member and perhaps asked to join the church board.

Too often the church today has offered a good message of salvation apart from lordship. For the sake of not deceiving people, for the sake of many who otherwise might someday hear "depart from Me," for the sake of the strength of the church, and for the sake of truly walking in the blessings of God, let's forsake our inadequate, "good" gospel message and return to the tree of life—the biblical message of salvation.

6

OUR INTERNAL GPS

I've got my eye on the goal,
where God is beckoning us onward. . .
—PHILIPPIANS 3:14 THE MESSAGE

To fall in love with God is the greatest
romance; to seek him the greatest adventure;
to find him, the greatest human achievement.
—ST. AUGUSTINE OF HIPPO

O ur foundation is the lordship of Jesus Christ. All aspects of our lives should be built upon this firm footing. If so, they will last. If not, they will eventually erode or pass away.

The next stage of building a house is the framework, and every aspect of this phase is built upon the foundation. This part of the construction process holds everything together. The flooring, walls, ceilings, cabinets, lights, trim, windows, bathtubs, and all the other finishing materials need a strong framework to last. With a solid foundation and strong framework we can build an enduring, successful house: *life*.

Your Internal GPS

To introduce this second aspect of a thriving life of faith, we'll divert away from the building illustration to a different analogy.

Let's begin with a question. What is your ultimate goal? In other words, what desire outweighs all other desires? Can you be honest? If so, you'll not end up in a place you don't want to find yourself.

Look at it like this. If the GPS on your smartphone is set for the airport but you actually desire to go to the mall, you'll moan in frustration when your GPS announces, "You've arrived at your destination," as you approach the airport terminal and see signs listing airlines instead of department stores.

In disbelief you'll protest, "What happened? How did I end up here?" It's quite simple. Your GPS took you where it was programmed to go.

The apostle Paul stated his "GPS setting": "I *press* toward the goal for the prize of the upward call" (Philippians 3:14). He knew what he was after, and his GPS was set. Even if he met resistance, roadblocks, or strong adversity, he would *press* through all of it and not be detoured to an alternate endpoint.

What is your internal GPS set on? Is it to have a lot of friends? Is it to be popular? Is it to enjoy a certain lifestyle? Is it to be the best in your field of work? Is it health and happiness?

You may respond, "I would like all of these." Most of us desire these things, but what single desire outweighs all others? It's important to make this distinction because it will ultimately determine your destination. The road to different endpoints may be the same at times, but inevitably there will come a point in your journey when the pathways will split and you will have to choose one way or the other.

So what's your zenith destination? If your ultimate goal is to be morally pure, ethical, a good person, healthy, and financially secure, then you may end up in the same place the rich young ruler found himself: possessing all these traits but still lacking the most important thing.

If your ultimate goal is to have a lot of friends, then you may find yourself like Aaron, Moses's brother: at the bottom of the mountain with plenty of social activity—even being the center of attention and facilitating your community—but all the while drifting away from the heart of God. The golden calf you build may appease your friends and acquaintances, but you'll sadly discover in the end it steered both them and you away from what was best.

If your passion is to be a well-known speaker, artist, or leader, or simply to have a certain number of followers on Twitter or Facebook, you may attain this status even in Christendom but end up like a man named Uzziah of Israel who was the best-known individual in the nation but died in isolation (see 2 Chronicles 26).

Your internal GPS setting may be more noble and benevolent. You may focus on giving generously to the poor and needy. This goal is attractive to many in our day, and it should be. People light up when we report the efforts Messenger International employs to help the poor, needy, and victims of social injustice. Yet Paul writes to the Corinthian church that he could give all he owned to the poor and still be found wanting (see 1 Corinthians 13:3).

You may strive to be the most generous giver in your community—an honorable goal. However, a man named Ananias and his wife, Sapphira, were members in good standing in the church of Jerusalem. On a certain day they gave a large chunk of the proceeds from selling a valuable plot of land. They desired to demonstrate their commitment to build the house of God. They anticipated accolades, but instead fell into judgment (see Acts 5). Their end was tragic.

There was a time when I considered myself noble and godly. Every day during an eighteen-month span, I got up at 5 a.m. and prayed until 7 a.m. A good portion of this time was consumed by crying out requests like, "Lord, use me to lead multitudes to salvation, to speak the Word of God powerfully, to bring nations into Your kingdom, to heal the sick and get people free." I asked persistently and passionately for these things morning after morning.

Months passed and one day God spoke to my heart: "Son, your prayers are off target."

I was stunned! What could be better, nobler, and more pleasing to my Creator than what I was asking for? I wondered if I had misunderstood what was spoken to my heart. How could all those wonderful spiritual goals be off target?

Immediately, I again heard the Spirit of God. "Judas left all he had to follow Me. He was one of the elite twelve. He preached the kingdom of God. He healed the sick, gave to the poor, and got people free. Judas is in hell."

I trembled, in shock and dumbfounded. I realized Judas had attained all I was crying out for but was forever lost. Perhaps if he'd examined his internal GPS more carefully, his ending wouldn't have been so disastrous.

I realized I could unknowingly be in the same category as Judas. I earnestly inquired, "What should be my targeted goal?"

Another Rich Young Ruler

This time God showed me another rich young ruler—not the one who came running to Jesus, but rather the one who was raised as a prince in Egypt, which at the time was the most powerful nation on earth. His name was Moses.

Consider Moses's life. He was brought up with no lack of money, food, clothing, material possessions, or education. His position was highly coveted, for he had the best of everything. No one in the world possessed anything he couldn't have. Moses wore the latest designer clothes, could shop at any time with an unlimited budget, and probably had all the "toys" available at that time. He possessed the chariot that today would be a Maserati, Lamborghini, or Ferrari, along with every model of Harley-Davidson. And if he didn't want to drive himself, there was a limo driver on constant call.

Moses never had to scrub a toilet, wash out a bathtub, mow a lawn, clean a car, straighten a room, wash dishes, do his laundry, or perform any other household chore because he had servants and attendants for all those jobs.

He had royal chefs who would whip up anything his palate craved. The finest foods of the land were his to enjoy.

His work was fun. If he wanted to, he could lead troops, design buildings, or plan great parties. If he wanted to play, he'd enjoy a day of competition and an evening of the finest amusement. He could fill his days however he desired.

He was also the most eligible bachelor in the land. He could date and marry any girl who caught his eye—and even request to meet women from other nations. In fact, if Moses wished, he could build a harem of wives and concubines.

If Moses wanted to be generous, he could give large gifts. He could summon Secret Service agents, police, or soldiers to protect his friends. He could help the poor or neglect them. He could influence the entertainment of his country by requesting the finest performers and actors to charm him. Nothing was withheld from him except the king's throne. To most, his life would have seemed a coveted utopia, yet he wasn't satisfied. We read:

> By faith, Moses, when grown, refused the privileges of the Egyptian royal house. He chose a hard life with God's people rather than an opportunistic soft life... (Hebrews 11:24–25 The Message)

Moses chose to walk away from what the most affluent nation on earth could offer. Why would he forsake such a lifestyle? Couldn't he find contentment in serving God while still living in Pharaoh's palace? No. Moses's internal GPS dictated that his true desire couldn't be attained where he currently resided, for the writer of Hebrews records about him:

> He thought it was better to suffer for the sake of Christ than to own the treasures of Egypt, for he was looking ahead to his *great reward*. (Hebrews 11:26 NLT)

What great reward? When I pose this question to audiences, most respond that it was the Promised Land. But if this is so, then we must ask, what did a land of milk and honey have to offer that the fertile land of Egypt didn't? In this era Egypt was rich in natural resources and agriculture. Was the Promised Land that much better? Could Moses build a nicer house in this new land than the palace where he already resided? I think we can confidently answer no to these questions.

So what was the reward Moses sought? He didn't exactly know it the day he left the royal house, but he knew there was more—much more in fact. He was on his way and would later discover what exactly he was seeking.

Look at it like this. You love warm weather and the beach and despise snow and cold. It's midwinter and you're currently residing in Vermont. It's

20 degrees below zero, and you long for what you love. So you start driving south on Interstate 95, heading in the direction of warmth. You don't know exactly where you're headed, but you know it's far better than freezing in the snow. In the middle of the trip, at a gas station, you notice a flyer with a picture of Palm Beach, Florida. You smile and say to yourself, "That's it!" Immediately, you program the address on the flyer into your GPS. You are now headed for the specific beach of your dreams.

This is similar to what happened with Moses. He left the palace knowing there was more, but he didn't find his reward until forty years later on the backside of the desert at a bush where he met God and experienced His presence. Once this happened, Moses's internal GPS was firmly set. God's presence was his reward, and the proof of it would come later, after he'd led Israel out of Egypt.

Refusing God's Offer

For Moses, times were difficult and filled with stress. The arid desert he and the people of Israel journeyed through was loaded with great challenges that could often be alleviated only by divine intervention, which frequently seemed delayed. To make matters worse, his national approval rating was at an all-time low. In the midst of these turbulent times God spoke to Moses:

> "Leave this place, you and the people you brought out of Egypt, and go
> to the land that I promised to give to Abraham, Isaac, and Jacob and to
> their descendants. I will send an angel to guide you, and I will drive out
> the Canaanites, the Amorites, the Hittites, the Perizzites, the Hivites,
> and the Jebusites. You are going to a rich and fertile land. But *I will not
> go with you myself...*" (Exodus 33:1–3 TEV)

Think about the circumstances Moses and the people face every day. They've had no variety of conditions—no beautiful valleys, streams, forests, fruit trees, freshwater springs, fertile soil, or pastures for grazing their livestock. It's been quite some time since they've seen any markets, shopping, or new clothing. Their diet is unaltered: strange bread that appears on the ground six days a week, and periodically some quail for meat. To relate, try eating the exact same bread, nothing else, for a few months. You'll understand at that point.

Life's been tough. Slavery in Egypt was terrible, but wandering in the wilderness doesn't seem any better. However, the people have a hope: their own land, the land of promise—Canaan. God has told them for years that it's a rich and fertile land, one that flows with abundance. All they've known is giving their strength and best efforts to building cities for the Egyptians and getting undesirable leftovers. Soon they'll have the capability of constructing beautiful houses, towns, and cities of their own—a new culture unique to their heritage, providing a noteworthy inheritance to pass on to their children and children's children.

Now God has instructed their leader, Moses, to take them into this Promised Land. He declared there would be a choice, mighty angel to guide and protect them. This warrior angel would drive out any and all foes. However, there was one catch: God Himself would not go.

Can you imagine hearing these words? What you and your ancestors have waited centuries for is now being offered by God Himself. Four hundred thirty years of homelessness, struggle, survival, and lack can now come to an end with this offer. Surely Moses will accept, hurry down the mountain, and announce the grand news to the national assembly. The people will finally laud him as a great leader, and his approval rating will climb to an all-time high. They'll all celebrate and begin their journey to their long-awaited promise.

This is exactly the way it would have played out if the "acceptable" good was the targeted goal. However, listen to Moses's reply to God's offer:

"If Your Presence does not go with us, do not bring us up from *here*."
(Exodus 33:15)

As a reminder, where was *here*? It was the place of lack, adversity, stress, and hardship—*the desert*. Moses gave a reply that's perplexing, even mind-boggling, to the average person. In essence he declared, "If I have to choose between Your presence and Your blessing, I'll take Your presence—even if it's in a place of lack and hardship—over Your blessing in a great environment."

Was Moses delusional? Had the desert sun distorted his sense of judgment? No. His internal GPS was set on what was best. It was directing him to make the best choice even when God was offering him a *good* choice, one that common sense and uncomfortable circumstances would have dictated he accept.

Moses's targeted goal—his reward—was to know God intimately. You can never truly *know* someone unless you spend time in their presence. You can *know about* someone in the absence of their presence, but if you don't spend time in a person's presence, you cannot truly know the person intimately. This was Moses's highest reward. To him nothing was of greater value and nothing could deter him, not even a good offer by God Himself. Can you imagine the pleasure this brought to God?

You may question, "Why would God be pleased with His offer being turned down?" I'll answer this with an illustration from my own life.

Lisa and I were on a trip and had a few free days together. There was an amazing golf course nearby. I love playing golf and experiencing great courses. Some friends had invited me to play this course, but I only had a few days to be with Lisa.

My amazing wife sincerely stated, "John, go play."

I responded, "No, honey, I'd rather spend the time with you."

Those few days ended up being wonderful. Lisa's delight at my choosing her over golf set it up, because she knows how I love the game and time with friends. Lisa made the offer, she was sincere, and she wouldn't have changed her mind if I had accepted. However, deep in her heart, she secretly hoped I'd choose her over golf.

This is the same principle revealed with Moses. God made him an offer, one He was willing to back. He would send an angel who would safely bring Moses and the people to the land of promise. However, that trip would have been without God's presence. I believe God made the sincere offer with the unspoken desire that Moses would choose Him over immediate relief from the desert and an easier life in a rich and beautiful land.

Moses declared two things in turning down God's offer. First and foremost, that time in God's presence was more valuable than time enjoying His blessing apart from His presence. Second, that Moses believed in God's flawless integrity. Even though entering the Promised Land would be on hold, Moses knew God would eventually bring Israel there. He knew God would keep His Word. Had Moses's internal GPS not been set correctly, given the circumstances, he certainly would have made a different choice.

Programming the GPS

What originally prompted Moses to set his internal GPS in such a way when all the other Israelites were so different in their motives? A brief look at previous choices and behavioral patterns reveals the answer.

A question I periodically ask an audience is, "What destination was Moses headed for when he led Israel out of Egypt?"

Every time, the majority responds, "The Promised Land."

Is this correct? Over and over when Moses went before Pharaoh, he relayed these words from God to the king of Egypt: "Let my people go, so they can worship me in the *wilderness*" (Exodus 7:16 NLT; also see Exodus 5:1; 8:1, 20; 9:1, 13; 10:3). Seven times, when he told Pharaoh where Israel was going, Moses coupled worship and the wilderness. Not once is the Promised Land mentioned.

Moses's objective was to lead the people to meet with and worship God in the wilderness at Sinai. Why would he want to bring them out of Egypt straight to the *Promised Land* before initially leading them to the *Promiser?* This would have promoted the promises over the presence of God and encouraged an incorrect GPS setting.

Sadly, ministers and teachers in our time have promoted the promises option. I recall in the 1980s and 1990s hearing much more about what Jesus would do for us than about who He is. This type of teaching produced disciples who set their internal GPSs on the blessings of God over His presence. This is no different than a woman marrying a man for his wealth. She may love him, but it's for the wrong reasons.

I find an amazing contrast between Israel and Moses. If you consider Israel's life in Egypt, they were harshly abused to say the least. They lived in slums, ate stale food, and wore threadbare clothing. Their entire lives were spent building someone else's inheritance. They had scars on their backs from the taskmasters' whips, and their sons were killed by Pharaoh's military.

Israel was miraculously delivered from Egyptian bondage, but after only a short time of desert expedition, they repeatedly complained and stated their desire to return to Egypt. They made comments such as, "Would it not be better for us to return to Egypt?" (Numbers 14:3) and, "It would have been better for us to serve the Egyptians" (Exodus 14:12).

Now consider Moses's comfortable and lavish Egyptian lifestyle, which I previously described. He too left Egypt and similarly came under all the same harsh conditions of the desert, yet he never once complained or spoke of returning to Egypt! Why? The answer is simple. Moses had one encounter with the presence of God at the burning bush. He was privileged to hear the Word of God straight from the Creator. Israel had a similar opportunity but drew back from it. Let me explain.

"Brought You to Myself"

Once out of Egypt, Moses brought the nation to Mount Sinai, the same location where he had met with God at the bush. When they arrived, God instructed Moses to tell the people:

> "You have seen what I did to the Egyptians, and *how* I bore you on eagles' wings and *brought you to Myself*." (Exodus 19:4)

Look at His words "brought you to Myself." Ponder this statement. It's staggering when you think about its true meaning. God, the Creator of the universe, made it clear the chief purpose of bringing Israel out of Egyptian bondage was to bring them all to Himself. He was seeking out a personal and intimate relationship with them.

We must remember, God is relational and has a Father's heart—He always has and always will. He yearned to know His children as a father or mother yearns to develop a relationship with a newborn child.

God had revealed Himself to Moses at the bush. He gave Moses the privilege of experiencing His presence. That one experience alone created such an appetite in Moses that he never had any interest whatsoever in returning to Egypt, even as good as his lifestyle had been there. This encounter influenced him significantly and firmly set his internal GPS.

Moses wanted Israel to experience what he'd experienced, but what's staggering is that God also desired this. Since He had already spent time with Moses at the bush, Moses could introduce God to the people and the people to God.

Think of it like this. There are three people, named Jordan, Abigail, and Susan. If Jordan and Abigail have met and Jordan and Susan know each other, Jordan is the one who will introduce Abigail to Susan. Moses had met and spent time with God. He had also spent time with Israel. Therefore he would be the one to facilitate the meeting of God and the people. God told Moses to prepare the introduction with this message:

> "'…You're special: a kingdom of priests, a holy nation.' This is
> what I want you to tell the People of Israel." (Exodus 19:5–6
> The Message)

They were all special to Him, and He desired every one of them to be priests—people who could directly approach Him on behalf of themselves or others. In essence He was offering them an inside friendship. What a privilege! Then God stated:

"Go to the people. For the next two days get these people ready to meet the Holy God. Have them *scrub their clothes* so that on the third day they'll be fully prepared, because on the third day God will come down on Mount Sinai and make his presence known to all the people." (Exodus 19:10–11 The Message)

God did come down on the mountain on the third day, but the response of the people was heartbreaking. They withdrew from Him instead of drawing close to Him. They cried out to Moses, "You speak to us, and we will listen. But don't let God speak directly to us, or we will die!" (Exodus 20:19 NLT)

The people of Israel couldn't handle God's presence *because they still had Egypt in their hearts.* They still loved their own interests over His. Knowing Him intimately was not a priority. His manifest presence merely exposed their internal GPS setting, and they weren't willing to change it.

Look again at God's instructions, which included a command to scrub their clothes. What's with that? Is God a stickler for physical hygiene? To find the answer we must remember that often in the Old Testament, outward actions were meant to convey spiritual realities. Egypt's filth still clung to the people's garments. It had to be removed before the people could enter God's holy presence.

Egypt was symbolic of the fallen world's system. People of this world live for the indulgence of the flesh, the gratification of the eyes, and for status, reputation, and prominence—"the pride of life" (see 1 John 2:16). Knowing God isn't the focus. Rather, "How can I benefit?" is the emphasis.

God's Not Looking for Gold-Diggers

Often while traveling, I'll observe an older, wealthy man with a woman who's striking in appearance and in the neighborhood of fifteen to twenty-five years younger than him. Most often the man's out of shape and could be mistaken for the woman's father. Why is she living with or married to him?

In rare cases the two are genuinely in love. However, most often this isn't the case—the woman is what's known as a "gold-digger." This is a slang or derogatory term used for a young lady who isn't interested in a man for who he is but rather for the lifestyle he can provide. She wants access to his wealth and influence. However, this isn't one-sided, for the man's primary interest isn't the woman but what she can do for his egocentric personality. He wants to project an image of still being young and on his game and, of course, enjoy good sex.

Simply put, each selfishly seeks what the other can provide rather than genuinely caring for the other person. On some level, each knows what the other is doing but tolerates it in order to continue to satisfy their own lust and pride. A lasting relationship is not the motivating factor; rather, the motive is self-centered gratification.

Recently my wife and I were in a furniture and home accessories store. Other than the sales lady, the only other couple in the shop was an old man and a young woman. At first I thought they were father and daughter, but in listening to their conversation with the sales lady, I discovered this wasn't the case. They were a couple shopping for their newly purchased house.

We were in the store with them for over twenty minutes, which gave me plenty of time to observe them. My attention was captured by their strained and superficial interaction. It was obvious they had little in common and possessed completely different interests. The absence of love and joy in their lives was glaringly apparent. She could barely look him in the eye and had a sullen countenance. She was wearing super-tight clothes and a lot of makeup. He carried himself in a youthful, hip way and acted like a high roller. He made it clear by the way he spoke to the sales agent that money was not an object for him.

Seeing this couple caused me to realize how special my relationship with Lisa is. I care for her very much, and it's not based on her physical appearance, although she's beautiful. Lisa cares deeply for me. We are best friends and love spending time together. I felt sorry for the couple at the store because of the obvious lack of love in their relationship. I don't bring this up to judge them; it is my hope that they will grow in their love for one another and enjoy each other's company. However, this is not usually the case because the relationship is based on the wrong foundation.

The people of Israel carried this type of relational filth from Egypt, and God had no desire for something superficial. He desires authentic relationships, not gold-diggers. The world's motivation, which still clung to the hearts of the Israelites, is not capable of producing genuine relationships since the motives are self-seeking. Israel could only know God if they cleansed themselves of this filth.

However, Israel couldn't rid themselves of their desires as Moses did. His passion was for a genuine relationship with God. Israel wanted benefits from God. It was that simple.

How about Today?

We're now in New Testament times, so has anything changed? Can someone carry the filth of the world in their heart and still have a genuine relationship with God? Does the grace of Jesus Christ eradicate the necessity of cleansing ourselves from the world's filth? A set of scriptures rarely emphasized nowadays specifically speaks to this:

> As God said: "I will live in them and walk among them. I will be their God, and they will be my people. Therefore, come out from among unbelievers, and separate yourselves from them, says the LORD. Don't touch their filthy things, and I will welcome you. And I will be your Father, and you will be my sons and daughters, says the LORD Almighty."
>
> Because we have these promises, dear friends, let us cleanse ourselves from everything that can defile our body or spirit. And let us work toward complete holiness because we fear God. (2 Corinthians 6:16–7:1 NLT)

There is so much to unpack in these few verses. First, notice the words "as God said." When did God first state these words and what was their context? Paul is quoting God's statement to Moses at the mountain of His presence:

> "I will live among the people of Israel and be their God, and they will know that I am the LORD their God. I am the one who brought them out of the land of Egypt so that I could live among them." (Exodus 29:45–46 NLT)

God repeated what He had stated in Exodus 19: His desire for authentic relationship. This was His pursuit, but Israel did not reciprocate. Only certain individuals, such as Moses, David, Daniel, Isaiah, and a handful of others, could have an intimate relationship with God because they chose to rid themselves of the world's motives of self-gratification. Now Paul uses these exact words to address us, those who have been washed by the blood of Jesus Christ and saved by the grace of God.

Again, we are told, "I will live in them and walk among them. I will be their God, and they will be my people. …Don't touch their filthy things, and I will welcome you." The words are no different than what God spoke to Israel, but now He is expressing them to a new people—*us*. His desire for intimacy has not changed, but it can't happen if we still have the filth of the world on our garments. He welcomes us into a relationship of closeness, but it's not unconditional. Once again He makes known His disdain of a gold-digger relationship.

God is not blind to our inner motives. He tells us to cleanse ourselves from all filth, not just of the flesh but even of the heart and spirit. He knows whether we have the filth of Egypt on our garments (live for self-gratification) or if, like Moses, we seek His desires over our own. So just as Moses instructed Israel to cleanse their garments in order to meet and have an intimate relationship with God, we too are told by the apostle Paul, "Let us *cleanse ourselves* from everything that can defile our body or spirit. And let us work toward complete holiness because we fear God." Cleansing ourselves from the filth of the world's system ensures our internal GPS will not be compromised and choose what's good over what's best.

To maintain the most beneficial internal GPS setting—toward a close relationship with God—it would seem the word *holiness* is the key factor. In the next few chapters we will unpack this exciting reality.

7

JEALOUS FOR US

"To whom will you compare me? Who is my equal?"
asks the Holy One. Look up into the heavens. Who
created all the stars? ...calling each by its
name. Because of his great power and incomparable
strength, not a single one is missing.
—ISAIAH 40:25-26 NLT

Your Lord is very jealous of your love,
O believer. Did he choose you? He cannot
bear that you should choose another.
—CHARLES SPURGEON

There is nothing more fulfilling and beneficial than being in God's presence. Ponder it for a moment: it's not just being in the company of a notable athlete, renowned scientist, famous artist, popular celebrity, or powerful world leader, but of the Creator of everything both seen and unseen. He is the One who imagined and brought forth a universe so vast that human minds can't comprehend its vastness, yet so detailed that tiny, complex atoms are the building blocks of all physical life and matter. These atoms are so minute that, as mentioned in a previous chapter, it would take billions of them to form a one-inch line. Even after extensive research, scientists still don't fully comprehend them.

There is absolutely no beneficial wisdom, knowledge, or understanding of any sort outside of God. There's nothing He needs to learn, because He truly knows it all—even the end from the beginning. Mighty angelic beings continuously stand before Him, covering their faces and crying out in awe of the progressive revelation of who He is. No wonder the wisest men and women of generations past have pursued the privilege of enjoying His company.

It's staggering that any human being can be in the presence of such a Being. What's even more astounding is that He desires our presence even more than we desire His. The apostle James states:

> Or do you think that the Scripture says in vain, "The Spirit who dwells in us *yearns* jealously"? (James 4:5)

To *yearn* means to have an intense longing or desire for something. When I think about this magnificent Person yearning for me, I so agree with what David said: "How precious are your thoughts about me, O God. They cannot be numbered! I can't even count them; they outnumber the grains of sand!" (Psalm 139:17–18 NLT) David was speaking of God's thoughts toward you and me as individuals, not toward all His people collectively. His thoughts about you outnumber every grain of sand on this planet! Think of all the sand on every beach, desert, golf course, and playground. That's a lot of sand—and a lot of thoughts.

Allow me to bring this into perspective. I'm deeply in love with my wife. We've been married for over thirty years. I've had many fond thoughts about her—countless, in fact. However, if I were able to number every thought I've had in the past three decades, I wouldn't fill even a shoebox full of sand, for scientists estimate that there are an average of 1.8 billion grains of sand in one cubic foot of beach!

Let's think this through a little further. Have you ever encountered a person who exaggerates? Perhaps he's a fisherman. You know the drill. He makes the declaration, "I caught a fish this big!" while stretching out his arms to illustrate the size of his catch. Yet if you had actually seen the fish, you would know it was significantly smaller.

Or how about the guy who pulls statistics out of the air, embellishing a number to make a point. He boldly announces, "Ninety-nine percent of all males don't like chick flicks." He's never seen any official poll or statistic but exaggerates to justify his disdain for this genre of movies.

Or how about the person who says, "I'm praying for you," yet if the truth were told, he may have prayed one time—and that half-heartedly. I'm guessing everybody exaggerates now and then, but let's be honest: an exaggeration is a lie. But here's an incredible truth: God cannot lie! (See Numbers 23:19 and Titus 1:2) If He were to lie, He would have to submit to the "father of lies," who is Satan—and that will never happen.

If God states that His thoughts about you outnumber every grain of sand on this planet, you can bank on it.

Can you comprehend how much He thinks about you? Consider your own thought life. Do you think excessively about someone you don't desire to be with or close to? Neither does He! The Spirit of God who dwells in us *yearns*—longs for and desires our company intently. Simply put, God wants to know you intimately, as a very close friend.

God's Jealousy

Let's look again at James's words: "Do you think that the Scripture says in vain, 'The Spirit who dwells in us yearns *jealously*'?" The key word is *jealously*. What's the implication here? Allow me to illustrate. Would my wife be intimate with me—share the secrets, longings, and desires of her heart—if I were pursuing a relationship with another woman? No way! If we look at this verse in context, the words just before this statement read:

> Adulterers and adulteresses! Do you not know that friendship with the world is enmity with God? (James 4:4)

The gist of this is, "Are you seeking friendship with the world? If so, you're an adulterer!"

James was writing to Christians only, for fifteen times in this book he says "my brethren." His statement is clearly targeted to those with a relationship with God, who have received Christ Jesus into their lives. Here is the truth: we commit adultery against God when we court the world.

Continuing with my illustration, if I were to pursue a relationship with another woman, not only would Lisa not want to share intimately with me, but she would also be angry and jealous—and rightfully so. I made the commitment to be hers and only hers. I'd have broken my promise and lied on top of it.

James prefaces his statement with, "Do you think that the Scripture says...?" He was actually referencing many scriptures, not just one. God repeatedly declares of Himself:

"...I, the Lord your God, am a jealous God..." (Exodus 20:5)

"...The LORD, whose very name is Jealous, is a God who is jealous about his relationship with you." (Exodus 34:14 NLT)

"God, your God, is not to be trifled with—he's a consuming fire, a jealous God." (Deuteronomy 4:24 The Message)

There are numerous other scriptures referring to God's jealousy. Bottom line, they all deal with our relationship with Him.

Before going any further, allow me to clarify: God's not saying He's jealous *of you*; rather, He's jealous *for you*. There is a huge difference. He desires your success, He wants you to be great, He's delighted for you to have abundance, and His will is for you to be productive (see Joshua 1:8; Proverbs 4:8 NLT; Matthew 25:29; and John 15:8). His jealousy solely refers to His desire to be close to you. He's not willing to share you with another lover, which is chiefly the world. James was simply reminding believers of how God views unfaithfulness. If we commit adultery against Him, His anger will burn in jealousy. This is no trivial matter.

But anger isn't the only emotion caused by unfaithfulness in a covenant relationship. Too often have I heard a brokenhearted spouse share with me the shock, disappointment, bewilderment, grief, and anger surging within them. They've been ultimately abandoned and betrayed by the one they gave their life to, and the gamut of feelings hits them in the deepest places of their soul. I've listened to a wife in utter confusion cry out, "Why would my husband do this when I've born his children and given him the best years of my life?"

Can you imagine how God feels? Can you imagine the emotions that surge through His soul when we are unfaithful? Paul writes, "For I am jealous for you with the jealousy of God himself" (2 Corinthians 11:2 NLT).

Paul, speaking on behalf of God, reflects God's feelings for us when we pursue someone or something in His place. Jeremiah does the same: "My grief is beyond healing; my heart is broken" (Jeremiah 8:18 NLT). We must remember we are created in His image, so as we feel, God feels!

God is jealous because He's given His life for us. He's sacrificed everything to make a lasting relationship possible. His heart and soul are deeply angered and grieved when we are unfaithful to Him. Listen to His words:

> "…My people have forgotten me. How you plot and scheme to win
> your lovers. Even an experienced prostitute could learn from you! And
> yet you say, 'I have done nothing wrong.'" (Jeremiah 2:32–33, 35 NLT)

Most often, we're unaware if we're committing adultery against Him, let alone of the gravity of our unfaithfulness. It takes truth to open our eyes. Our hearts grow insensitive to His broken heart and grieving soul. God asks, "Are they ashamed of their disgusting actions? Not at all—they don't even know how to blush!" (Jeremiah 6:15 NLT) Just as Jeremiah and others had to point out Israel's unfaithfulness, Paul and James did the same in the New Testament.

The World

In continuing to unpack James's crucial statement, the Greek words for *friend* and *friendship* are *philos* and *philia* respectively. A few of the words used to define *philos* are *fond*, *friendly*, and "to associate"; and *philia* is defined as "a friend" or "to befriend." Of *philia*, W.E. Vines states in his comprehensive dictionary, "It involves 'the idea of loving as well as being loved.'" Think of this in light of Jesus's words:

> "The *world* would love you as one of its own if you *belonged* to it, but
> you are no longer part of the world. I chose you to come out of the
> world, *so it hates you*." (John 15:19 NLT)

You no longer belong to the world, though you once did. You now belong to God. The former person who lived in your body died the moment you gave yourself to Jesus. A brand-new creation came forth. You were reborn as one who's in covenant relationship with God.

Jesus stated that a true mark of one who belongs to Him is to be hated by the world. Honestly ask yourself, "Am I hated by the world?" Are the Christians you know hated by the world? If we are, then how can we live, operate, and be fruitful in the world? How can we reach the world? Wouldn't we influence the lost more effectively if the world loved us? These tough questions need to be addressed, and we will address them in the coming chapters.

The apostle John covers the flip side of Jesus's statement. He boldly commands us, "Do not love the world or the things in the world. If anyone loves the world, the love of the Father is not in him" (1 John 2:15).

Jesus, James, and John all used strong language regarding a person in relationship with God who's connecting with the world and vice versa. They attached the concepts of friendship, loving the world, and the world loving us with ideas such as adultery, hatred, enmity, and God's love not being in us. Before continuing to comment on these confrontational statements and what friendship with the world implies, we should first establish what the world is.

The Greek word for world is *kosmos*. It is defined as "the present world, the present order of things, as opposed to the kingdom of Christ; and hence, always with the idea of transience, worthlessness, and…irregular desires."[9] Let's discuss each of these terms.

Transient, the root word of *transience*, is defined as "not lasting, enduring, or permanent." If we were to step back and view our society over time, we'd see it's constantly changing. Change, for the most part, is good; it means progress, development, and growth. However, moral change most often veers away from what is authentically good to God.

In our society, *what's morally acceptable and commonplace today* often *was uncommon and regarded as morally and socially wrong yesterday.* To illustrate, let's look at an obvious trend. Take a typical PG–13 rated movie. Masses line up at the box office for the latest release. Yet more often than not, the blockbuster will be filled with blatant immorality. It will portray fornication, homosexuality, or adultery as desirable. Often it will include indecency, theft, murder, and even witchcraft. And it's not the "evil" characters in the story engaging in these behavioral patterns but the heroes and their companions. Often the dialogue is plastered with an array of profanity, including God's name used in vain.

We've come to just accept, even expect, this in many movies. However, if this exact movie had been shown in theaters back in the 1950s, general audiences would have been appalled! Americans would have been outraged by the foul language, nudity, and display of blatant immorality. The national outcry would have been, "Why does this film portray two unmarried people living together—even showing them in bed together—as acceptable? Why is this portrayed as a normal lifestyle? Unbelievable! Shameful! Outrageous!" Then the general public would have boycotted the movie.

So what's happened? Has God introduced a new standard of what's normal, acceptable, and good? Have the lines shifted? Have we grown more mature? Were we just too stiff back in the fifties? Is this progress?

If we look at actual real-life statistics, we discover the drastic change in movies is only a reflection of the changing moral standards of society. A recent study showed that the number of young women living with their boy-friends has more than tripled since 1982.[10] *US News & World Report* reported that between the years of 2006 and 2010, nearly half of women (48 percent) between the ages of fifteen and forty-four lived with a partner before getting married, an 11 percent jump since 2002 and a 41 percent jump since 1995.[11] I could continue to give such statistics about our *transient* culture, but that's not my focus here.

The world also fosters *worthlessness*. There are developments and changes that occur in our society that are valuable. The advancements we've experienced in science, technology, communications, medicine, and so on bring usefulness to humanity by increasing our ability to be productive. This is in line with God's first command to "be fruitful and multiply" (Genesis 1:22).

However, do our moral changes add value? Or are they based on greed, lust, or status? Have we enhanced a child's upbringing by subjecting them to be raised by two ladies or two men professing marriage? Is this arrangement better for the child than a nurturing mom and masculine dad, or has this change been made to satisfy *irregular desires* (the final characteristic in our definition of *kosmos*)?

Does a man and woman living together, as opposed to committing to marriage, foster security for children, or is the arrangement for the sake of satisfying the parents' self-seeking desires and lack of commitment? Does bending the truth and using deceptive techniques to increase sales benefit the customer or satisfy the greed of the seller? Does legalized recreational marijuana enhance brain cell activity? Don't published scientific studies commonly report the depletion of brain cells from the use of this drug? Do any of these commonplace irregular desires bring us closer to our Creator?

Scripture tells us the course of the world is set by lawless spirits craftily working through the citizens of our generation (see Ephesians 2:2). Simply put, *kosmos* is the culture that is created by darkened minds. The apostle John leaves no room for questions when he writes, "The world around us is under the control of the evil one" (1 John 5:19 NLT). It progressively drifts further and further from God's heart and authority. For the most part its appearance is not blatantly contrary or evil; rather, its changes are masked as *progress* or *good*. But the sad truth is the world seduces its inhabitants away from the heart of their Creator.

The *New International Encyclopedia of Bible Words* takes our definition deeper. It states, "Worldliness is not a matter of engaging in those practices that some question. It is unthinkingly adopting the perspectives, values, and attitudes of our culture, without bringing them under the judgment of God's Word."[12] Simply put, with worldliness, we're the source for setting the standard of what is considered good and evil. The perspectives, values, and attitudes that set the bar are rooted in the indulgence of the flesh, gratification of the eyes, and longing for status, reputation, and prominence:

> Do not love this world nor the things it offers you, for when you love
> the world, you do not have the love of the Father in you. For *the world
> offers only* a craving for physical pleasure, a craving for everything we
> see, and pride in our achievements and possessions. These are not from
> the Father, but are from this world. (1 John 2:15–16 NLT)

Notice the words "the world offers only." This summarizes how to detect the world's influence—or in alignment with James's words, how to spot the adulterous ones who seek you out.

Please hear me, dear Christ follower: *the world is seeking you out.* The world's invitation into a relationship is frequently accompanied by enticing speech, logic, flattery, opportunity, power, influence, and—always—promises of personal gain and/or pleasure. It's no different than the serpent's alluring approach to Eve. It's no different than an adulterous woman who has set her sights on the man of her desire. She makes it appear that it's about him, when in reality it's all about her web. That web secretly traps her targeted victim so that she can carry out her desire on him.

The world's web covertly traps its victims—those who profess Christianity—so it can fulfill its desire to lure believers away from the presence, life, and blessings of God. The writer of Proverbs bluntly declared the world's bedroom is the den of death and its way is the road to hell. He warns that *many strong men and women have been slain by its alluring power* (see Proverbs 7:21–27).

What the World Isn't

When it comes to defining the world, so much emphasis has been placed on form rather than motive. My heart has grieved when hearing the thought processes of sincere believers who were raised in or are currently trapped in *legalism*. Legalism is spoken of frequently, and the term is often used loosely, so before continuing, let's define it. The dictionary defines *legalism* as "strict adherence...to law or prescription, especially to the letter rather than the spirit." It's further defined as "the judging of conduct in terms of adherence to the precise laws."

Many of us have heard horror stories that accompany this lifeless form of Christianity. Pastors pound the Bible on their pulpits, declaring regulations and rules to strictly observe and obey. They label women as worldly if they wear pants, fashionable outfits, jewelry, makeup, piercings, or short, stylish, or colored hair. Men don't escape their soapbox sermons either: up-to-date fashions are scrutinized, along with piercings and length of hair.

It doesn't stop there. Condemnation is administered for being seen at parties with sinners. Those who attend movie theaters or other entertainment events are criticized. Friends outside acceptable circles are frowned upon, and any attempt to reach out to the lost in a creative manner is often tagged as backsliding. Included in the list of don'ts are dancing, attending certain social functions, all forms of secular music, the use of television, atmosphere enhancers such as lights or smoke machines in church—and this is just the short list of the regulations required to "follow Jesus and stay free from the world."

I've just listed some of the obvious targets of legalists; however, there are more subtle forms of legalism that are equally dangerous. These are imposed—and often self-imposed—criteria that people strictly adhere to in order to earn salvation, grow spiritually, or judge the outward appearances of others. A sampling of these would include praying long hours, fasting, or reading prescribed daily portions of the Bible. Of course these are all inherently advantageous practices, but they shouldn't be done with the intent of earning some form of spiritual superiority.

It could be we struggle to accept forgiveness, so we succumb to the urge of punishing ourselves in some fashion to make up for the wrong we've done. This takes the focus off the blood of Jesus and puts it right back on our works.

Legalism could manifest in believing we have greater access to God because we serve diligently in ministry or the church. Or we believe our prayers are heard quickly because we haven't committed any significant sins lately. The unspoken mindset is that we can fill our spiritual bank accounts with good behavior, deeds, or works. Legalism doesn't allow a person to rest or enjoy life due to the driving pressure to be constantly busy in "serving God," whether it's in church administration, volunteering, or giving resources to the poor. Love is not the motivation; attempting to earn God's favor is.

A classic example of this type of legalism is the Pharisee who judged the town's notorious sinner by comparing his own lifestyle to that of the tax collector (equivalent to a modern-day mafia member). The Pharisee superficially thanked God for his own good behavior: he didn't sin, didn't cheat people like the mafia man did, didn't commit adultery, fasted and prayed regularly, and gave generously to the synagogue. Ironically, at the very moment the spiritual leader was boasting about his behavior and pointing out the syndicate leader's shortcomings, that notorious sinner was in the back of the synagogue calling out to God for mercy. Jesus said it was that second man who was justified, not the "perfect," rule-keeping leader.

This type of legalism is heavily rooted in the spirit of the world, as it focuses on status, pride, or the self-gratification that accompanies following the regulations set by oneself or others. It veers away from dependency on

God's ability in our lives as it turns our focus on ourselves. It also robs us of the joy that accompanies God's presence.

A friend of mine who is a businessman is very effective in reaching out to people. He was brought up in legalism but has been freed from it. He once told me, "John, I thought anything that was fun or brought laughter or joy was of this world, and it was viewed as strictly off-limits." His pastor and leaders focused on a person's outward appearance, not the inward disposition of the heart. His church had very little influence on anyone outside their group. Sadly this church's leaders didn't really hear Paul's words: "For the Kingdom of God is not a matter of what we eat or drink, but of living a life of goodness and peace and *joy* in the Holy Spirit" (Romans 14:17 NLT).

There's great and enduring joy when we are in the Spirit. Joy is attractive to the lost, as the world doesn't possess it. Jesus was attractive to all who were sincere, even the most notorious sinners in society. Anyone trying to earn their salvation or grow in Christ through legalistic teachings or beliefs doesn't possess true joy. They live in a very small world because those who don't think exactly like they do are filtered out.

It would have been good if this businessman's leaders had meditated more on Paul's words in another letter:

> You have died with Christ, and he has set you free from the spiritual
> powers of this world. So why do you keep on following the rules of the
> world, such as, "Don't handle! Don't taste! Don't touch!"? Such rules
> are mere human teachings about things that deteriorate as we use them.
> These rules may seem wise because they require strong devotion, pious
> self-denial, and severe bodily discipline. But they provide no help in
> *conquering a person's evil desires.* (Colossians 2:20–23 NLT)

Interestingly, Paul attributed legalistic rules of devotion, self-denial, and severe bodily discipline to the powers of this world. Not that licentiousness, sexual immorality, murder, theft, drunkenness, and so forth are not sinful. It's just a different form of worldliness. Those who are bound by legalism often don't realize that the world they preach so strongly to stay away from is the same system holding them in bondage.

The key to Paul's statement is found in the words "conquering a person's evil desires." Legalism doesn't clean up a person's heart—and the heart is the world's target, which the forces of this world want to infect. This is why we are told, "Guard your heart above all else, for it determines the course of your life" (Proverbs 4:23 NLT).

Jesus states, "A good man out of the good treasure of his heart brings forth good things, and an evil man out of the evil treasure brings forth evil things" (Matthew 12:35). It's all about what we inwardly store up and view as valuable. Clean up the heart and the outer life falls into place, in perfect alignment with what God considers good.

To sum it up, the world's grip is not outward but inward. It comes down to the desires, intentions, and motives of the heart and mind. This is the battlefield; this is where the web is spun. This is where friendship or adultery with the world begins and is eventually consummated. And it can happen as easily with a person who rarely attends church as with one who never misses a service and is heavily involved in ministry.

With a better grasp on what the world is and is not, let's turn our attention to *friendship*. How do we enter a relationship of friendship with the world? How do we commit adultery with it? This will be our focus in the upcoming chapter.

8

FRIENDSHIP

...Our friendship with God was restored
by the death of his Son...
—Romans 5:10 NLT

Whatever your heart clings to and
confides in, that is really your God.
—Martin Luther

Friends. We all have and enjoy them. As a young boy, two of my closest friends were Danny and Glenn. I spent most of my free time with them. We played sports, rode bikes, explored, made up games, went to town, or just sat and talked. Our chats revolved around what was important to us: other friends, girls, academics, social events, athletics, career plans, and a host of other topics. Our friendship was, for the most part, healthy. We encouraged each other to be better, stronger, and wiser and to reach our potential. We'd protect each other, do favors for one another, and help each other through difficult situations. Simply put, they were my favorite people to be with.

How about you? Think of your friends in years past. Ask yourself, what are the key elements of a friendship? I'm sure you'd agree enjoying time together, relating to and understanding each other, and sharing common interests all stand out. Love, trust, respect, humor, and mutual attraction are also vital. There are certainly more components, depending on the individual; however, for all of us the most important aspect is we enjoy being together.

Scripture speaks positively of friendships. One of my favorite verses is, "Just as lotions and fragrance give sensual delight, a sweet friendship refreshes the soul" (Proverbs 27:9 The Message). We were not created to fly solo; companionship invigorates us. It was the chief element missing in God's original creation. He declared, "It is not good that man should be alone" (Genesis 2:18). We were created in His image, which includes desiring and enjoying friendship.

But there's a flip side. Jesus, James, and John speak *unfavorably* of a particular friendship. Listen again to the apostle's words: "You adulterers! Don't you realize that friendship with the world makes you an enemy of God? I say it again: If you want to be a friend of the world, you make yourself an enemy of God" (James 4:4 NLT). His tone isn't just unfavorable but direct, blunt, and strong! So let's ask, what are the indicators of entering a relationship with the world?

The Classic Affair

In the last chapter we learned the word *philia* is defined as "to be a friend" or "to befriend" and carries the idea of "loving, as well as being loved." The *Encyclopedia of Bible Words* further states, "In the Greek world the idea of friendship was well developed. Philia…was used in the broad sense of 'acquaintance,' as well as in the more intimate sense of a personal and deep bonding of real affection." In essence, this word James uses applies to a broad spectrum of friendship. We all know there are levels of relationships, and the friendship James speaks of runs the gamut. Subsequently, the full spectrum of friendship is directly connected to unfaithfulness.

Committing adultery against God is little different from the typical scenario of a married man's unfaithfulness, so let's review the steps in a common affair. In most cases the husband and his mistress don't end up in bed together on the first encounter. There's a courting involved; it can be intentional or unintentional.

It begins with simply meeting each other and getting *acquainted*. It can happen by way of social media or in person. A spark is initiated by the acquaintance. Often the man's interest is fostered from unfulfilled intimacy with his spouse. In less frequent cases it's solely driven by his desire for more physical and emotional connection. The initial interactions seem harmless, but with each contact, the interest of both parties escalates. Eventually they exchange cell phone numbers and email addresses.

The attraction continues to intensify as the man interacts with the woman through texting, emailing, phone calls, or simply "bumping into" her. This deepens their level of conversation. They long for each other, but neither admits it. The unspoken attraction adds to the thrill of the developing relationship. They've far surpassed the appropriate level of friendship.

Eventually plans are made to take it a step further—to get coffee, lunch, or meet in a secluded place. It's usually at this point their feelings for each other come out.

She's now constantly on his mind, and he yearns to be with her. He dreams and plans how they can get away without his wife and friends knowing. His heart no longer longs for his wife but for this woman. In the company of his wife, he's actually not present, for his thoughts and imagination are with his mistress. It's only a matter of time before they end up in bed together.

Where did it begin? It started with inappropriate thoughts and conversations in the acquaintance stage. At what point did it become adultery? Was it when they exchanged personal contact information or met together alone? Or was it when he first touched her? Their first kiss? Or did it occur when they undressed and had sex together?

It actually happened before any of these markers. Jesus sheds light on this when He emphatically states, "But don't think you've preserved your virtue simply by staying out of bed. Your heart can be corrupted by lust even quicker than your body" (Matthew 5:28 The Message). The heart is where we live; outward actions simply follow. Adultery commenced once the man's affections swung toward the woman—somewhere in the *acquaintance* stage.

Friendship with the World

The world lures us away from our "first love" in a similar fashion. It begins by stirring our interest. The calling card can be humor, pleasure, comfort, excitement, intrigue, success, or anything that is appealing. No different than in the example I just gave, the acquaintance stage can happen by way of the media or in person. It often occurs due to lack of fulfillment in our relationship with God. We have lost the thrill of His friendship. Our times of fellowship with Him are dry and dull. Our need for companionship draws us elsewhere.

The world's attraction grows with invested time. Before long our thoughts and emotions are hooked. If we examine Paul's words to two different churches, we'll discover a warning that, if heeded, will protect us from slipping into adultery with the world:

> If then you were raised with Christ, *seek* those things which are above, where Christ is, sitting at the right hand of God. *Set* your mind on things above, not on things on the earth. (Colossians 3:1–2)

Did you read his words carefully? If not, look at them again and pay particular attention to the two italicized words, *seek* and *set*. Our mind is *set* upon what we *seek*.Before I comment further, let's closely examine Paul's words to the Romans. Again, look for the word *set*:

> For those who live according to the flesh *set* their minds on the things of the flesh, but those who live according to the Spirit, [*set* their minds on] the things of the Spirit. For to be carnally [fleshly] minded is death, but to be spiritually minded is life and peace. Because the carnal [fleshly] mind is enmity against God... (Romans 8:5–7)

As a point of interest, notice the word *enmity*. It's the exact Greek word used in James 4:4: *echthra. Strong's* defines it as "hostility...a reason for opposition." Once again Paul addresses a believer who is connecting with the world.

It's not only my love for Lisa that keeps me from committing adultery against her. It's also my not wanting to face her wrath. I would become the target of her hostility. I don't want the one I love hostile, angry, and disappointed with me. However, that would be small in comparison to what Paul and James speak of, for no Christian in their right mind would want to face God's hostility. (Remember, James and Paul are speaking to believers.)

Jonah faced God's hostility, and he ended up in big fish vomit. Samson faced it, and he fell into slavery and lost his sight. Eli faced it, and he died the same day his sons were taken from the earth. There are other examples like Saul, Balaam, Joab, Alexander the coppersmith, and many more. Getting God upset is a bad idea.

If you desire more examples, in the New Testament consider Jesus's comments to the churches in the book of Revelation. These were actual churches with born-again believers. To one church that compromised their relationship, He threatened to remove their lamp stand—their light (see Revelation 2:5). Another church was forewarned that God would "fight against them" (see Revelation 2:16). Another church was threatened by God with "a sickbed" and "great tribulation" (see Revelation 2:22). Another was warned that He'd "come upon them as a thief" (see Revelation 3:3), and yet another was told that He'd "vomit" them out of His mouth (see Revelation 3:16). Bottom line: you don't want to face God's hostility!

In Romans 8:5, notice the phrase "set their minds." The key word is *set*. Let's think this word through. Suppose it's wintertime and your home thermostat is *set* at 70 degrees Fahrenheit. The temperature outside is −5 degrees Fahrenheit. In a rush, a member of your family leaves and doesn't securely shut the front door. He or she drives away, and only minutes later the wind blows the front door wide open. You're in another part of the house, and before long you feel that the temperature in your house has dropped drastically. You start searching for an explanation and find the front door wide open with frigid air pouring in. You immediately shut the door, but by now the temperature in your house is below 60 degrees. Then what happens? Once the temperature drops, the thermostat signals the furnace to turn on until it restores your house to the *set* temperature. Without any conscious involvement on your part, the temperature returns to 70 degrees.

Let's return to our example of the man who commits adultery. Years earlier, when courting his wife, his affections and desires were *set* on her. He dreamed of being with her, of being intimate with her, and eventually of how he would ask her to marry him. She was on his mind when he woke up, when he was at work, when he was stuck in traffic, and especially when he laid in bed at night. Simply put, when he didn't have to use his mind for a specific purpose, his thoughts would revert to where they were set: on her.

His buddies would catch him periodically drifting from their conversations. They'd even say, "Hey, man, where are you?"

Embarrassed, he'd casually respond, "Sorry guys, I've got a lot on my mind." He avoided the truth in order to not catch grief from his friends by admitting he was thinking about her. His thoughts were *set*.

But years later, after the engagement, after the wedding, after a few children are born, he finds himself in an adulterous affair with another woman. The same pattern had developed. His mistress was constantly on his mind. When thinking wasn't required, his thoughts returned to their *default setting*. Even when in the company of his wife, his affections were with his mistress. He sought out and longed for her because his mind was *set* on her. Just as a thermostat automatically restores the temperature of a house to where it's *set*, even so the mind will default to where it's *set*.

How does this relate to the believer? When first saved, we are overwhelmed with love. We think about Jesus when we wake up, at breakfast, in the car, on the job, during lunch, after work, when alone, and especially lying in bed at night. We long for our fellowship times with His Spirit. We anticipate with excitement attending the next service, reaching out and sharing Jesus with others, or talking to a fellow Christian about God's ways. Simply put, He consumes our thoughts; our affections are set on Him.

Time passes. We used to anticipate going to a service, experiencing His presence, worshiping Him, and hearing His Word. Now we are physically there, but we're really not present. Our thoughts easily drift to our favorite sports team, the sale at the nearby department store, an upcoming date, the business deal hanging in the balance, the party we've been invited to, and other things. What's happened? Do our thoughts really drift or does our mind go where it is *set*, to what we passionately are *seeking* after? Have we unknowingly acquired other lovers?

My Story

Let me share my story. I attended Purdue University, and during my sophomore year, two of my fraternity brothers came to my room and shared Campus Crusade's Four Spiritual Laws. My spiritual eyes were opened, and I gave my life to Jesus. In no time I was ablaze with passion for God. He was so real, and I was deeply in love with Jesus and profoundly grateful for the freedom He had given me. I shared Him with everyone who would listen, and even with those who wouldn't listen! My fraternity brothers tried to blackball me (throw me out of the fraternity) because I'd discuss Jesus with people at all our parties.

There were girls affiliated with our fraternity who we called "little sisters." Two of them were biological sisters, and between them they had slept with roughly half of the sixty guys in our fraternity. If any of the brothers wanted sex, they knew these girls were the quick and easy option.

A couple of us led one of these girls to Jesus, and within twenty-four hours she had led her sister to the Lord. Without us saying anything about their promiscuous behavior, they immediately stopped having sex with the fraternity brothers. Instead, they started witnessing to the guys they had slept with. The frat brothers were furious. I was seen as the ringleader, because by this time I was leading an all-campus Bible study right in our fraternity house.

Eventually, the vice president came to my room and said, "John, we are going to blackball you." Then he said—these were his exact words—"Why can't you be like the rest of the Christians in this fraternity?" He was speaking of the other guys who attended church on Sunday but were fornicating with their girlfriends, getting drunk at our parties, and participating in other lewd behavior that was the norm in our house.

It was a rough time, but even though the second-in-command in our fraternity had promised to oust me, it never happened. Interestingly enough, they couldn't get enough votes to blackball me. We had led too many to Christ, and they stood with me.

Several months after meeting and falling in love with Jesus, football season rolled around. I was now a junior and, as in years before, I had season tickets to our games. During the previous two years, I hadn't missed one of them, but now I was so excited about Jesus I used the time during the football games to study my Bible. The fraternity house was quiet because all the guys were at the game. It was a chance for some great times of prayer and fellowship with God. No one had said to me, "You shouldn't go to the football games," and I never thought attending a game was wrong. In fact, the next year I went to many of the games. I didn't go my junior year because it was an opportunity to be with God. I passionately wanted to know Him. My mind was set on things above.

By the time I graduated from Purdue with a mechanical engineering degree, many of my fraternity brothers and other students had come to know the Lord—including my wife-to-be, Lisa, who at the time was regarded as one of the wildest girls on campus. My passionate love for Jesus was contagious, and people either loved me or hated me. There was no middle ground: if you met John Bevere, you would find out soon enough where his mind and heart were set because the passion just poured out of me. I was no different than someone who is an avid fan of a sports team or a guy who's fallen head over heels in love with a girl.

I moved to Dallas, Texas. Six months later Lisa moved to Dallas too, and we were married soon afterward. I worked for Rockwell International as an engineer. Once again I met up with guys who didn't like my passion for Jesus. They thought I was too outspoken and couldn't understand why I didn't share in their lewd jokes, off-color discussions, and happy hour ventures after work. But being in a professional environment, my viewpoints and behavior were tolerated more than at the fraternity.

Twenty-two months later I was asked to join the staff of our church. It was one of the largest and best-known churches in America and had international influence. The church had over four hundred employees to support its ministry outreaches, and being asked to come on the team was almost surreal to me. It seemed like the next best thing to going to heaven! I thought my persecution was over because now I would be working with Christians. No more would I face the intense battles previously fought in my fraternity and at Rockwell International.

At that time the Dallas Cowboys were one of the best teams in the National Football League. I really wasn't much of a fan of them since I'd grown up in Michigan, but I heard the guys on staff talking about the Cowboys every Monday. They would gather with their coffee and talk with such passion about the stats of the previous day's game, the great plays, and the victory or loss.

Out of curiosity I started watching the Cowboys on TV. It started out with watching a quarter or two of a game. I liked watching the Cowboys because they were exciting. There was another benefit: it gave me the opportunity to intelligently discuss the games with the guys at the church office.

It all started out seemingly innocent and harmless. But after time, my interest in the Cowboys became stronger, and I started watching entire games. I found myself talking to the TV with great passion, cheering, and sometimes yelling at the players. It eventually got to the place that I didn't miss a game or any portion of one. Even in the offseason my coworkers and I continued conversation about the draft and how great the Cowboys would be the next year. I thought about the team quite often, even when I wasn't discussing stats with the guys. I was now a full-blown fan!

Once the next season arrived, I was consumed with excitement. Every Sunday after service I would rush home and flip on the TV before even removing my church clothes. Sometimes I would just sit there glued to the television even though I was in uncomfortable clothes (a suit and tie) and needed to use the bathroom. I didn't want to miss a single play.

At halftime I would go to my room and change. If Lisa needed help with something, forget it. "Honey, the Cowboys are playing." We'd eat at halftime or, even better, after the game—never while they were playing.

Now I knew all the stats. I'd carefully examine them, and I constantly thought about how the Cowboys could do better. I was the one leading the conversations at work. I would brag about different players' performances on game day. The conversations weren't just on Monday but throughout the week. There were some people at my church who had season tickets, and I jumped at every invitation to go to a game.

Let's fast-forward to the next season, a year later. A short time earlier I had prayed something I thought to be quite simple and seemingly insignificant. However, I didn't realize it would change my life. My prayer was, "Lord, I ask that You would purify my heart. I want to be holy, set apart for You, so if there's anything in my life not pleasing to You, expose and remove it." I had no idea of the depth of this prayer and what would be uncovered.

The football season was coming to a close, and the playoffs were approaching. It was the day of a crucial game. The Cowboys were playing the Philadelphia Eagles. The winner of the game would go to the playoffs and the loser was out. I was glued to the television, not seated on the couch but standing on my feet. The game was too close for sitting. It was the final quarter with only eight minutes left in the game. The Cowboys were behind by four points, and their star quarterback had the team moving down the field. I was now pacing the floor between plays, yelling in frustration at poor performances or reacting with exuberant joy over great plays. The suspense was exhilarating.

All of a sudden, without any notice, the Spirit of God prompted me to pray. A sudden urge overwhelmed me: *Pray, pray, pray!* It was a burden, a strong and weighty feeling deep in my heart. I had come to recognize that this urging happens when the Spirit of God desires you to pull away and pray.

Lisa was not within earshot, so I said out loud, "Lord, there are only eight minutes left in this game. I'll pray when it's over." The urge continued; it didn't let up.

A few minutes went by. Still looking for relief, I exclaimed, "Lord, I'll pray for five hours when this game is over. There are only six minutes left!"

The team was moving the ball down the field. I just knew they would come back and win this important game. However, the urge to pray still didn't lift off me. In fact, it was stronger. I was frustrated. I didn't want to pull away from the game. I said aloud, "Lord, I'll pray the rest of the day—even through the night if that is what You desire!"

I watched the rest of the game. The Cowboys won, and the stadium was electric with excitement. I joined in the crowd's jubilation. However, I had made a promise to God. I immediately turned off the television. I went straight up the stairs to my office, closed the door, and got down on the carpet to pray. But the urge to pray was no longer present. There was no longer a burden. There wasn't even a slight feeling. There was nothing.

I tried to work it up. I tried to pray, and my words were stale and flat. It didn't take long to realize what had happened. I had chosen the Dallas Cowboys game over God's request. I dropped my face into the carpet and moaned, "God, if anyone asked me, 'Who is more important in your life, God or the Dallas Cowboys?' I would without hesitation respond, 'God, of course!' I just showed who was more important. You needed me, but I chose the football game over You. Please forgive me!"

I immediately heard in my heart, "Son, I don't want your sacrifice of five hours of prayer. I desire obedience."

Divided Loyalty

I was overcome with sorrow for being unfaithful to the One who'd given His life for me. It was all for the sake of something of this world—what feeds the hearts, souls, and thoughts of those who have no other source of life. My affections were clearly set on a football team.

In light of this, look carefully at James's words again:

> You adulterers! Don't you realize that friendship with the world makes
> you an enemy of God? I say it again: If you want to be a friend of the
> world, you make yourself an enemy of God. What do you think the
> Scriptures mean when they say that the spirit God has placed within us
> is filled with envy [*jealousy*]? Come close to God, and God will come
> close to you. Wash your hands, you sinners; purify your hearts, *for your
> loyalty is divided between God and the world.* (James 4:4–5, 8 NLT)

My loyalty was divided. Loyalty is identified by the decisions we make,
not merely by the words we speak. There are plenty of men and women who
claim to be loyal, but their actions prove otherwise. Could this be why God's
Word states, "Many will say they are loyal friends, but who can find one who
is truly reliable?" (Proverbs 20:6 NLT)

Back then I would have stated with conviction, "Jesus is most important
in my life, more than anything or anyone else!" However, my choice proved
otherwise. Actions are a higher level of communication than our words.

The apostle John gives the New Testament version of Proverbs 20:6:
"Let's not merely say that we love…let us show the truth by our actions"
(1 John 3:18 NLT). The truth is, the Dallas Cowboys had taken the place
of my first love. I had provoked the Spirit dwelling in me to jealousy. Even
though I had read the warning in Scripture, I was blind to the words. God
was merciful and showed me my error.

John also writes:

> Dear children, keep away from anything that might take God's place in
> your hearts. (1 John 5:21 NLT)

This is not James warning us but John the Beloved. It should be pointed
out that these are the final words he wrote in his lengthy letter. In those days
the apostles couldn't call, text, Facebook, or overnight a letter to those they

loved. A letter was rare and took a lot of effort to be delivered. So if you were writing an inspired letter from the Holy Spirit, He would most likely save the most important piece of information for the end.

To join in with James and John, Paul also scribes a warning to not allow the world to take the place of our loyalty to Jesus. He says:

> You can't have it both ways, banqueting with the Master one day and slumming with demons the next. Besides, the Master won't put up with it. He wants *us*—all or nothing. Do you think you can get off with anything less? Looking at it one way, you could say, "Anything goes. Because of God's immense generosity and grace, we don't have to dissect and scrutinize every action to see if it will pass muster." But the point is not to just get by. We want to live well... (1 Corinthians 10:21–24 The Message)

I'm in awe of these verses. They are so appropriate for the day we are living in. I also like the way the New Living Translation frames Paul's words: "Do we dare to rouse the Lord's jealousy? Do you think we are stronger than he is? You say, 'I am allowed to do anything'—but not everything is good for you" (verses 22–23). Once again, we hear of God's jealousy for us.

No More Football?

The question may now arise, should I not watch any professional sports? Should I not partake of anything the world consumes? If so, how can I live and function in this world?

Allow me to frame the answer like this. As a married man, am I to remove myself from any contact with any woman other than my wife? The answer is no. I am in the company of women continually. I sit on flights next to them—as I currently type this book, a lady is sitting next to me on my flight. I work with women. I interact with women in many other places and circumstances.

As a married man, I try to be friendly to women, in particular because so many of them these days have been mistreated by males. Too often females have been reduced to pieces of meat to satisfy a man's lust or have often not been seen as equal to a man. That infuriates me, as I know God created both men and women in His own image. He's gifted both men and women; He's given the mind of Christ to His covenant men and women alike. He's not partial to a man over a woman, so why have we been that way even in the church?

However, I'm careful to not open my heart and affections in a romantic or inappropriate way toward another woman. I have a covenant with Lisa. When I married her, I declared goodbye to every woman on the planet, romantically speaking. So I have a proper way of relating to all other women.

Let's compare this to a friendship with the world. I can still enjoy watching football, although it's hard to keep my interest up for a full game. The passion is just not there as it was back when my mind was set on the Cowboys. My affections lie with fulfilling the desires of our Lord. Loving and caring for my family, working to help others, working for our ministry, and heeding the wisdom and counsel of God are the things that have my full attention and affection.

Have there been times when other things have gotten out of place in my life? Oh yes! And because I've asked Him to, the Holy Spirit has helped me recognize those things. Golf, food, movies, and even the work of the ministry are a few of the things I've had to address and even cut off for a season to get my affections back in the proper place.

When my love for golf was out of place, the Holy Spirit prompted me one day to give my entire set of clubs to another pastor. Why did the Spirit ask me to do that? Simply put, golf wasn't out of place in the pastor's life, but it was in mine!

After a year and a half of my not playing, the Lord put it on the heart of a professional golfer to give me thousands of dollars' worth of his golf gear. I was puzzled. This professional golfer, a man of prayer, said, "John, I know I'm supposed to do this."

A few months later, a pastor who helped start what is now the largest church in the world in South Korea told me God had put it in his heart to give me a set of clubs. At this point, I was really confused! I asked the Lord, "What do I do with these sets of clubs?"

"Go play golf," I heard in my heart.

"But You had me give all my clubs away a year and a half ago."

I heard God say, "Golf is no longer out of place. It's now recreation and enjoyment for you."

I've played the game ever since. God has used this game in a wonderful way to bring rest and refreshment, and as an avenue for me to connect with my sons, other church leaders, and ministry partners. In fact, in the three years before the writing of this book, over three million dollars for missions outreaches have been donated to Messenger International through golfing with friends and partners and our Messenger Cup golf tournaments. If I had totally cut golf off for the rest of my life, this wouldn't have happened.

We should never be frightened when the Lord requests obedience. It's actually easy to obey when His request lines up with our passion; otherwise, it's drudgery.

Godly Sorrow

James clearly outlines what provokes jealousy in the Spirit of God: friend-ship with the world. I've covered one aspect of what this friendship entails, and there are others. In the next chapter, I'll discuss its root cause, but at this point it's important to address how to respond if our affections are mis-directed. Let's examine James's counsel to believers who've slipped into an inappropriate relationship with the world:

> Wash your hands, you sinners; purify your hearts, for your loyalty is divided between God and the world. Let there be tears for what you have done. Let there be sorrow and deep grief. (James 4:8–9 NLT)

Once God revealed what I'd done in choosing the Cowboys over prayer, I experienced sorrow and deep grief. I realized I'd hurt the One who gave His life for me with an inappropriate "relationship."

I recently talked with a man who had committed adultery against his wife and been restored. He shared with me how he'd sinned over the course of six months, and while telling me, he wept profusely. He's a strong man—a former college football player, a successful businessman, and definitely not the crying type. I was amazed while observing this "man's man" weep. He didn't weep from not feeling forgiven by God or his wife. In fact, his marriage was now stronger than at any time before. He wept over the fact that he had done this to the person he loves deeply; he grieved that he had brought such pain to her. It was admirable to see the depth of his emotion and care for her.

This man's behavior displayed a truth. It's the same behavior a true believer should have over entering an inappropriate relationship with the world. As James writes, "Let there be sorrow and deep grief."

This man attributed no blame to his wife and was truly sorry. It was refreshing to see his genuine humility. I've spoken to others who've committed adultery against their spouses, and their responses were different. Somehow in their "confession" or "testimony" they eventually intermingled their spouse's lack of affection or faults as part of the reason for the adultery.

Scripture speaks of *godly sorrow* and *worldly sorrow* (see 2 Corinthians 7:10). King David exemplified godly sorrow; he was in deep grief because he had hurt the One he loved by committing adultery and murder. He cried out, "Against you, and you alone, have I sinned; I have done what is evil in your sight" (Psalm 51:4 NLT). He cried out and mourned on his face for days and didn't care what those who served him thought about how he was grieving. He wasn't trying to save face; he was heartbroken. And then he was restored.

King Saul was different. He too hurt God's heart by choosing to feed on what the world feeds on—gratification and pride—instead of obeying God's Word. He too was sorry for what he'd done, but his sorrow included the fact that he was caught, was embarrassed publicly in front of those who were to respect him, and faced possible consequences to his rule. Saul's sorrow was worldly. He didn't come away clean, as did David or the former football player. Saul was deceived and polluted in his thinking. It was altered for a short time, but eventually his true motives manifested: pride and self-gratification. His mindset never truly changed.

The apostle Paul declared, "For the kind of sorrow God wants us to experience leads us away from sin" (2 Corinthians 7:10 NLT). This sorrow is God-given; it is rooted in our love for Him. If we love what He can do for us more than we love Him, then our behavior will be no different than Saul's.

In the next two chapters we'll see how friendship with the world affects our experiential relationship with God. We will uncover how substituting good for God has cost us greatly, both on a personal and a corporate church level. But before turning the page, it would be good to take time to pray and ask God to help you identify any inappropriate relationship with the world in your life.

Father, in the name of Jesus, I ask that You would search me and know me, that You would examine my ways and motives. If there is anything in my life that is replacing my affections and love for You, please expose it by Your Spirit. I'm leaving nothing covered. May I truly become and remain Your lover, one who has embraced self-denial for the purpose of following and serving my Lord Jesus Christ. I ask this in Jesus's name. Amen.

9

THE AVOIDED TRUTH

...Work at living a holy life, for those
who are not holy will not see the Lord.
—HEBREWS 12:14 NLT

How little people know who think that
holiness is dull. When one meets the
real thing...it is irresistible.
—C.S. LEWIS

Holiness. Mention the word and watch people recoil and quickly change the subject. For many it carries a bad taste because it's not "cool" and might put a damper on life. All too often it's viewed as synonymous to earning salvation through works, or it seems to be an aspect of legalism. If holiness is brought up, often you'll hear the rebuttal, "I'm free and living in God's grace. Don't attempt to bring me under the law."

However, New Testament holiness is not even remotely connected to works of the law or legalism. It's actually a magnificent way of life that is desirable on many levels. In our time, without a doubt, it's vastly misunderstood.

Why Don't We Talk about It?

Why would any child of God want to avoid discussing holiness when we're emphatically told, "Pursue...holiness, without which no one will see the

Lord"? (Hebrews 12:14) Did you grasp the directness of this statement? No holiness equals no seeing the Lord! That deserves my full attention; how about you?

Consider the president of the United States. Because I'm a citizen of this nation and he's our national leader, I have a "relationship" with him. I am under his governing authority and affected by his decisions, as are 320 million other Americans. But even though I have this relationship with the president, to this day I've not been granted the privilege of a personal audience with him. In fact, in my fifty-plus years as an American, I have never seen one of our presidents in person.

On the other hand, there are other Americans who do get to see the president on a regular basis; they are his friends or work closely with him. In either case, they know the man in the White House much better than I do.

Similarly, there are millions of Christians who are under the rulership of Jesus Christ. He is their professed King. He protects, provides for, and loves them and answers their requests. However, the question is, do they see Him? In other words, do they experience His presence? According to Scripture, we all should be experiencing it. The book of Hebrews states, "We are able to *see* Jesus" (2:9 AMP). Paul elaborates on this privilege:

> …All of us who have had that veil removed can *see* and reflect the glory of the Lord. (2 Corinthians 3:18 NLT)

"The glory of the Lord" is a phrase often misunderstood, and we typically don't use it today. We would more likely say "the greatness of the Lord." In our lingo, Paul is saying, "All of us who have had that veil removed can *see* the greatness of the Lord."

Jesus also identifies those who will see or experience His presence. His exact words at the Last Supper were, "In just a little while the world will no longer see me, but you're going to see me because I am alive and you're about to come alive" (John 14:19 The Message).

There are two clear facts here. First, a very real aspect of Christianity is seeing Him. Second, we are able to behold Him in a way the world cannot.

Why is it important to see God? First, as with the president, if we don't see Him, we can't know Him. We can only know about Him.

There's a second reason that's equally important. Without beholding Him, we cannot be changed or transformed into His likeness. In the same verse as quoted before, Paul mentions that those who see the Lord "are being transformed into the same image from one degree of glory to another" (2 Corinthians 3:18 ESV). Transformation is crucial in the life of a believer.

Have you encountered someone who professes to know Jesus Christ, and has done so for some time, but lives as if he or she has never met Him? Why is this? This person is simply not experiencing the process of transformation. They are not being changed into His likeness.

Paul prophesied that our days will be difficult. Interestingly, he wrote that these stressful times will not result from persecution for our faith, as in his day, but from professing Christians who don't keep the words of Jesus. They will still behave just like those who have no relationship with God. They will still love themselves and their money, disobey their parents, communicate in a crude manner, refuse to forgive, seek fame and reputation, betray their friends, love pleasure more than they love God—the list goes on. Paul clearly stated, "They will hold to the outward form of our religion, but reject its real power" (2 Timothy 3:5 TEV). The power they will reject is grace's ability to transform us, a core reality of true Christianity. The Amplified Bible states, "Their conduct belies the genuineness of their profession."

These professing believers are deceived, for they will be "always learning and never able to come to the knowledge of the truth" (2 Timothy 3:7). As I said before, there is one major problem with deception: it's deceiving! We can fully believe we are fine with God when in reality we're not. Many such "believers" attend churches, conferences, worship nights, Bible schools, and connect groups. They love learning but remain unchanged in character and behavior.

The Bottom Line

Here's the bottom line: only those who walk in holiness can see God—can *enter His presence.* Jesus couldn't have made it any clearer when He said, "A little while longer and the world will see Me no more, but you will see Me. Because I live, you will live also. He who has My commandments and keeps them, it is he who loves Me. And he who loves Me…I will love him and *manifest* Myself to him" (John 14:19, 21).

The word *manifest* is defined as "to make clear or evident to the eye or the understanding; show plainly." *The Complete Word Study Dictionary* defines this word, *emphanizo*, as "to make apparent, cause to be seen, to show." It is even more specific in stating, "Of a person…meaning to let oneself be intimately known and understood."

Jesus stated that only those who keep His commandments are the ones He will make Himself apparent to. They will be the ones who see Him, who enter His presence and thereby come to know Him intimately. *This privilege is not promised to all believers*, only to those who pursue obeying His Word—those who pursue holiness.

In the 1980s I was asked to host the senior pastor of the largest church in the world. His name is Dr. David Yonggi Cho, and he is from Seoul, South Korea. At the time there were 750,000 people in his church. One of my responsibilities in hosting him at our church in America was to drive him from the hotel to a service. I'd only been a Christian a few years, so it was overwhelming to get this privilege.

Dr. Cho travelled with approximately fifteen businessmen from his church. The lead businessman approached me on the day of the meeting and said, "Mr. Bevere, you are the one who will drive Dr. Cho to the service tonight, is that correct?"

"Yes, sir."

With a solemn gaze, he said, "Mr. Bevere, I have important matters to discuss with you. First and foremost, do not speak to Dr. Cho during the car ride to the meeting. He doesn't like talking before he ministers." This was not the only instruction, but it was the top priority on the list.

I drove up to the hotel that night and waited in the vehicle until the men who traveled with Dr. Cho opened the car door. Dr. Cho climbed in the front seat beside me and the presence of God filled the car. It was overwhelming. God's majesty and love were very real and apparent.

As I drove, tears streamed down my face even though I'm not much of a crier. Halfway to the auditorium, we stopped at a traffic light and I couldn't stand it any longer. I did what the lead assistant had told me not to do. I reverently said to my passenger, "Dr. Cho, the presence of God is in this car."

He looked at me and said, "Yes, I know."

I spent a lot of time with this man during his visit. We played golf together. I drove him to other functions, ate with him, and brought him to and from the airport. In every situation, whether in the public eye or not, Dr. Cho was godly, reverent, sincere, and humble in attitude and action. I pondered the hours he spent each day with the Lord. It was obvious why the presence of God was so strong on his life. He truly pursued adherence to the words of Jesus.

I've often experienced the presence of the Lord in similar ways in services, during prayer, while reading the Word of God, or just going about my day. I understand why Moses left everything for this magnificent presence. There have been seasons in my life when His presence has been aloof, sometimes due to my not keeping His words. Other times I was in the heat of trials. I understand the latter is unavoidable, but the former is preventable.

To *manifest* doesn't just mean "to see" but also carries all of what being with Him entails. To manifest means to bring from the unseen into the seen realm, from the unheard into the heard, and from the unknown into the known. It's when God makes Himself known to our minds and senses. He gives intimate understanding, knowledge, and insight into Himself and His ways. The writer of Hebrews described these privileged ones as those "who have consciously tasted the heavenly gift and have become sharers of the

Holy Spirit" (6:4 AMP). Even though His manifest presence is accessible to every child of God, only those who obey His words (walk in true holiness) experience this privilege.

Paul quotes God's audible words to Moses. This statement is an unchanging truth that spans throughout not only the old covenant but also the new. It's directed toward those who are already His:

> Come out from among unbelievers, and separate yourselves from them, says the LORD. Don't touch their filthy things, and I will welcome you.
> (2 Corinthians 6:17 NLT)

It's clear. God welcoming us into His presence is conditional, not automatic. We have to fulfill His request before being granted an audience with Him. Paul's statement is perfectly aligned with Jesus's words. *The Message* Bible paraphrases this verse:

> "So leave the corruption and compromise; leave it for good," says God. "Don't link up with those who will pollute you. I want you all for myself."

Paul then gives our proper response to God's conditional promise:

> ...Let us cleanse ourselves from everything that can defile our body or spirit. And let us work toward complete holiness because we fear God.
> (2 Corinthians 7:1 NLT)

Once again, we find the purpose of pursuing authentic holiness is the honor of being welcomed into God's manifest presence.

Atmosphere or Presence?

After seeing all these quotes in the New Testament from the apostles, Jesus, and the Father, we must ask, why isn't this important aspect of New Testament Christianity discussed, taught, and proclaimed more frequently? Could it be the enemy has devised a clever plan to encourage us to embrace a salvation devoid of genuine holiness, which would keep us from beholding Him and thereby make it impossible for us to be transformed? This crafty strategy of the enemy has occurred not only on a personal level but corporately too. In regard to our gatherings, could it be that we have substituted *atmosphere* for the *presence of God*?

One of the great advances the church has made in the past twenty years is to create better atmospheres in our worship services. Years ago, when you entered a typical church, you were often faced with a substandard building, outdated décor, and a wearisome service. Our music was repulsive, the messages quirky and irrelevant, and our clothes—to say the least—very unfashionable. We allowed practically anything in music performance or the message to the congregation as long as it was done "in the name of the Lord." To put it frankly, to society we appeared completely inept. There were scattered exceptions, but this was the norm a couple decades ago.

Due to wise leadership, we've changed this paradigm. Now we play remarkable music, truly inspired and relevant. We've designed church buildings that are comfortable, with state of the art sound and lighting. Our services are tight and relevant, and we've created attractive, fun children's areas and teen auditoriums. Many church foyers now have coffee bars, smartly arranged areas for people to connect, and well-stocked bookstores. We conduct our services so they're no longer loathsome to the lost. Simply put, we've created great atmospheres in our meetings, and I believe God is pleased with this excellence.

But have we made externals our end goal? Atmospheres are good to create an introduction to what's truly important: the presence of God. Atmospheres are man-made. Hollywood, Las Vegas, Disney, Broadway, and others in entertainment industries are masters at evoking emotions. Have we settled into their methods? Are we satisfied with only stimulating the feelings of the people who attend our services? Is the true presence of God filling our sanctuaries, or are we simply doing in the realm of Christianity what others are so good at elsewhere?

Here is the reality: *to be changed, we need His presence!*

Could this be why we have people who are excited about Christianity, love worship, and continue to learn but are not being transformed? If so, the consequences are costly. These people will not be conformed to the image of Jesus. Years ago we tolerated bad atmospheres, but I recall often being in services filled with the awesome presence of God. I couldn't always articulate how it happened, but I was truly changed.

So the question is, why can't we have both atmosphere and presence? We don't have to choose! However, to have God's presence, we must pursue holiness.

On another front, the clever plan of the enemy to design a Christianity devoid of holiness has made the gospel of Jesus Christ appear to be a powerless religion to many who are lost, thus making following Jesus unattractive—when in reality it's the most fascinating life possible.

What Is Holiness?

So what is true holiness? The Greek word is *hagios.* Thayer's *Greek–English Lexicon of the New Testament* lists one definition as "set apart for God, to be, as it were, exclusively his." In light of this meaning, allow me to quote God's words again: "Don't link up with those who will pollute you. I want you all for myself" (2 Corinthians 6:17 The Message).

When Lisa and I were married, she became exclusively mine and I became exclusively hers. She was committed to me, to live for me, and I to her. Prior to meeting and marrying Lisa, I didn't factor in her desires or wishes; I simply didn't know her. Lisa doesn't like dark furniture, watching professional sports or certain types of movies, listening to jazz or big band music, eating Thousand Island dressing or blue cheese, and a host of other things. I liked, did, listened to, or ate most everything on that list! However, after we got married I avoided these things, as I knew they didn't please her. There were plenty of other things we could enjoy together.

More than this, I stayed away from inappropriate contact with other ladies. Before we were married I had a lot of friends who were female, and it was normal for me to entertain, hang out with, and even date these girls. But the day I said "I do" to Lisa was the day my relationships with those other females forever changed.

To sum it up, I was passionately in love with Lisa; it was now a pleasure to live for her desires and no longer just my own.

I've observed husbands who have little regard for their wives' wishes; they think selfishly. They may technically be married, but these husbands and wives are not experiencing close intimacy. When we enter the covenant relationship of marriage, we sign up to serve our spouses for the rest of our lives. There isn't any room for selfishness in a good marriage.

Before we entered into a covenant relationship with Jesus, we were of this world and loved by it. It was perfectly normal for us to live motivated by what gratified our flesh and stimulated our eyes. We pursued status, reputation, and anything else that would serve our pride and selfishness.

Now that we've met and entered into a relationship with Jesus, we must honestly ask, are we living for ourselves or for Him? We can be technically "related" to Jesus but not be experiencing intimacy with Him (lacking His manifest presence)—no different than the husband who lives selfishly in his marriage.

Paul writes, "Those who receive his new life will no longer live for themselves. Instead they will live for Christ" (2 Corinthians 5:15 NLT). This is the only way to experience a healthy relationship (or marriage) with Him.

If we review the behavior James identifies as committing adultery with the world, we find he's confronting believers who've reverted back to living *selfishly*:

> …If your heart is full of…*selfishness*, don't brag or lie to cover up the
> truth. That kind of wisdom doesn't come from above. It is earthly and

selfish and comes from the devil himself. Whenever people are…*selfish*, they cause trouble and do all sorts of cruel things.

…Why do you fight and argue with each other? Isn't it because you are full of *selfish* desires that fight to control your body? You want something you don't have, and you will do anything to get it. …But you still cannot get what you want, and you won't get it by fighting and arguing. You should pray for it. Yet even when you do pray, your prayers are not answered, because you pray just for *selfish* reasons. *You people aren't faithful to God* [you're adulterers and adulteresses]! Don't you know that if you love the world, you are God's enemies? And if you decide to be a friend of the world, you make yourself an enemy of God. (James 3:14–16, 4:1–4 CEV)

Notice the word *selfish* is used frequently in these verses? James does that because there are two kinds of behavioral patterns: *giving* and *taking*. That's it. Taking is self-seeking, worldly, and unfaithful to God. The believer who's motivated to live this way is identified as an adulterer or adulteress. Jesus's commandments are not top priority in this scenario. Instead, *what I want* is the priority.

The world is driven by selfishness, and so is the believer who is unholy. He or she is not fully devoted to God but is self-centered in conduct. Therefore he or she is lured by what gratifies the flesh and the eyes or gives status and reputation.

The motivation behind sin is selfishness. The man who steals does so for himself. The man who lies does so to protect or benefit himself. The man who commits adultery against his wife considers not his wife and children but his own passion. The man who murders does so for himself. The man who disobeys authority does so because he believes he knows better and wants better for himself. The man who pursues popularity and fame does so to appease his insecurity and pride. In the incident when I was watching the football game and refused to obey God's word and turn off the television and pray, I did so for myself.

A New Nature

The citizens of this world are bound to such behavior because they are ruled by fleshly (selfish) appetites and desires. The believer has been liberated from this slavery (see Romans 6:11–14). The Son has truly made us free!

In the Old Testament, God's people were told not to commit sins, but they couldn't obey because their nature was sinful (selfish). The Old Testament decisively proves that man can never live *good* in God's eyes in his own ability. People are bound to their fleshly appetites and cravings, contrary to God's desire.

As new creations, we now have a new nature. We are alive inside, recreated in the image of Jesus with the inward ability to live the truly good life. Look at Paul's words:

> With the Lord's authority I say this: Live no longer as the Gentiles do,
> for they are hopelessly confused. Their minds are full of darkness; they
> wander far from the life God gives because they have closed their minds
> and hardened their hearts against him. They have no sense of shame.
> They live for lustful pleasure and eagerly practice every kind of impu-
> rity. (Ephesians 4:17–19 NLT)

The unbeliever is enslaved to the appetites of his flesh. His spirit is dead—lifeless. He has no inward ability to live *good* before God. I find it puzzling when Christians are shocked by the behavior of nonbelievers. They fail to realize that an un-regenerated person only does what is normal according to his nature. He sins. He's selfish. If he has strong willpower, he can put on a good front and even appear unselfish. But make no mistake about it; he's bound to his fallen nature.

Paul goes on to distinguish a true believer:

> Since you have heard about Jesus and have learned the truth that
> comes from him, throw off your old sinful nature and your former

way of life, which is corrupted by lust and deception. Instead, let the Spirit renew your thoughts and attitudes. Put on your new nature, created to be like God—truly righteous and holy. (Ephesians 4:21–24 NLT)

Unlike the unsaved person, the believer has been given a new inward nature. We are instructed to submit to it, to live a holy life. The Christian has a choice that the unbeliever doesn't possess. A Christian can yield to the powerful inward nature of the new creation or continue submitting to the flesh's desires. The decision is ours.

Position versus Behavior

At this juncture it's important to ensure clarity. There are two important aspects of holiness, and the New Testament speaks of both. Confusion always results from lumping the two together.

The first entails our *position* in Christ. Paul writes, "Even before he made the world, God loved us and chose us in Christ to be *holy* and without fault in his eyes" (Ephesians 1:4 NLT). This holiness is solely due to what Jesus did for us and speaks of our place in Christ. We never could have earned this position by our behavior; it's His gift to us.

When Lisa became my wife, it wasn't something she earned but rather a position she received because I gave my heart to her. In our covenant, she did the same thing for me. Period.

The second aspect of holiness is the *behavior* that results from holding this position. Once Lisa became my wife, her conduct reflected her loyalty to me. She no longer flirted or sought relationships with other men. Her actions corresponded to her unwavering relationship as my wife. And of course as her husband I did the same.

This aspect of our relationship with God is what I'm describing here. Peter affirms this:

So you must live as God's obedient children. Don't slip back into your old ways of living to satisfy your own desires. You didn't know any better then. But now you *must be holy in everything you do*, just as God who chose you is holy. For the Scriptures say, "You must be holy because I am holy." And remember that the heavenly Father to whom you pray has no favorites. He will judge or reward you according to *what you do*. So you must live in reverent fear of him during your time as "foreigners in the land." (1 Peter 1:14–17 NLT)

It's clear that Peter is talking to God's children, not the lost. We are told God will judge or reward us according to *what we do*, which is referring to our *actions*, not our *position* in Christ. The blood of Jesus forgives our sins, but there is a certain judgment that will occur with God's children in regard to *what we do*. Paul affirms this in 2 Corinthians 5:9–11. To willfully live in disobedience is not an insignificant matter. If we are truly His, we should passionately want to not hurt His heart by living in sin.

As did James and Paul, Peter affirms that our old ways of living were motivated by selfish desires, and he urges us to be holy in everything we *do*. Let me reiterate: he's talking about our *behavior and lifestyle*, not our *position* in Christ. In the same passage, another translation states that we must "be holy in all our conduct and manner of living" (verse 15 AMP). There's no gray area or confusion about what Peter is referring to. In agreement with Paul, Peter simply announces that if we have been saved by grace, we are enabled by the gift of our new nature to live differently than the world, to live a holy life.

Recall Hebrews 12:14, which charges us to pursue holiness. I recently discovered a sermon on this verse by Charles Spurgeon that arrested my attention. This excerpt will show you why:

There has been a desperate attempt made by certain Antinomians to get rid of the injunction [to pursue holiness] which the Holy Spirit here means to enforce. They have said that this is the imputed holiness of Christ. Do they not know, when they so speak, that, by an open perversion, they utter that which is false? …We are to follow holiness,— this must be practical holiness; the opposite of impurity, as it is written, "God hath not called us unto uncleanness, but unto holiness." …This is another kind of holiness. It is, in fact…practical, vital holiness which is the purport of this admonition. It is conformity to the will of God, and obedience to the Lord's command.[13]

Wow! Clearly the church isn't experiencing a weakened idea of holiness for the first time, for Spurgeon taught this in the 1800s. But when our understanding is based in the truth of Scripture, we can see that holiness relates both to who we are in Christ and to how we live on His behalf.

Here's the important point: neither our *position* in Christ nor our *behavior* is due to what we've earned or produced by our own merits or strength. Both are products of what's freely given to us. However, in regard to our lifestyle, we have to cooperate with or yield to our new nature to produce good behavior.

Another Definition of Holiness

As we've now seen, holiness means more than merely being His. It speaks of conduct that is morally acceptable to God. This brings us to another definition of holiness. The Greek word *hagios* also describes "pure, sinless, upright" behavior. This meaning of the word scares some people, but it shouldn't. I can explain what I mean by telling an embarrassing story that happened in my childhood.

In our family I was the only boy out of six children, so my jobs were all the outdoor chores: washing the car, mowing the lawn, raking leaves, shoveling snow, and so forth. Since my friends and I loved sports, our normal pattern was to hurry through our chores to make time to compete in a game.

It was springtime, and the grass was growing again after a long winter. My friends and I had arranged a ball game after school. I had let the lawn get a little out of control, and the grass was long. My dad had instructed me the previous night that I had to mow the lawn before I could play with my buddies—and the chore needed to be done before he got home from work.

I hurried home from school, changed clothes, and pulled the lawn mower out of the garage for the first time that spring. I knew I had to move fast, as my friends would soon be ready to play. I pulled the mower's start cord more than once. The engine didn't turn over and ignite. I pushed the choke button a couple times to get additional gas in the carburetor chamber. I continued pulling the cord over and over and got the same result: nothing.

I thought, *I've probably flooded the carburetor and need to wait a few minutes for it to drain.*

I waited and in the meantime checked the oil. I then rechecked all the switches to make sure everything was set to the start position. Everything looked good; I just needed to wait out the few minutes. I did, and I tried again—but still the engine did not start.

I was now frustrated, so I checked the spark plug to see if it was dirty. But it looked good. *What's wrong?* I thought. I was getting more upset by the minute. If the lawnmower didn't start, I wouldn't get the grass cut, I wouldn't satisfy my dad, and I couldn't go play with my friends.

What can I do? I thought. *If I bring the mower to the shop, it will be dark before it's fixed and I'll miss the game. Maybe I can borrow someone else's lawnmower, but that will take a lot of time.* We had a pair of hand shears, but it would take me until late at night to hand cut every blade of grass; and even if I did, they would all be uneven and the yard would look horrible. That was an impossible idea.

I was angry at the piece of junk. *It's going to cost me some fun,* I thought. The mower was broken and I knew it. I was faced with an impossible situation. There would be no way I could get the grass cut and meet my friends on time.

Then my buddy who was going with me to play came over and said, "Ready, John?"

"No. My dad told me I had to mow the lawn before I can go, and the lawnmower won't start," I said. "There's no time to get it fixed, borrow one, or cut the lawn by hand. I'm not going to be able to play today."

My friend, who was a little wiser than me, said, "Let me look."

"Sure, go ahead!" I was desperate.

The first thing he did was open the gas tank. He looked in it, started laughing, and said, "There's your problem, John. You don't have any gas in the tank."

I was embarrassed but relieved, too.

You knucklehead, I thought, *That should have been the first thing you checked!* I immediately filled the tank, and the mower started right away. I quickly mowed the lawn, and we headed out to play with our other friends.

How does this relate to holiness? When we see the words *pure, sinless*, and *upright* as the definition of holiness, we get frustrated and think, *It's not possible.* That's because we try to imagine living this way in our own strength. It's like trying to cut the entire yard of grass with hand shears in time for a game: utterly impossible! It will be dark outside before you're done with a fraction of the yard.

But we have a new nature, which can be compared to possessing a lawn-mower. However, without gas in the tank, we are just as bad off as we were without the lawnmower. We need gas in the tank to make it run.

In the next chapter we will find out what fuels our new nature—what gives us the ability to walk purely before God.

10

THE FUEL

...We make known to you the grace of God
bestowed on the churches of Macedonia...
that according to their ability, yes,
and beyond their ability...
—2 Corinthians 8:1-3

...*Be ye perfect* is not...a command to do
the impossible. [God] is going to make us
into creatures that can obey that command.
—C.S. Lewis

To pursue holiness is not an end in itself; it's the gateway into the presence of Jesus. The Master makes it clear: "The person who has My commands and keeps them is the one who [really] loves Me...and I [too] will love him and will show (reveal, manifest) Myself to him. [I will let Myself be clearly seen by him and make Myself real to him]" (John 14:21 AMP). We intimately come to know the Master when we keep His words.

The writer of Hebrews affirms this: "Pursue...holiness, without which no one will see the Lord" (Hebrews 12:14). It's simple: no holiness, no seeing Jesus—no entering His presence!

Holiness is about being exclusively His, set apart for Him. It also means to be "pure, sinless, upright." Both definitions go hand in hand. To belong to Him is to live for Him, to please Him in our behavior. Colossians 1:10 states

He desires "that you may walk (live and conduct yourselves) in a manner worthy of the Lord, fully pleasing to Him" (AMP). After all, He's returning for a glorious church, "not having spot or wrinkle or any such thing, but that she should be holy and without blemish" (Ephesians 5:27).

Interestingly, this is the single description of those He's returning for. Think of it—Scripture doesn't identify His Bride as being powerful, relevant, organized, leadership-driven, well connected, worshipful, or joyful. All those are great traits, but the predominant characteristic He wants in His Bride is that she be "holy and without blemish."

Another interesting fact is that holiness is the predominant quality that describes God Himself. The prophet Isaiah and the apostle John each wrote about seeing God's throne room. Both men could not help but notice the mighty angels who've surrounded Him for ages and are still crying out, "Holy, holy, holy" (see Isaiah 6:3 and Revelation 4:8). They don't shout "faithful" or "loving" or "kind" or "generous." He has all of these wonderful characteristics, but *holiness* trumps them all.

Two Options

The charge to be *pure, sinless,* and *upright* arouses the age-old question: "But how can we live this way?" We tried and failed miserably in our own strength. We wanted to obey the law of God residing within our conscience (see Romans 2:14–15), but we repeatedly failed.

But then came *grace*. We couldn't earn it by good behavior and still can't. We didn't deserve it and still don't. God's gift completely forgives us and will continue to when we fall short. We have been saved from our sins!

Even though we have this wonderful knowledge, we are still frustrated by our inability to keep His instructions. Why is it such a struggle? We have been born again with a new nature, so why do we keep failing?

At this point we think we may have an option, one that gives us an out. We can teach that holiness refers only to our position in Christ and altogether neglect the scriptures calling us to holy behavior, thus alleviating any conviction. We can excuse our lack of transformation because, after all, we are only human and will continually make mistakes. Our focus will be solely on an abbreviated doctrine of grace—how it covers all sins past, present, and future. If we teach and believe only this, we foster a false security, for we've silenced our consciences. Yet if we listen more carefully to our hearts, we will hear them crying out, "There must be more!"

Sadly, many of us have settled for this option and, in doing so, neglected a boatload of New Testament scriptures calling us to a godly lifestyle. I could list many pages of scripture on this topic, but allow me to start with just one passage:

> My dear children, I am writing this to you so that you will not sin. ...
> And we can be sure that we know him if we obey his commandments.
> If someone claims, "I know God," but doesn't obey God's command-
> ments, that person is a liar and is not living in the truth. But those
> who obey God's word truly show how completely they love him. That
> is how we know we are living in him. Those who say they live in God
> should live their lives as Jesus did. (1 John 2:1, 3–6 NLT)

John didn't write, "Don't worry if you sin because, after all, we're human." No, he bluntly writes "that you will not sin." This should be our target. If we miss it, we do have the blood of Jesus that cleanses us. Our goal, however, is to live just as Jesus did. And according to Scripture, it's not an impossible goal. So a choice to overlook repeated sin due to "human nature" doesn't align with John's words or numerous other New Testament scriptures.

Is there something missing? Would God not have foreseen our dilemma and already devised a plan? In fact, He did! It's the option less spoken of, but it aligns perfectly with the overall counsel of the New Testament. It's the aspect of grace many are unaware of. It's the fuel that powers our new nature. To put it simply, grace empowers us to live the good life.

The Unknown Truth of Grace

In 2009 a survey was conducted with thousands of Christians across America. Those surveyed were born-again, Bible believers from various churches. The question asked in the survey was, "Give three or more definitions or descriptions of the grace of God." The overwhelming majority of the responses were *salvation, an unmerited gift,* and *forgiveness of sins.*

It's good to know American Christians understand we are saved only by grace. Salvation doesn't come by the sprinkling of water, belonging to a church, keeping religious laws, doing good works that outweigh the bad, and so forth. Most American evangelical believers are well established in these foundational truths about God's grace because they've been emphasized from our pulpits, and I believe God is pleased with this.

However, the tragedy is that only 2 percent of the thousands surveyed stated that grace is God's *empowerment.*[14] Yet this is exactly how God has defined and described His grace. He says:

> "*My grace* is all you need, for *my power* works best in your weakness."
> (2 Corinthians 12:9 TEV and NLT)

God refers to His grace as His empowerment. The word *weakness* means "inability." God is saying, "My grace is My empowerment, and it is optimized in situations beyond your ability."

The apostle Peter defines God's grace the same way. He writes, "Grace and peace be multiplied to you…as His divine power [*grace*] has given to us all things that pertain to life and godliness…" (2 Peter 1:2–3). Once again grace is referred to as "His divine power." Peter states that every resource or ability needed to live a godly, holy life is available through the empowerment of grace.

But the fact that the survey revealed only 2 percent of American Christians know this truth is a huge problem. Allow me to explain. In order to receive from God, we must believe. This is why New Testament scriptures are called "the word of faith" (see Romans 10:8). Simply put, if we don't believe, we don't receive.

Here's one basic example of this. Jesus died for the sins of the whole world. However, only the ones who believe are those who are saved. So here's the huge problem: we can't believe what we don't know. If 98 percent of Christians don't know that God's grace is His empowerment, then 98 percent are attempting to live holy in their own ability. This leads to frustration and defeat. Their new nature isn't empowered; in other words, there's no gas in their tank!

Let's take this one step further by going to the Greek. The word that is most frequently used for *grace* in the New Testament is *charis*. This word is defined by *Strong's Exhaustive Concordance* as "gift, benefit, favor, gracious, and liberality."

If you take this initial definition and couple it together with selected scriptures from the books of Romans, Galatians, and Ephesians, you'll pinpoint the definition of grace the majority of America is familiar with. However, *Strong's* continues its definition: "the divine influence upon the heart, and its reflection in the life." We see there is an outward reflection of what is done in the heart, which speaks of the empowerment of grace.

In the book of Acts, Barnabas came to the church of Antioch, and when he arrived he "saw the evidence of the grace of God" (Acts 11:23 NIV). He didn't hear about grace; rather, he saw the evidence of it. People's outward behavior verified grace's empowerment in their hearts.

This is why the apostle James writes, "Show me your faith [grace] without your works, and I will show you my faith [grace] by my works" (James 2:18). I inserted the word *grace* for *faith* because it is by faith (believing God's Word) that we access the grace of God: "We have access by faith into this grace" (Romans 5:2). Without faith—without believing—there's no empowerment (grace). James emphatically states, "Let me see the evidence of empowerment." It's the true indicator we've received grace through believing.

Grace is a *gift*. With what we've just learned, let's expand this understanding further. Salvation is a *gift of grace*. Forgiveness is a *gift of grace*.

Healing is a *gift of grace*. Provision is a *gift of grace*. Receiving God's nature is a *gift of grace*. Empowerment is a *gift of grace*. All of these are manifestations of His favor upon our lives, each undeserved and unmerited.

In regard to empowerment, *grace gives us the ability to go beyond our natural ability.* We didn't have the ability to deliver ourselves from hell; grace did. We shouldn't live in freedom, but grace enables us. We couldn't change our nature; grace did. We don't have the ability to live holy, but grace enables us. No wonder we call it amazing!

A Thought-Provoking Question

Recently, in prayer, the Lord asked me, "Son, how did I introduce *grace* in My book, the New Testament?"

As an author who's written over a dozen books, the question carried significant meaning to me. Let me explain. Whenever I'm bringing up a new term in a book, one that most are not familiar with, I want to give the primary definition when I introduce it. Later in the book I can give secondary definitions. So when a new term is introduced in the book of an experienced author I assume it carries the primary definition.

My response to the Lord's question was, "I don't know."

So without hesitation, I quickly went to my Bible concordance and found out how God introduced grace in the New Testament. Here is what I discovered: "Of His fullness we have all received, and grace for grace" (John 1:16).

Notice John wrote "grace for grace." I have a friend who lives in Athens, Greece. He's a man who was born there and not only speaks Greek as his primary language but also has studied ancient Greek. He's one of my go-to people when it comes to the Greek language. He shared with me that the apostle was actually communicating that God has given us "the richest abundance of grace." In other words, the apostle John was stating that the overflow, or abundance, of what grace does for us is it gives us the fullness of Jesus Christ! Did you hear that? *The fullness of Jesus Christ Himself!* That says a lot, especially concerning nature, ability, and power!

Let's highlight the magnitude of this statement through a couple of examples. Suppose I approach a high school basketball player. He's not a starter on his team; in fact he sits on the bench until there are two minutes left in the game and the team is either twenty points ahead or behind.

I pull him aside and say, "We now have the scientific means of being able to put on you the fullness of LeBron James," who is, of course, one of the greatest to ever play the game.

What do you think his response would be? He'd say, "Yes, right away! What exactly do I need to do?"

Once we did this—you guessed it—he'd not only start on his high school team, but his team would win the state championship. He would get a full-ride scholarship to a university and eventually be the first pick in the NBA draft.

Or suppose I approach a struggling businessman and say, "We have a new scientific means of being able to put on you the combined fullness of Donald Trump, Steve Jobs, and Bill Gates."

What do you think his response would be? "I want it. Let's do it!" he'd cry out excitedly. What would he do after receiving these men's full abilities? He'd start thinking of ways of investing that he'd never thought of before and would become very successful.

Grace hasn't given us the fullness of LeBron James, Steve Jobs, Donald Trump, Bill Gates—or Albert Einstein, Johann Sebastian Bach, Roger Federer, or any other great men or women in history. No, it gives us the fullness of Jesus Christ Himself! Do you comprehend the magnitude of this?

So maybe it comes as something of a surprise, but in the New Testament, God didn't introduce grace as a free gift, salvation, or forgiveness of sins! Let me be clear. I'm forever grateful for these amazing benefits, but they are brought out later in the New Testament. God introduced grace as the impartation of the fullness of Jesus Christ. That speaks of possessing His nature and empowerment! This is why John boldly declares, "As He [*Jesus*] is, so are we in this world" (1 John 4:17).

Have you ever heard a minister say, "We are really no different than sinners, we're just forgiven," or "We are just unworthy worms," or "We are humans with a sin nature and bound to it"? How can anyone who reads the Bible say these things! Even the natural world teaches us better.

Have you ever heard of a lion giving birth to a squirrel? Have you ever heard of a thoroughbred racehorse giving birth to a worm? Yet Scripture states that we are bone of His bone and flesh of His flesh (see Ephesians 5:30). We are told, "Beloved, now we are children of God" (1 John 3:2). Not *later*, when we get to heaven, but *now* we are the sons and daughters of God. How could God give birth to an unworthy worm? We're born of God—we have His seed within us, we have His divine nature. As He is, so are we in this world! Not in the next life, in *this world*!

Let's look at Peter's words again:

> May God give you *more and more* grace…by his divine power [grace],
> God has given us everything we need for living a godly life. (2 Peter
> 1:2–3 NLT)

When it comes to empowerment, the gift of grace is not a one-time occurrence at the moment of salvation. It is something we need continually; we need "more and more grace." This is why we are told, "Let us therefore come boldly to the throne of grace, that we may…find grace to help in time of need" (Hebrews 4:16). It's the fuel we need in our tank!

Now listen to what James says to believers after exposing their self-seeking, adulterous lifestyle:

> You adulterers! Don't you realize that friendship with the world makes
> you an enemy of God? …But he gives us *even more grace* to stand against
> such evil desires… So humble yourselves before God. (James 4:4, 6 NLT)

Read these words again carefully: "He gives us *even more grace* to stand against" selfish desires. The Amplified Bible renders it as, "But He gives us more and more grace." This unmerited empowerment gives us the ability we didn't previously possess: the capacity to live a holy life.

This grace, extended to those who humble themselves by believing His Word, infuses the *strength* of His divine nature into our being. The proud focus on their ability; the humble depend on God's empowerment. David's oldest brother, Eliab, was a proud man who didn't depend on God's empowerment but faced the giant Goliath in his own strength (see 1 Samuel 16–17). David was a humble man who confronted the giant in God's strength. We know what the outcome was in each situation.

Jesus exemplified depending on God's grace. In the Garden of Gethsemane, He was in the middle of a huge fight. His flesh wanted out of what His Father commanded, but He humbled Himself in prayer while His disciples slept. He cried out for the fuel to get through His greatest battle against selfishness. It was a time of need, and He came boldly to obtain His Father's empowering grace to get through the fight. The disciples failed, but not without first being warned by Jesus: "The spirit is willing, but the body is weak" (Matthew 26:41 NLT)!

In my story about needing to cut the grass before playing ball, I didn't buy or deserve either the lawnmower or the gas. They were both gifts from my dad. The lawnmower could represent our brand-new nature, which we need to be given only one time. Possessing it gave me the potential to cut the lawn. But without the gas, I was just as bad off as when I didn't have the mower. The gas represents the *empowerment* of grace. The gas is not a one-time gift—I needed more of it each time I mowed the lawn.

Grace gave us His nature when we were saved, but we need more and more grace to empower our nature so we can live as Jesus did.

Dos and Don'ts

Let's revisit Paul's words to the Ephesians. They'll take on greater meaning after what we've just discussed.

> With the Lord's authority I say this: Live no longer as the Gentiles do,
> for they are hopelessly confused. They have no sense of shame. They
> live for lustful pleasure and eagerly practice every kind of impurity. Put
> on your new nature, created to be like God—truly righteous and holy.
> (Ephesians 4:17, 19, 24 NLT)

There should be a distinct difference between the lost and believers, not just in what we believe but in the way we live. This is because we have a new nature. But we have to put it on. In other words, we have to humble ourselves by believing in and yielding to grace's empowerment. Look at it like this. My dad could give me a lawnmower, but it would be no good if I didn't put gas in it, start it, and use it. This is putting on our new nature. *We use it!*

Paul continues to describe what this looks like practically:

> So stop telling lies. Let us tell our neighbors the truth, for we are all
> parts of the same body. And "don't sin by letting anger control you."
> Don't let the sun go down while you are still angry, for anger gives a
> foothold to the devil. If you are a thief, quit stealing. Instead, use your
> hands for good hard work, and then give generously to others in need.
> Don't use foul or abusive language. (Ephesians 4:25–29 NLT)

I've heard it said, "The Old Testament is filled with dos and don'ts, but the New Testament is all about grace." It's even taught now in conferences and churches that the grace of God frees us from commandments, and many firmly believe it. Yet Jesus said only those who hear and keep His *commandments* will experience His manifest presence. These teachers think they are freeing their audiences, when in reality they're steering people away from what brings us into the presence of God. It's heartbreaking.

It's a fact: Jesus gives us commandments. He commissions us, "Go therefore and make disciples of all the nations…teaching them to observe all things I have *commanded* you" (Matthew 28:19–20). Not "all things I've *suggested* to you."

In these days, many love His words that speak of sovereignty but take lightly His words that call for godly conduct. God truly is sovereign, but without an awareness of humankind's freedom of choice, we can reach the place of viewing His words commanding godly behavior as mere suggestions.

Commandments

The apostles gave Jesus's commandments to us. Let me repeat John's words: "We can be sure that we know him if we obey his commandments" (1 John 2:3 NLT). Then he goes on to say, "Loving God means keeping his commandments" (1 John 5:3 NLT).

Paul writes, "For you know what *commandments* we gave you through the Lord Jesus" (1 Thessalonians 4:2). His very next words: "God's will is for you to be holy" (1 Thessalonians 4:3 NLT). We are expected to keep Jesus's *commandments* in order to live holy.

Peter makes crystal clear the command to live holy. He identifies the tragic reality that people will fall away from the faith in the latter days. He writes that they will "reject *the command they were given to live a holy life*" (2 Peter 2:21 NLT). Not only are we given commandments in the New Testament, but they specifically fall under the label of "the command…to live a holy life."

If we examine the apostle Paul's words in Ephesians 4:25–29, we see direct commands to live holy:

Don't tell lies.

Don't sin by letting anger control you.

Don't steal.

Don't use foul or abusive language.

Can we honestly say there are no don'ts in the New Testament? These certainly sound like don'ts to me. Do they to you?

Look at it like this. When I was a child, my dad told me, "Son, don't run out in the street to get a ball without looking both ways." That was a don't, but he wasn't being hard or negative. He was simply giving me this command so that I wouldn't be suddenly killed and could live a long life.

God is simply telling us what not to do so that we can live full, productive, and long lives. And what's even better, we have the divine nature and the fuel of grace to fulfill the commands.

Stop Telling Lies

Let's discuss each of the *don't* behaviors I've just listed.

I've heard and witnessed the consequences of many heartbreaking accounts of dishonesty among Christians in my travels. I recently took fifteen entrepreneurial businessmen to Machu Picchu for a four-day hike on the Inca Trail. It was an amazing time of sights and ministry and—to put it mildly—a very challenging workout.

In hiking a few hours with each man, I heard recurring stories of their experiences with other Christian businessmen who lied to make a sale or deal. Empty promises and unfulfilled commitments seemed to be a common occurrence, rather than the exception, when dealing with a brother in the faith. I was told of Christians using substandard materials, breaking codes, violating rules, offering services that weren't fulfilled, neglecting warranties, and more.

One of the men relayed a story about a fellow homebuilder. The two men were building in the same development. This "brother" dug holes on other owners' lots—including those of the man hiking with me—where he dumped waste materials. Then he covered them up instead of paying to have the materials properly hauled off. I heard worse stories on this trip, but this one particularly stood out because the "brother" was the worship leader of an evangelical church in the community.

Lying doesn't just occur in the marketplace but also in government, education, ministry, and medicine and among family members and friends. We lie to save face, protect our reputations, propel ourselves to desired positions, or expedite a desired end. Lying is attractive; it can speed up the process of something we should be trusting God to provide.

How often do we tell people we are praying for them when we aren't? We promise our children something and don't follow through on it. We cancel engagements after giving our word. We exaggerate to make our point. These are all lies and inevitably result in people getting hurt.

Let me reemphasize this important point: the benefit of keeping the commands of Jesus is the *promise of His presence*. The psalmist confirmed this truth by asking, "Who may enter your [God's] presence?" (Psalm 15:1 NLT) He then gave the answer: those who "keep their promises even when it hurts" (verse 4). *The Message* Bible records it as, "Keep your word even when it costs you."

If we overlook Paul's commandment to the Ephesians to not lie, we can turn to James's command. He writes, "Don't cover up the truth with boasting and lying" (3:14 NLT). And Paul gave a similar command to the Colossians: "Don't lie to each other" (3:9 NLT). Imagine this! Paul, the one who God used to bring the richest revelation of grace, gave us a *don't* command. If we isolated many statements in the New Testament—by Paul as well as by other apostles—we could accuse them of being anti-grace, when in fact they're not.

If our entire discussion is centered only on grace covering us, without teaching believers the empowering behavior that accompanies grace—in this case, not to lie—we'll inevitably have a church that justifies this behavior to meet a desired end. Does an unbalanced teaching and belief about grace without emphasizing holiness open us up to this? Does it teach us to ignore our consciences?

Don't Let Anger Control You

Next on the list: *don't sin by letting anger control you*. I've beheld the faces of women and men who live with an angry spouse. I've heard the accounts of the fear that fills a home when these professing believers go into fits of rage.

How about the children living with parents whose anger has become abusive and destructive? Property damage and even physical harm result from such outbursts. The victims live in terror of the next outbreak. Anger destroys the atmosphere of the home, which is no longer a refuge. In church on Sunday, all about this family may seem well, but it's a front. Sadly, we've chosen to take lightly or ignore this commandment.

This directive is not isolated. There are more commands to forsake anger in the epistles. Paul writes, more directly: "Get rid of all bitterness, rage, anger, [and] harsh words" (Ephesians 4:31 NLT). James commands, "You must all be…slow to get angry. Human anger does not produce the righteousness God desires" (James 1:19–20 NLT). Paul again commands the Colossians, "Get rid of anger [and] rage" (3:8 NLT).

Let's ask once again, do these all sound like don'ts from men who received the revelation of God's grace? Have we missed something here?

Don't Steal

Quit stealing. How often do we borrow money and not pay it back? How often do we get into enormous debt? We believe God's blessing will eventually manifest, so we continue ignoring wisdom and fall further into debt. We may eventually declare bankruptcy, an accepted term that frees us from admitting we've not paid back what we owe to others.

How often have we used our company's resources for personal use? That's called embezzling. We'll confidently declare, "I'm a Christian saved by the grace of God." But we're not obeying the commands of Jesus given through His apostles.

One pastor I worked with attended every service, saw miracles occur, and bragged to me about how easy it was for him to pray during an extended fast. But the whole time, he was embezzling thousands of dollars from the church. Eventually he was caught. This is only one story about Christians stealing and somehow justifying it.

How many of us have cheated on our tax returns, refraining from reporting some of our income? In this case, yet another commandment of Paul is ignored: "Pay your taxes" (Romans 13:6 NLT). We justify our theft because of the "bad job" our civil leaders are doing. But when will we learn that two wrongs never make a right?

Don't Use Foul or Abusive Language

The Amplified Bible states the next command like this: "Let no foul or polluting language, nor evil word nor unwholesome or worthless talk [ever] come out of your mouth" (Ephesians 4:29). All too often I've ministered to those who've been verbally abused by other believers. They've been torn down by cutting and hurtful words. Their souls were wounded, and it takes time to be healed.

Numerous times I've heard worthless conversation among believers, even off-color stories and jokes in ministry offices. The use of profanity from the pulpit is no longer unheard of.

Recently I sat at dinner with a young couple who oversee a great church. They admire and look up to a certain global ministry. They were given the opportunity to have dinner with one of this organization's renowned leaders. During the course of the meal, he used hardcore profanity several times. The couple was still in shock months later.

We've Undersold Grace

What's happened? Have we become so cool that we've thrown out godly behavior? Have we sacrificed our witness to become more relevant? I'm 100 percent in favor of being relevant, progressive, and forward in our thinking, but not at the expense of compromising the Word of God.

We must ask this question: the apostles saw it as necessary to give commands leading us to godly behavior, so why aren't we vocalizing them? Do we know more than them? Do we know more than Jesus?

Could it be the enemy has seduced us as he did Eve? This time it's a little different. Eve was well aware of the command not to eat the fruit of the tree of the knowledge of good and evil. The enemy had to risk exposure by directly contradicting the Word of God. That was a delicate task for him.

We've made it easier for the devil. We've just conveniently left out some of God's words. Do you recall how God commanded, "Of every tree of the garden you may freely eat; but of the tree of the knowledge of good and evil *you shall not* eat"? (Genesis 2:16–17) By contrast, some today would have said, "Of every tree of the garden you may freely eat." Period. End of story. They leave off the command that "you shall not"—the *don't*—related to behaviors that are ungodly.

In essence, we've undersold the grace of God. We've declared rightly that it saves, forgives, and is a free gift of His love. However, we've not declared that it has changed our very nature and empowers us to not live as we used to. We've avoided telling people that they're now empowered to forsake ungodly behavior. The result of such silence is that believers are ignorant of godliness and missing out on God's presence.

Our Actions Matter

Recently I was in the middle of my morning Bible reading. At that time I was reading from Psalms and Hebrews. I had finished my portion in Psalms and was turning to Hebrews when I strongly sensed the Holy Spirit saying, "No, don't read Hebrews. Read Revelation."

I had started reading Revelation a few weeks earlier, also by the Holy Spirit's prompting. I read the first couple chapters, but I'm sad to say I lost interest. The next day I returned to my scheduled reading. Now, two weeks later, I returned to the place where I'd left off in chapter three. I was about to be floored by Jesus's words to the church in Sardis:

> "I know all the things you do, and that you have a reputation for being alive—but you are dead." (Revelation 3:1 NLT)

First, notice Jesus states "I know the things you do," not "the things you believe." He doesn't say "I know your intentions." In another translation He says "I know your works." It is clear that He's referring not to the church's positional righteousness but to their outward holiness—their works, behavior, life choices, and so forth.

He identifies this church as having a reputation of being alive. What would give this impression? Could it be that it's growing and popular, the meetings are exciting, and the atmosphere is electric? Remember, we can inadvertently substitute atmosphere for presence. If you attend a pop concert, there are crowds, contagious enthusiasm, and great anticipation for a fabulous evening, but are these shows in line with God's heart?

An important question in deciphering whether a congregation is alive or dead is, are we obeying the words of Jesus, or are we developing a tightknit community that is actually straying from His commands? Another question we should ask is, are we proclaiming truth that addresses the condition of the heart, resulting in changed behavior, or messages that stroke our emotions and stimulate our intellects?

Following this opening declaration, Jesus goes on to say:

"Wake up! Strengthen what little remains, for even what is left is almost dead. I find that your actions do not meet the requirements of my God." (verse 2 NLT)

Again Jesus identifies their actions, not their beliefs. As stated earlier, there are dos and even don'ts in the New Testament; these commands address our actions. According to Jesus, this church is not pursuing and embracing a lifestyle of holiness. He then states:

"Go back to what you heard and believed at first; hold to it firmly. Repent and turn to me again. If you don't wake up, I will come to you suddenly, as unexpected as a thief." (Revelation 3:3 NLT)

Remember, Jesus is addressing the church, not the city, of Sardis. But if His words were only meant for this historic church, they would not be in Scripture. The fact that they are means they have prophetic application today. And they apply to believers, just as they did when they were first spoken. These words are addressed to us, for the Word of God is alive. So henceforth I will refer to Jesus's statement in that context.

Jesus instructs us to go back to what we first believed. In other words, we've strayed from holy living. We've devised a doctrine of grace that permits us to live no differently than the nonbelievers in our community do. It's a seemingly good teaching, but is it God's Word?

Jesus tells the church to repent and return to His words. There are modern teachers who declare that once we are Christians, we no longer need to repent because all our sins past, present, and future are automatically forgiven. If this is the case, why does Jesus tell us, His church, to repent and return to Him?

If you look at the unbalanced "grace" teachings that are attracting multitudes today, many of them are propagated by leaders who were actually brought up hearing legalistic, skewed messages on holiness. Yes, holiness has been misrepresented in many circles, but that doesn't change the fact that it is fundamental to Christianity. Throughout the history of the church, the call to a holy life has been an essential part of our collective mission and our individual assignments. We must return to our foundation: what we "heard and believed at first."

Jesus continues:

> "Yet there are some in the church in Sardis who have not soiled their clothes with evil. They will walk with me in white, for they are worthy." (Revelation 3:4 NLT)

Notice the words "soiled their clothes." Remember Paul's words that prepare us for the presence of God: "Let us cleanse ourselves from all filthiness of the flesh and spirit, perfecting holiness in the fear of God" (2 Corinthians

7:1). Jesus is correcting the course of the church with a call to return to holy living and to not soil the clothing of the flesh and spirit with ungodly life-styles. This keeps us in a ready state for both His presence and His return, for He later states, "Blessed are all who are watching for me, who keep their clothing ready" (Revelation 16:15 NLT). He concludes with:

> "All who are victorious will be clothed in white. I will never erase their
> names from the Book of Life, but I will announce before my Father
> and his angels that they are mine. Anyone with ears to hear must listen
> to the Spirit and understand what he is saying to the churches." (Reve-
> lation 3:5–6 NLT)

To have your name erased from the Book of Life is quite a serious matter. Yet these words are straight from our Savior's mouth. It's important that we listen and pay careful attention to what the Spirit of God speaks through the written Word of God, and that we not overlook these statements that may not line up with what we previously believed or what is commonly taught.

God has made us righteous; we could never do anything to earn this position in Christ. However, a corresponding lifestyle of holy behavior is obviously very important in His eyes.

Paul writes, "For God has revealed his grace for the salvation of all people. That grace instructs us to give up ungodly living and worldly passions, and to live self-controlled, upright, and godly lives in this world" (Titus 2:11–12 TEV). That's a clear directive. So why are we not heralding this truth from our platforms?

Let's never stop teaching that we can't earn God's favor, forgiveness, or salvation. Let's keep shouting that good news. However, let's quit underselling His grace. Let's proclaim its entire truth!

11

GOOD OR BENEFICIAL?

You say, "I am allowed to do anything"—
but not everything is beneficial.
—1 Corinthians 10:23 NLT

. . .Entire sanctification is not only essential as
the condition of entering heaven, but. . .
it is also necessary for the highest results
of the Christian life on earth.
—Dougan Clark

As a minister who frequently speaks and "gives out," it's especially re-freshing to hear messages from other men and women of God. Re-cently I was enjoying such an occasion. The pastor who was speaking is well respected in our nation, oversees a large church, and is known for his insights on local church development. His message was interesting, encouraging, and eye-opening. Thousands were listening intently in the auditorium.

At one point he made a comment that seemed good, wise, and humble, but it didn't sit right. He said, "What I'm about to say may sound a little negative. I usually don't speak this way because I don't convict people with my messages. I leave all conviction to the Holy Spirit."

I tried to shake the agitation in my spirit but couldn't. In the past I'd heard other leaders say similar words. The logic seemed sound, so why was

I troubled? I then thought of the apostle Paul's words to a young apprentice named Timothy. After the service I looked up the verse:

> Preach the word! Be ready in season and out of season. Convince, rebuke, exhort... (2 Timothy 4:2)

Let me first share the context of this scripture. At the time when Paul wrote this letter, Timothy was pastoring the large church in Ephesus. This chapter in the New Testament contains the final written words of Paul, not only to his young apprentice but also to all of us. I would imagine he had a sense of finality and chose his topic and words very carefully.

I didn't want only surface knowledge of what Paul meant by "convince, rebuke, exhort," so my search began. I first went to the Amplified Bible for clarification, but before I could get to the verse quoted above, the previous verse grabbed my attention:

> I CHARGE [you] in the presence of God and of Christ Jesus, Who is to judge the living and the dead... (2 Timothy 4:1)

The word *charge* is translated in all capital letters; I've not made a mistake. This was done for emphasis. I contacted my friend Rick Renner, a longtime scholar of the Greek language, and inquired about the exact meaning of this. His response:

> The Greek word "CHARGE" is *diamarturomai*—a word that was used when officials took an oath of public office. The person who gave them the oath of office would call upon all the gods to watch and listen—placing great seriousness upon the one taking the oath—and then the one giving the oath of office would "charge" them to do their job responsibly and to remember that the gods were watching. In the context to Timothy, Paul was saying (paraphrase): "I call upon God to watch as you receive the words I am about to speak to you..." It was a solemn, solemn word that told Timo-

thy he better be serious about what he was about to hear because God Himself was watching and listening—and that is why the rest of that verse talks about judgement...Paul wanted Timothy to understand the seriousness of what he was about to say and what he was about to hear. This word "charge" is a word that would have placed great responsibility upon the receiver.

Paul was very strong with this young pastor (and with us), making sure his command was not seen as optional. As Rick stated, Paul made this charge in the presence of God and Christ Jesus. In other words, God would judge Timothy, along with any other minister, if he didn't heed this mandate. Here is the mandate:

Herald *and* preach the Word! Keep your sense of urgency [stand by, be at hand and ready], whether the opportunity seems to be favorable or unfavorable. [Whether it is convenient or inconvenient, whether it is welcome or unwelcome, you as preacher of the Word are to show people in what way their lives are wrong.] (2 Timothy 4:2 AMP)

A minister of the gospel is "to show people in what way their lives are wrong." That stands out!

My immediate thought about the message I'd heard was, *No wonder the pastor's statement didn't sit right.* It seemed good, but it actually wasn't the truth. Either knowingly or unknowingly, he had chosen what seems good over God. This leader placed the responsibility on the Holy Spirit, but Paul clearly states the responsibility is actually ours

Recently a very popular pastor and his wife were being interviewed on an international news program. The correspondent brought up the subject of sexual immorality, and their response was, "It's not our place to tell anyone how they should live."

I know this couple loves people. They want to see the lost hear the gospel and come to know Jesus. Their vision is great—it would be fabulous if all ministers had their passionate resolve. However, do we alter our direct charge from *God* to "show people in what way their lives are wrong" and replace it with our *good* philosophy of "not telling people how they should live"?

Was this the tactic of the apostles? On one occasion Paul declared his strategy to an unsaved king:

> "And so, King Agrippa, I obeyed that vision from heaven. I preached first to those in Damascus, then in Jerusalem and throughout all Judea, and also to the Gentiles, that all must repent of their sins and turn to God—and prove they have changed by the good things they do." (Acts 26:19–20 NLT)

To tell the unsaved to *repent of their sins,* and then after conversion to *prove they have changed,* is directly dealing with *how they should live.* Sadly, the evangelistic philosophies of Paul and the couple who were being interviewed are completely opposite. One is *God's;* the other is *good.*

Paul demonstrated his resolve to adhere to divine strategy when the opportunity arose to speak to another notable, unsaved leader and his wife. Examine his tactic by the subjects he discussed:

> A few days later Felix and his wife, Drusilla, who was Jewish, sent for Paul and listened to him talk about a life of believing in Jesus Christ. As Paul continued to insist on right relations with God and his people, about a life of moral discipline and the coming Judgment, Felix felt things getting a little too close for comfort and dismissed him. "That's enough for today. I'll call you back when it's convenient." (Acts 24:24–25 The Message)

Felix sent for Paul because he and his wife were interested in hearing Paul's message about eternal life. Two of the main topics he addressed with this unsaved couple were moral discipline and the coming judgment. So strong were Paul's words that it made them very uncomfortable. How does this stack up against our modern-day tactic of ministering to the lost? There are some church leaders whose primary goal is to get seekers back to the next Sunday's service. Of course getting people to return to church the following Sunday is commendable, but it isn't the ultimate aim. Paul's goal wasn't to create in people a desire for another meeting; it was to speak the truth faithfully.

Recently I attended a popular young pastor's meeting. He was conducting a road tour proclaiming his message of God's love. Over a thousand people had gathered into a packed auditorium to hear him. The atmosphere was electric; people were excited to hear this young leader's words. Prior to his message, the audience was informed twice—by the leader's manager and the leader himself—that we would hear only "good news" and he would speak nothing "negative" that night. "Good news" was set up as the opposite of "negative." However, there are times when good news initially seems negative, especially if it brings a course correction in our lives. But if that course correction saves us from the way of death, then how should we view it?

Once on the platform, this pastor connected with the audience using clever humor for the first twenty minutes. He then shared about Jesus's passionate love for us. It was a heart-warming and encouraging message. Then he offered the opportunity for salvation without calling the seekers to make a course correction—to forsake their love for the world or disobedience to God. Nothing was said about repentance of sin, a foundational teaching that has to accompany salvation (see Hebrews 6:1). Many responded to his offer that night.

Was this pastor's message in line with Paul's message to King Agrippa or to Felix and Drusilla? Was his message in line with the words of Peter, who sternly told those who desired salvation, "Repent of your sins and turn to God, so that your sins may be wiped away"? (Acts 3:19 NLT) Did the seekers leave the meeting that night saved?

Opposite Extremes

Let's again ask, why is it so easy to swing the pendulum to the complete opposite side—so far from the legalism we despise to the point that now we omit key elements of the gospel?

Many of today's leaders were raised up by what are now viewed as stern church fathers. In the twentieth century, these fathers weren't afraid to confront and expose sin; they called us to holy living. In those years there weren't nearly as many megachurches as today. The firm, convicting messages from Scripture often turned insincere seekers away.

At some later point, as a strategic countermove, some leaders resolved that large followings could be built by turning to exclusively *positive, uplifting messages*. We downplayed conviction, rebuke, and correction while searching the Bible for encouraging messages. We stopped telling people how their lives were not in obedience to God's Word. This has become our strategy in the twenty-first century. Yet hear the continuation of Paul's mandate to Timothy:

> [...You as preacher of the Word are to show people in what way their
> lives are wrong.] And convince them, rebuking and correcting, warning
> and urging and encouraging them, being unflagging and inexhaustible
> in patience and teaching. (2 Timothy 4:2 AMP)

Here's what the three critical Greek words in this passage—*elegcho, epitimao,* and *parakaleo*—mean. *Strong's* definition of *elegcho* is to "convict, tell a fault, rebuke, reprove." *The Complete Word Study Dictionary* is more specific in its definition: "In the New Testament, to convict, to prove one in the wrong and thus shame him." That's strong!

The second word, *epitimao,* is defined as "(straightly) charge, rebuke." That's direct! The third word, *parakaleo* is defined as "to comfort, to encourage." That is the uplifting aspect; it's indeed necessary.

Focusing on the first two words, Paul commanded ministers to preach messages that will convict, rebuke, reprove, tell a fault, and prove one in the wrong. In hearing these words defined, we have to question the paradigm of present-day leadership in the Western church. Is today's strategy the wisdom of God or the wisdom of *good*? In traveling full time to conferences and churches for over twenty-five years, I can honestly say we've drifted over to the *good*.

I could share countless stories along these lines, but allow me just one more. I was asked to speak to a very large church in the northwestern part of the United States. I admire its leader and his work and was looking forward to time with him, his wife, their leadership team, and the church.

A few weeks before the event, I got an email from the pastor that said, "John, we are looking forward to you coming and speaking into the life of our church. As you prepare your messages it would be good for me to share with you our culture. We are a positive church; our people are not accustomed to hearing negative messages. So when you address our congregation, please keep your messages along an encouraging, positive theme."

The question again arises, how does this "wisdom" stack up with what Paul just *charged* Timothy to do? To compare, I'll list in the original language the "positives" and what we'd today view as "negatives."

Positive: 1) *parakaleo*: comfort, encourage

Negative: 1) *elegcho*: convict, tell a fault, rebuke, reprove; to prove one in the wrong

              2) *epitimao*: (straightly) charge, rebuke

There are three commands from Paul. Two of the three are considered "negative" and only one is "positive." Let me put it another way: 67 percent are "corrective" and 33 percent are "affirming." I am not implying 67 percent of our messages should be corrective. However, what we should ask is, are we out of balance? If our aim is 100 percent encouraging and uplifting teaching in our churches, then could we now have an increasingly positive people who believe they're on target with God, while in reality they are straying further and further from His character and presence?

The Essence of the Command

The writer of Hebrews informs us:

> No discipline is enjoyable while it is happening—it's painful! But afterward there will be a peaceful harvest of right living for those who are *trained* in this way. (Hebrews 12:11 NLT)

There are two important points here. First, discipline is *painful*! Encouragement is not painful; rebuke, correction, and exposing a fault are. Second, the discipline the writer of Hebrews spoke of is *training* for holy living.

The question we now should ask is, how does God train us? If we return to what Paul wrote to Timothy, it all comes together:

> Every Scripture is God-breathed (given by His inspiration) and profitable for instruction, for reproof and conviction of sin, for correction of error and discipline in obedience, [and] for *training* in righteousness (in *holy living*, in conformity to God's will in thought, purpose, and action), so that the man of God may be complete and proficient, well fitted and thoroughly equipped for every good work. I CHARGE [you] in the presence of God and of Christ Jesus, Who is to judge the living and the dead, and by (in the light of) His coming and His kingdom: Herald and preach the Word! (2 Timothy 3:16–4:2 AMP)

Again, did you note the words *reproof, conviction of sin, correction of error*, and *discipline in obedience*? Did you also note that Scripture *trains us in holy living*, and that Paul then commanded Timothy and us *to preach the Word* (Scripture)? Putting it all together, here is in essence what's being commanded:

> *Timothy, and any other minister of the gospel, here's a fact: divine discipline is painful, but it trains us for holy living. God administers this discipline (training) through the inspired spoken Scriptures, which also properly equip the man or woman who is to speak for Him. Therefore, preach the Word— the Scripture. For you, as a messenger of God, are to show people in what way their lives are wrong. This is accomplished by properly using Scripture to lovingly administer reproof, conviction of sin, rebuke, correction, discipline in obedience, and encouragement. This is the divine process of training the hearers for holy living.* (paraphrase)

I realize this is so diametrically opposed to our twenty-first century church culture that it may be shocking. But do we want a strong church or a misled church? Do we want to cultivate healthy or deceived people? These instructions are given so we don't unknowingly drift from God's heart. If we are going to walk securely with Jesus, we must be grounded in Scripture. It's impossible to reconcile our present culture with the directives of the New Testament. Let's make the change and observe the emergence of a healthy church!

Desirable or Beneficial?

Paul, by insight from the Spirit, foresaw ministers and others not heeding this command and foretold the fallout that would occur:

> For the time is coming when [people] will not tolerate (endure) sound
> and wholesome instruction, but, having ears itching [for something
> pleasing and gratifying], they will gather to themselves one teacher after
> another to a considerable number, chosen to satisfy their own liking
> and to foster the errors they hold. (2 Timothy 4:3 AMP)

Welcome to that time! Let's ask, what's more desirable: an encouraging, happy, positive, lighthearted message? Or a message of warning, rebuke, correction, telling faults, and conviction?

Everyone, including me, would much rather be spoken to with content reflecting the first type of message. I'm a positive person, so I naturally gravitate toward the upbeat message. If given a choice, any normal human being will do the same.

If there are two churches next to each other, and you know in one of them you might hear words that will deal pointedly with your sinful behavior, and in the other you will only hear an uplifting, encouraging word, you'll pick the latter. This is what Paul said would eventually happen—people would choose *good* over God. The correct question is not what is more desirable, but what is more beneficial?

Let's be honest. Most people don't want to hear about this critical choice between messages. But consider this example. A man named Steve has been diagnosed with cancer. The tumor is in its early stage, and having it surgically removed could easily thwart its threat. The doctor says, "We can remove it with a simple procedure."

Steve then goes for a second opinion. This second doctor doesn't heed medical research or the instruction he received as a medical student. He just loves being a doctor and helping people his way. He tells Steve not to worry. Everything is fine and he has a great life ahead. This doctor enthusiastically states, "Steve, your health is in a good place."

Steve leaves the second doctor relieved. He thinks, *What a nice doctor. He spoke well of me. I'm so encouraged.* Now he's actually a little upset at the first doctor for being so negative and asking him to go through a procedure that would be inconvenient, painful, and expensive. He made Steve aware that his condition was serious. His manner was blunt and he wasn't particularly encouraging.

Thanks to the second opinion, Steve believes he has nothing to be concerned about. However, two years later Steve is very ill and just weeks away from death because the small tumor grew to life-threatening size. It invaded many crucial organs of his body. No treatment will help Steve now.

Two years earlier, it was easier to listen to the positive doctor. But what was more needed then—the truth or flattery, the corrective measure or the positive talk? Steve was told he was healthy, when in fact he wasn't. It's too late to go back. He wishes he had listened to the truth.

Could this be where we are spiritually in the Western church, both as leaders and church members?

There was a time in Israel's history when the religious leaders adopted an exclusively positive ministry. They avoided confrontation and only spoke in an uplifting manner. God declared His view of their messages: "They offer superficial treatments for my people's mortal wound. They give assurances of peace when there is no peace" (Jeremiah 8:11 NLT). Interestingly, the message they spoke was in essence no different than the one the second doctor gave Steve.

"I Don't Like His Messages!"

Not embracing the correction of truth is an age-old problem. In a different time period, a king of Israel planned an endeavor. He called in hundreds of spiritual advisors and asked them if his plans would be successful. These advisors were given a great opportunity to speak truth to the king, but one by one they responded, "Yes, you will succeed." They further predicted the good that would come out of his venture.

The king of Judah was also present, and his heart was tender toward God. He longed for truth, which gave him discernment. He didn't sense the Lord's voice, even though all the spiritual advisors were saying the same thing. He kept searching for the word that would resonate with his sensitive heart.

Finally, the king of Judah asked Israel's leader, "Are there no other advisors who will speak accurately?"

The king of Israel replied, "As a matter of fact, there is still one such man. But I hate him. He never preaches anything good to me, only doom, doom, doom" (1 Kings 22:8 The Message). Nevertheless, to appease his fellow ruler, Israel's king requested that this "negative" advisor be brought before the royal assembly.

This prophet's name was Micaiah, and the king's messenger who found him said, "Look, as one man the other prophets are predicting success for the king. Let your word agree with theirs, and speak favorably" (1 Kings 22:13 NIV).

Micaiah's reply was, "As surely as the LORD lives, I will say only what the LORD tells me to say" (1 Kings 22:14 NLT). He did just that, and it was a corrective word that angered the king. But as it turned out, all the positive advisors were wrong about the outcome while Micaiah was accurate.

Where are these advisors or ministers like Micaiah today? Why aren't we hearing their protective convictions and warnings on a more regular basis? Why aren't their books calling us to holiness bestsellers? Why are they not the most popular conference speakers? Why aren't they the most watched on YouTube?

God made His leadership directive clear through the apostle Paul, yet we teach otherwise. I actually had a very prominent pastor say to me one day at lunch, "John, if you look at the majority of the pastors in our country with successful churches, they are preaching messages of hope, grace, and encouragement." One of his associates added further, "John, you may want to reevaluate what you've been teaching on the subject of grace." He was struggling with the empowering, transformation aspect of grace.

We do need hope and encouragement, but we also need correction, discipline, and conviction. This is what Paul *charged* Timothy with. Why does it have to be all or none? Why do we have to swing the pendulum to the complete opposite side? Let's offer all of what Paul told Timothy.

The Key Ingredient

Let me give you another illustration. A sly, crooked used car salesman will tell you what you want to hear. He'll smile, laugh with you, tell you how good a guy you are, and that because you're so sharp, the car you picked is the best deal on the lot. You may think, *Wow, even my wife doesn't speak this encouragingly to me!* The reason is that your wife *loves* you; this man is *flattering* you to get your money. This brings us to the most important ingredient in framing our messages: *love*. In the body of Christ, our messages must be bathed in love and come from a compassionate heart.

A young man once approached me at my resource table after a meeting. He smiled and said, "Like you, I'm called to speak prophetically, bringing correction to the church."

The way he said this made me feel uncomfortable. I sensed he wanted to tell people off more than he had genuine concern for their welfare.

"Do you want to know the secret to speaking prophetically?" I asked him. He lit up, anticipating a tip for successful ministry.

"The entire time you bring a corrective or challenging word," I said, "you must absolutely love the people you are addressing."

He looked at me with a stunned expression. After a few moments he responded, "I think God has some work to do in me." I was proud of him for admitting it.

Often I too have wrestled with speaking confronting messages. I love people dearly, I love the church, and I love God's leaders. As I write this book or speak correctively, my heart aches because I want to encourage and affirm. But on the other hand, I know that true love doesn't flatter; it's truthful. It speaks what is needed to bring health to the hearers. Paul writes that we are to speak the truth in love, and that doing so will cause the hearers to grow and mature in Christ (see Ephesians 4:15).

There have been ministers who proclaimed corrective messages, emphasizing holiness in a mean-spirited way. They had little or even no compassion for those they addressed. That's so tragic and costly. All of us must be motivated, moved, and even consumed with love for the people we address, or we should not speak at all. We should passionately yearn for their well-being more than anything else. We don't speak out of an "I told you so" or "I know more than you" or "I'm better than you" attitude. We must communicate fervently, wanting the best for them. We must esteem our audience or those we meet in a variety of settings as more important than ourselves. This is the heart of God, Jesus Christ, and the Spirit.

HOLY LIFE COACHING

A life coach is a person whose job is to improve the quality of a client's life. In a way, the apostle Paul instructs us to be spiritual life coaches. By following God's prescribed ways, we improve the quality not only of our lives but also of the lives of those we coach.

We can't improve on God's ways. Adam and Eve attempted and failed miserably. They were the first of many who tried this folly. So as coaches, we are not only to instruct, but also to warn and correct. By not correcting, we permit those we coach to continue down a path of sorrow and destruction. Again, for this reason Paul urges Timothy, "You as preacher of the Word are to show people in what way their lives are wrong" (2 Timothy 4:2 AMP).

At the onset of Paul's letter to the Ephesian church, he speaks of our new nature coupled with empowering grace. The combination of these two characteristics positions a believer for a transformed life. This gives the believer the ability to identify with Christ as well as stay out of harm's way.

Paul then gives a list of commands that define this life. They are not burdensome or impossible, as were the Old Testament commands. They're merely the behavior expected of us because we have a new nature.

Now let's read the remainder of his list:

> Let there be no sexual immorality, impurity, or greed among you. Such
> sins have no place among God's people. Obscene stories, foolish talk, and
> coarse jokes—these are not for you. Instead, let there be thankfulness to
> God. ...Don't be drunk with wine... (Ephesians 5:3–4, 18 NLT)

Again this looks like a list of don'ts. To reiterate, it's not a list of commands that, if kept, will save us. Rather, it is a list to keep us out of an adulterous relationship with the world so we can remain in the manifest presence of Jesus. Allow me to list all the sinful behaviors again.

Those discussed in a previous chapter were:

- Don't tell lies.
- Don't sin by letting anger control you.
- Don't steal.
- Don't use foul or abusive language.

The remainder of the list is:

- Don't be sexually immoral.
- Don't be impure.
- Don't be greedy.
- Don't tell obscene stories.
- Don't talk foolishly.
- Don't tell rude jokes.
- Don't be drunk with wine.

The New Testament is a message of grace, but for a message many say doesn't contain commands or don'ts, this list—from just one of the twenty-seven New Testament books—is getting long! What's even more ironic is that the apostle who was given the deep revelation of grace compiled the list! Are these commands to be ignored or taken seriously?

No Sexual Immorality

The first item on our new list is *no sexual immorality*. As sons and daughters of God, we are not to commit adultery, engage in homosexuality, or engage in any sexual activity unless we are married.

All too often I've encountered couples living together who profess Christianity. This is not a rare occurrence—it's actually rampant in the church. Many of these couples attend evangelical churches, are outspoken in their faith, and are often exuberant over "what God is doing" in their lives. There's no hint of conviction, remorse, or sorrow. They simply don't believe that living together when unmarried is wrong. Why? Maybe they've not heard from the pulpit messages like those from Paul, Peter, James, John, and Jude, calling them to godly, chaste living. Their pastors' Sunday talks are uplifting and encouraging but not confronting or convicting. They are without the discipline of holy living.

In our society it is accepted, even considered a good idea, to live together, to have sex before marriage, and to unite as a homosexual couple. Sadly, as evangelicals, our knowledge of Scripture is often superficial. Without intently looking into God's Word, many of us have adopted our culture's ideas. The prevailing thought is, *If we are in love, why not live together?*

How about homosexuality? This too is rampant, but not just with those who've never been involved in the church. Just recently I was shown the Facebook page of a lady who used to be a department manager at a ministry. Now she's in love with another woman, and they've made plans to be married. I beheld with great sadness the pictures of their engagement and other intimate moments.

In the past, those who were backslidden in their relationships with God knew it. However, this woman spoke enthusiastically of God's love and her devotion to Him. How can she be married to another woman when Jesus clearly says, "Haven't you read in your Bible that the Creator originally made man and woman for each other, male and female? Because God created this organic union of the two sexes, no one should desecrate his art"? (Matthew 19:4, 6 The Message) Jesus states that marriage is for a man and a woman—the two sexes. Why isn't this woman aware that she's desecrating His institution? Has it not been made clear from the pulpit?

I understand society departing from God's original intent for marriage. The unsaved possess a sin nature. Lost men and women are without God in this world and have limited awareness of what is truly good and evil. Their behavior should not distress us, for they think and do what their nature dictates. What's troubling is believers adopting what the world calls good as acceptable to God. Statistically, there is a rise in churches that encourage the homosexual lifestyle and homosexual marriage. However, churches encourage it not only by what they say, but also by what they don't say. Listen carefully to these words:

> If a righteous man turns from his righteousness…he shall die; because
> you have not given him warning, he shall die in his sin and his righ-
> teous deeds which he has done shall not be remembered, but his blood
> will I require at your hand. (Ezekiel 3:20 AMP)

This speaks of warning a believer—a righteous man. If we don't warn believers about their sins, the consequences are serious.

You may counter, "But John, that's the Old Testament. How can you say blood will be required of a minister's hand in the New Testament era?"

I once spoke at a leadership conference where I had a pastor confront me over this issue. He was angry and said, "How dare you put others' blood on us! That's Old Testament stuff."

I said to him, "Would you open your Bible to Acts 20 and read the twenty-sixth and twenty-seventh verses to me?"

Here is what the pastor read back to me: "I am clean and innocent and not responsible *for the blood of any of you.* For I never shrank or kept back or fell short from declaring to you the whole purpose and plan and counsel of God" (AMP).

The pastor looked up at me in shock and said, "John, I've read this, but I've never seen this before." At the close of our conversation he said, "I'm so sorry for accusing you." I appreciated his honesty.

In this paragraph I want to speak directly to church leaders. These were Paul's words to his leaders at Ephesus, but we too will be found guilty if we who teach and preach don't declare the whole counsel of God to His people. If we only speak in an "uplifting" way, we withhold a large percentage of the counsel of God. Consequently, our people will gravitate toward what the world considers good, no differently than an undisciplined child will err toward folly. The bottom line: their blood will be on our hands.

Allow me to cite one more example. I watched a pastor announce to his people that he was a homosexual during a service broadcast on his megachurch's website. He told how he was tired of hiding; he didn't want others involved in this lifestyle to continue suffering conviction (he called it "condemnation").

He systematically listed every verse in the Bible revealing God's view of homosexuality and discounted it. Then he boldly told his viewers, "The apostle Paul was great with 'in Christ' realities but awful with relationships"—thus muting Paul's instruction about sexuality. The pastor proceeded to explain that Paul had messed up in the first chapter of Romans when he implied that if we didn't worship God we could end up in homosexuality (see Romans 1:21–27). According to this pastor, Paul's words couldn't be true because, in his words, "Half the worship leaders in America are homosexual." (I wondered what research had revealed that statistic?) While watching this man speak I counted several standing ovations from the congregation.

After I heard the pastor's twisted words, God spoke to me and said, "Read Romans chapter one." This is what I found:

That is why God abandoned them to their shameful desires. Even the women turned against the natural way to have sex and instead indulged in sex with each other. And the men, instead of having normal sexual relations with women, burned with lust for each other. Men did shameful things with other men, and as a result of this sin, they suffered within themselves the penalty they deserved. They know God's justice requires that those who do these things deserve to die, yet they do them anyway. Worse yet, they encourage others to do them, too. (Romans 1:26–27, 32 NLT)

How could this minister discount the scripture that declares homosexual behavior "shameful"? It doesn't take a spiritually minded person to know such sexual practice isn't natural. Even animals don't engage in such behavior. Why would we think God overlooks, approves, or encourages it?

Think of all the professing Christians hearing that pastor's message who battle the urge to succumb to this lustful desire and sinful lifestyle. Their consciences communicate to them, *It's wrong for a child of God to do this*. Yet sadly this pastor's words would be used to muffle their inward voice. Not only was he positioning himself for judgment, but he was also encouraging others to do the same.

How about the standing ovations from those in his church? The Amplified Bible states in Romans 1:32 that all who "*approve* and *applaud* others who practice" such things are under judgment.

What do we do with Paul's words?

Don't you realize that those who do wrong will not inherit the Kingdom of God? Don't fool yourselves. Those who indulge in sexual sin, or who worship idols, or commit adultery, or are male prostitutes, or practice homosexuality or are thieves, or greedy people, or drunkards, or are abusive, or cheat people—none of these will inherit the Kingdom of God. (1 Corinthians 6:9–10 NLT)

Obviously, there are other sins that are harmful. But we must not ignore what these verses say about wayward sexual practices.

The direction of the world is toxic. If we don't proclaim truth about sexual immorality from our pulpits, people will be unaware of what is godly behavior and will be fooled by the evil one. They will accept what the world identifies as good, thinking even God approves.

No Impurity

Next on the list of don'ts is *no impurity*. We are to stay away from all forms of pornography, lewd videos, or lustful thinking. Jesus says, "Anyone who even looks at a woman with lust has already committed adultery with her in his heart" (Matthew 5:28 NLT). The psalmist writes, "I will set no base or wicked thing before my eyes" (Psalm 101:3 AMP).

Pornography offers brief stimulation and satisfaction because it appeals to our flesh's desires, but it will corrode our ability to be intimate with our spouses and God. Eventually, it leaves us dissatisfied with our spouses—and ourselves, too. While it may seem like pornography ignites a spark, it actually lights a fuse that will eventually set off an explosion of confusion, guilt, shame, and insecurity.

Until recently, pornographic sites were the most popular online destinations—they've now been surpassed by social media sites. More than one in ten websites are pornographic. Over forty million Americans regularly visit these sites, and every second 28,258 Internet users are viewing porn.[15]

This is not an exclusively male issue. About one in five women view pornography online on a weekly basis, and many express feelings of helplessness regarding masturbation.[16] Both men and women feed their addictions offline with things like magazines or erotic books, the latter being especially popular among women.[17]

What about the church? *Christianity Today* magazine did a survey in which pastors were asked if they'd visited a pornographic website in the past year. Fifty-four percent answered yes. These are our church leaders! Other statistics show that 50 percent of all evangelical men are addicted to pornography,[18] and a poll reported on by CNN showed that 70 percent of Christian men struggle with it.[19]

So we must ask, have predominantly uplifting messages from the pulpit been the answer to this epidemic, which is now at an all-time high?

I struggled with pornography until I was twenty-seven, a time period that included my beginning years in ministry. I was sure that once I got married to a beautiful woman, the sin would stop; yet it didn't stop and even got worse. It put a wall between Lisa and me. I didn't get free until the fall of 1984, when I told a man of God about my addiction and he said, in no uncertain terms, "Stop it!" He rebuked me strongly. I didn't get an encouraging message from him! I received firm instructions and warnings that put a healthy fear of God in my life.

That man's words started me on a quest to seek God for liberty. Within nine months I was completely delivered and have walked in that freedom to this day. I discovered that the grace of God is so powerful! It can set free a man who had been bound to pornography since he was eleven years old. This is yet another reason I'm so saddened that ministers will not elaborate on the full benefit of the grace of God. If I hadn't discovered grace—not only as a free gift, forgiveness of sin, and salvation, but also as God's empowerment to live beyond my natural ability—I'd still be bound today.

No Greed

The definition of *greed* is "intense and selfish desire for something, especially wealth, power, or food." How often do believers twist and pervert into greed God's promise to help us be blessed, successful, and prosperous? Their focus is on "me" rather than on being equipped to serve and give to others. Greed is covetousness, and that is idolatry (see Colossians 3:5). When we are greedy, we put our desires, passions, appetites, fame, status, popularity, and financial lusts above God and others.

There are many stories that could be told about greed slipping into believers' lives. Balaam lost his relationship with God over it, as did Cain, Korah, and many others who at one time stood in God's presence. Many slip into greed because they are not warned. To warn in teaching or preaching is to depart from only giving positive and uplifting messages. But to help men and women become mature in Christ, we must not only *teach* but also *warn* (see Colossians 1:28).

As a child I enjoyed my parents' teachings but didn't care for their warnings. Yet I later learned it was the warnings that would save my life. If my father didn't warn me about the consequences of jamming a screwdriver in an electric outlet, I might have done so out of curiosity and electrocuted myself.

Paul said to one of his beloved churches, "Watch, and remember that for three years I did not cease to warn everyone night and day with tears" (Acts 20:31). Every day and night for three years! And he did it with tears! Are we warning people? What about daily? Or do we who preach and teach simply hope our encouraging messages will keep our hearers out of greed? Do we care? I haven't heard a message on avoiding greed in years!

Paul is the one who preached grace, yet he also is the one who passionately cries out to the Ephesian church—and to us—"Don't fall into greed."

Hear also the words of the apostle James:

What is causing the quarrels and fights among you? Don't they come
from the evil desires at war within you? You want what you don't have,
so you scheme...to get it. You are jealous of what others have, but
you can't get it, so you fight and wage war to take it away from them.
Yet you don't have what you want because you don't ask God for it.
And even when you ask, you don't get it because your motives are all
wrong—you want only what will give you pleasure. You adulterers!
(James 4:1–4 NLT)

Come on, James, don't be so negative! Was the apostle merely grumpy, stiff, and rigid? Or could it be that he really loved the people he wrote to? Is this why he spoke sobering truth instead of giving a popular and uplifting message? Could this be why God had him write part of the New Testament instead of selecting a more motivating speaker of his day?

No Inappropriate Communicating

Next on the list: *don't engage in foolish talk* or rude, obscene jokes or stories. This would include watching videos or listening to music or other audio of the same kind.

I've been asked to help young people on ministry teams who are bewildered by the fact that their leaders are using rude language, telling obscene jokes, or talking no differently than a lost person would. Why are the leaders doing this? Could it be we are not telling God's leaders and people, "This is not the behavior fitting for a kingdom citizen"?

Paul writes to the Colossians, "Let your conversation be gracious and attractive" (4:6 NLT). Our speech is to be full of grace.

Don't Be Drunk

Next: *don't get drunk*—not on beer, wine, or any other alcoholic beverage. (We can also apply this instruction to drugs, whether legal, illegal, or prescription.) Once again we are hearing the word *don't*.

Alcohol is seductive (see Proverbs 23:31–33). It can easily lure us to drink more without knowing when to stop. Alcohol has the capability to lessen, and eventually deplete, sound judgment. Restraints are compromised, and the natural protective functions of the heart and brain are disarmed. This could be compared to removing the firewall from a computer. We open ourselves to harmful thought processes as discretion wanes. In essence, alcohol removes the security system of our brains. Even if we can and do know when to stop, we may unknowingly inspire others to drunkenness. Let me share a story.

A lead pastor was drinking at a restaurant in his city. One of his members, a recent convert, was in the same restaurant. He was a wealthy businessman who, prior to being saved, struggled with alcohol. After his conversion, he avoided drinking and could be identified as one who had "barely escaped from a lifestyle of deception" (2 Peter 2:18 NLT).

Shortly after seeing his pastor drinking in the restaurant, this business-man went on a three-day drinking binge. During those three days he made some very unwise business decisions and, financially, lost almost everything. Even more devastating, he lost his marriage. When later asked why he had gone on the binge, his response was, "I saw my pastor drinking, so I figured, *If he can drink, so can I.*"

Of course this man is ultimately responsible for his bad choice, but shouldn't such an outcome make us all consider our influence on others?

In recent times, more ministers feel free to drink in public. Scriptures are cited to support their claim to this right. One is 1 Timothy 3:3, where Paul told Timothy that church leaders are not to be "given to wine." The Greek word Paul uses is *paroinou. The Complete Word Study Dictionary's* definition includes: "Pertaining to wine, drunken. The word does not include the re-sponsible and temperate usage of alcohol, rather it has in view the abuse or incessant use of it. The word-picture is that of an individual who always has a bottle (or wineskin) on the table and so signifies addiction." The New Liv-ing Translation version of this verse says that a church leader must "not be a heavy drinker" (1 Timothy 3:3 NLT).

In another letter Paul advised Timothy to "use a little wine for your stomach's sake and your frequent infirmities" (1 Timothy 5:23). Timothy was the equivalent of a lead pastor in Ephesus. The thinking of many minis-ters today is, *If a church leader was never to touch wine, as with a Nazirite's vow, Paul wouldn't have told Pastor Timothy to use it even for its healing properties.*

The most quoted scripture passage in this discussion is where Jesus turned water into wine (see John 2:1–11). The thought is, *Jesus wouldn't turn water into wine in a public setting if it were wrong to drink.*

If only these scriptures are considered, a person could argue that the pastor who drank in public was justified in what he did. However, we live in a society where alcoholism is widespread. In the United States, nearly

88,000 people die from alcohol related causes annually,[20] and alcoholism is the third leading preventable cause of death.[21] In 2007 *The Washington Post* reported that one out of every three Americans have, or have had, problems with alcohol.[22] The National Institute on Alcohol Abuse and Alcoholism reported that in 2012, 25 percent of people age eighteen or older reported they had engaged in binge drinking in the past month. That's staggering—one in four in just one month! I could give many more statistics, but the important point is that Americans have a propensity toward alcohol abuse.

Alcohol abuse is widespread not only in the United States. In 2012, 6 percent of the world's deaths (3.3 million) were attributable to alcohol consumption. Globally, alcohol misuse is the fifth-leading risk factor for premature death and disability. Among people between the ages of fifteen and forty-nine, it is the first![23]

Due to this epidemic, as responsible believers we must take our logic one step further and consider the broader implications of Paul's directive regarding the eating of meat sacrificed to idols. In his words, "If what I eat causes another believer to sin, I will never eat meat again as long as I live—for I don't want to cause another believer to stumble" (1 Corinthians 8:13 NLT). Paul made clear it's not a sin to eat meat sacrificed to an idol. However, if it causes a weaker brother to be offended and stumble, he said he would not eat it again.

An argument can be made supporting a Christian's right to drink small quantities of alcohol, but as believers—and especially those of us who are church leaders—do we want to take the chance of being a stumbling block or helping lure back into addiction those who have barely escaped the sin of alcoholism, especially when we live in a society that is riddled with such abuse? If the lead pastor who was drinking in the restaurant had lived by this wisdom, perhaps the businessman could have been spared from his tragic three-day binge.

We must flee any form of drunkenness. It's not the behavior befitting a child of God, and it is not a trivial matter. We are emphatically warned,

"Don't you realize that those who do wrong will not inherit the Kingdom of God? Don't fool yourselves. Those who indulge in sexual sin…or are thieves, or greedy people, or *drunkards*, or are abusive, or cheat people—none of these will inherit the Kingdom of God" (1 Corinthians 6:9–10 NLT).

One more important aspect should be considered in our discussion. We are in a spiritual race, and our Coach tells us to "strip off every weight that slows us down, especially the sin that so easily trips us up" (Hebrews 12:1 NLT). There are sins that more easily beset us than others, and it would seem from the statistics previously mentioned that alcohol abuse is high up on the list. So why flirt with something that has brought so many to ruin?

In conclusion, let's ask ourselves, why do we who have the genuine experience of being filled with the Spirit look to artificial means for peace or tension relief? Are we Spirit-filled in name only and not by experience, therefore needing assistance from substances?

Don't Be Fooled

We have looked at only this one chapter of the book of Ephesians. There are plenty of other commandments in the New Testament. Again, remember, this is not a list to keep in order to be saved; rather, this lifestyle is attributed to those who will live in the manifest presence of God.

Listen to how Paul concludes his list of don'ts:

Don't be fooled by those who try to excuse these sins, for the anger of God will fall on all who disobey him. Don't participate in the things these people do. …Carefully determine what pleases the Lord. Take no part in the worthless deeds of evil and darkness; instead, expose them. It is shameful even to talk about the things that ungodly people do in secret. …So be careful how you live. (Ephesians 5:6–7, 10–12, 15 NLT)

Don't be fooled by those who try to excuse these sins. The consequences are quite unfavorable. We must carefully, not casually, determine what pleases

God in our lifestyle. Many of us act as if we're on a playground when in reality we're on a battlefield. We're at war, there's a target on our heads, and the enemy works tirelessly to bring us down. But if we remain in the light, he will fail because of God's amazing grace on our lives.

I encourage you: Press into the high life. Depend on grace to live a godly, blameless life in the midst of a perverted, dying world. You have what it takes because God has freely given His divine nature to you. Don't squander or receive in vain the amazing grace of God.

13

OUR MOTIVATION

Therefore, I will always remind you about these
things—even though you already know them and are
standing firm in the truth you have been taught.
And it is only right that I should keep on
reminding you as long as I live. For our Lord Jesus
Christ has shown me that I must soon leave this
earthly life, so I will work hard to make sure you
always remember these things after I am gone.
—2 Peter 1:12-15 NLT

...We regard falling from God's
friendship as the only thing dreadful and
we consider becoming God's friend the only
thing worthy of honor and desire.
—Gregory of Nyssa

The call to live holy is not a suggestion or a recommendation. It isn't something we strive for but that is realistically unattainable. It's a command, one we're expected to fulfill.

The apostle Peter made clear that the reiteration of critical truths and commands made by our Lord Jesus Christ is vitally important. The concept of being reminded is mentioned three times in the four verses above. The people reading Peter's letter already knew what was written, yet he declared that even after he went to heaven, his readers must constantly review these important truths. Isn't it a good idea for us to also give more careful attention to the importance of his message?

At the beginning of his two letters, Peter writes, "You *must be* holy in everything you do" (1 Peter 1:15 NLT). Two statements of command are found frequently in Scripture: *should be* and *must be*. We are wise to adhere to the should bes. We are fools if we don't adhere to the must bes! Peter's statement was a *must be*.

The apostle was clearly speaking about our lifestyle. We should not be intimidated, scared, or discouraged by this. We are promised, "His commandments are not burdensome" (1 John 5:3). This means they are attainable and not unrealistic.

Peter continues to discuss, in the remainder of his first letter and more so in his second, what living a holy life means practically. He made statements such as, "I warn you as 'temporary residents and foreigners' to keep away from worldly desires that wage war against your very souls" (1 Peter 2:11 NLT).

The battlefield is our mind. It is our thoughts, emotions, and will that must be held in check. All sin begins in this arena. The battle usually occurs when we least expect it, and it frequently occurs when we are near unbelievers or compromising believers. Peter explicitly identifies this reality: "Be careful to live properly among your unbelieving neighbors" (1 Peter 2:12 NLT).

The apostle addresses our holy behavior related to government, employment, marriage, and other relationships. He speaks specifically of each but emphasizes that our greatest opportunity to give a strong witness will occur with ungodly neighbors, co-workers, and fellow students—especially those we used to hang out with before coming to Christ. He says:

> Of course, your old friends don't understand why you don't join in
> with the old gang anymore. But you don't have to give an account to
> them. They're the ones who will be called on the carpet—and before
> God himself. (1 Peter 4:4–5 The Message)

At the beginning of his second letter, Peter instructs us to "work hard to prove that you really are among those God has called and chosen. Do these things, and you will never fall away" (2 Peter 1:10 NLT). The things we are to practice to prove our authenticity include moral excellence, self-control, patience, endurance, godliness, kindness, and love. These are the fruits of grace we develop by faith. If we do these things, "Then God will give you a grand entrance into the eternal Kingdom of our Lord and Savior Jesus Christ" (verse 11).

Peter further warns of teachers who will arise who "cleverly teach destructive heresies" (2 Peter 2:1 NLT). They will attract a large audience: "Many will follow their evil teaching and shameful immorality" (verse 2). *The Message* Bible says of these false leaders, "They've put themselves on a fast downhill slide to destruction, but not before they recruit a crowd of mixed-up followers who can't tell right from wrong. They give the way of truth a bad name" (verses 1–2).

These teachers will be "among us"—in our conferences, churches, and connect groups. We are warned, "These people eat with you in your fellowship meals commemorating the Lord's love" (Jude 12 NLT; also see 2 Peter 2:13). There will be enough of the truth mixed in with their teaching that two things will happen.

First, people will no longer be able to distinguish between right and wrong. Behavior that draws us away from God's heart will be labeled as acceptable and, in some instances, even good. Adhering to and proclaiming God's Word will be viewed as legalistic and judgmental.

Along with causing a decaying "Christian" lifestyle, what is taught will act to silence discernment. These deceptive ministers and teachers will be gifted, excellent orators and will disarm and influence many. Since the *full* counsel of God's Word will no longer be held as the ultimate standard, the rate at which believers will be lured into disobedience will be at an all-time high.

The second consequence will be that the gospel will receive a bad rap. This can only happen if these teachers use enough language that aligns with the truth:

They have forsaken the right way and gone astray… (2 Peter 2:15)

These leaders began as godly Christ followers but didn't persevere, which explains why they know the language of Christianity but have compromised its integrity.

Peter points out that if we pursue holy living, we will never fall—we'll never succumb to the influence of these false teachers. Our safety lies in this. Then he bluntly writes of the victims who will be lured into the counterfeit teachings and lifestyle of these influencers:

> And when people escape from the wickedness of the world by know-ing our Lord and Savior Jesus Christ and then get tangled up and enslaved by sin again, they are worse off than before. It would be bet-ter if they had never known the way to righteousness than to know it and then reject *the command they were given to live a holy life.* (2 Peter 2:20–21 NLT)

This is startling, almost mind-blowing information and certainly worth reiterating. This great apostle speaks of people who will actually escape the grip of sin through receiving Jesus Christ into their life. But because of un-sound teaching, incorrect believing, and a loss of discernment, they will de-teriorate back into ungodly living. He actually states that they now are worse off than before they received Jesus, and that it would have been better for them to never have known the way of truth than to reject the command to live holy. How sobering!

Again, we see it is a *commandment* to live holy—and a critical com-mandment at that!

Two Unbeatable Forces

The Lord's commandments aren't burdensome because our new nature, cou-pled with grace's empowerment, enables us to keep them. But let's be realistic. We may possess this ability, but what motivates us to keep the command to live holy in the heat of the battle? The answer is two unbeatable forces.

Allow me to set up my explanation of the first force with a story. When I was a youth pastor back in the 1980s, I was preparing to speak for our weekly service. I sensed the Lord desired to speak to me, so I quieted myself and heard in my heart, "Read John 14:15."

I had no idea what John 14:15 said, so I quickly turned to it and noticed that in my Bible it began a new paragraph. I read Jesus's words: "If you love Me, keep My commandments..."

Then I read from the fifteenth verse down to the twenty-fourth verse. All ten of these verses related back to verse fifteen. The theme of this section is keeping Jesus's words. What I understood from these scriptures was simply, "By keeping My commandments, you prove you love Me." After I read the last verse, the Lord spoke to my heart: "You didn't get it. Read it again."

I read all ten verses again. Again the message seemed to be, "By keeping My commandments, you prove you love Me." Again I heard God's voice: "You didn't get it. Read it again."

Now my curiosity was really aroused. I read the ten verses again, only to hear the Lord give the same message: "Read it again." After this transpired seven or eight times, my frustration mounted.

I decided to slow way down and read these ten verses at a snail's pace. I'd read *if*, then stop, say it aloud, and think about it. Then I'd go to the next word, *you*, and repeat the same process. I continued like this to the end, which took a long time. After fifteen minutes or so, I finally finished the ten verses again and immediately heard the Spirit say, "You didn't get it. Read it again."

Exasperated, I cried out, "Lord, please forgive my ignorance! I must be stupid! Open my eyes to see what You're saying!"

Then I read verse 15 again: "If you love Me, *keep My commandments." I noticed an asterisk by the word *keep*. I went to the reference note in my Bible's margin and read that the more accurate translation is "you will keep."

After substituting this phrase in the place of the single word *keep*, the verse now read, "If you love Me, you will keep My commandments." When I read it this way, an explosion went off inside. I saw it now.

I then heard God say, "John, I wasn't saying that if you keep My commandments, you'll prove that you love Me. I already know whether you love Me or not! I was saying that if you fall head over heels in love with Me, you will be motivated to keep My commandments!" My original understanding had been legalistic. The new insight was about a love relationship, which is the key to motivation.

Passionate Love

Allow me to illustrate. Have you ever fallen in love? When I was engaged to my wife, Lisa, I was head over heels in love with her. She was constantly on my mind. I'd do whatever I could just to spend time with her. I recall one occasion when we were together for several hours. I finally said goodbye, but Lisa called me shortly afterward and said, "John, you left your jacket at my house." I was thrilled that I had forgotten it because that gave me the opportunity to see her again.

I replied, "Well, I guess I'll just have to come get it!" We both laughed. That led to several more hours together.

If Lisa needed something, no matter the inconvenience, I would get it for her if at all possible. If she had called me in the middle of the night and said, "Honey, I want an ice cream cone," I would have said, "What flavor? I'll be there in five minutes!" I would have done anything to fulfill any desire she had or any request she made of me. Here's the gist: *her wish was my delightful command.*

Because of my intense love for Lisa, it was a joy to do whatever she desired. What she asked for was never troublesome. I didn't respond to her wishes to prove that I loved her; I did it because I was in love with her!

This illustrates what Jesus was saying. Out of an intense love for Him, we find our delight in fulfilling His desires. His Word is not restrictive or burdensome but our consuming passion!

Let's move forward a few years into my marriage. I became heavily involved in the work of the ministry, and without my awareness, my love for Lisa began to wane. Now Lisa's wish was no longer my command. Often it was inconvenient, and sometimes it was burdensome. I had a totally different attitude in serving her. It wasn't done with excitement, as it was when we were dating. It was no longer, "What flavor? I'll be right over!" It was, "Really? Honey, I'm swamped with other things to do!" I wasn't seeking opportunities to spend time with her. I spent time with her because it was the right thing to do. My new passion was my work.

Listen to what Jesus says to a church:

"I know your works, your labor, your patience… Nevertheless I have this against you, that you have left your first love. Remember therefore from where you have fallen; repent and do the first works…" (Revelation 2:2, 4–5)

Look again at Jesus's statement: "I know your *works*… You have fallen; repent and do the *first works*." There are two different works spoken of. The first works were motivated by the church's passionate love for Jesus, no different from my attitude of, "What flavor do you want? I'll be there in five minutes." Now the church's works were out of obligation, no different a motive than, "Really? Honey, I'm swamped right now."

In regard to Jesus, it translates this way: When we first fell in love, we were excited to do anything for Him. Now the passion has waned; obedience has become duty.

How do we repair this shortcoming? We spend more time with Him in the Word, in prayer, and in worship. We turn our thoughts toward Him, not just in church or during our morning devotion, but continually acknowledging His presence throughout our day. We should also ask the Holy Spirit, our constant Companion, to fill our hearts afresh with the love of God daily (see Romans 5:5).

You can't love God too much; it will only add passion to your life. Never forget, "Love never fails" (1 Corinthians 13:8).

Holy Fear

The other motivating force is godly fear. It's the virtue Paul specifically cites to keep us on a holy track:

> Let us cleanse ourselves from all filthiness of the flesh and spirit, perfecting holiness in the fear of God. (2 Corinthians 7:1)

Holiness is matured in the fear of God. This single truth is seen throughout the New Testament.

Paul writes to a different church, "Work out your own salvation with fear and trembling" (Philippians 2:12). It takes deep reverence, trembling, and holy fear to obey God's commands. Peter writes, in regard to keeping the command to live holy, "So you must live in reverent fear of him during your time as 'foreigners in the land'" (1 Peter 1:17 NLT).

The writer of Hebrews urges us to pursue holiness with this statement: "Therefore, since we are receiving a kingdom which cannot be shaken, let us have grace, by which we may serve God acceptably with reverence and godly fear" (Hebrews 12:28). To fear God is the acceptable way to serve Him.

Many are confused about the fear of the Lord. Isn't *fear* what we were set free from? What place does this word have in our vocabulary now?

God is love. He is our Dad. Yet *fear* must be addressed because it's spoken of frequently in the New Testament.

Some have played it down by saying, "It only means to worship God." A world-renowned teacher once said this to me in the green room before I was to speak at a national conference in South Africa. My question about his definition was, "Why does Paul speak of fear and trembling four times in the New Testament if it is only about worship?" Trembling is a bit more than worship.

Strong's single definition for the Greek word *tromos* (trembling) is "quaking with fear." This being the case, we are told to "work out our salvation quaking with fear." There is a *profound respect* and even *healthy terror* involved here—a bit more to it than our common understanding of worship.

About the meaning of fear, you may hear this response: "That's an Old Testament teaching. We don't have to fear God because He's not given us a spirit of fear but of love." Those who say this have confused the spirit of fear with the fear of the Lord.

When Moses brought Israel to Sinai and God manifested His presence, the people of Israel ran back and frantically cried out to Moses, asking him to beseech God not to manifest His greatness to them. Hear Moses's reply to Israel:

> "Do not fear; for God has come to test you, and that His fear may
> be before you, so that you may not sin." (Exodus 20:20)

It sounds like Moses contradicts himself: "Do not fear... God has come that His fear may be in you." But he was simply differentiating between being *scared of God* and *the fear of the Lord*. There's a huge difference. Why would God want us scared of Him? It's impossible to have intimacy with someone you're scared of, yet God passionately desires to be intimate with us.

The person who is scared of God has something to hide, so consequently he or she is afraid of God. The first thing Adam and Eve did once they sinned against God was hide from His presence (see Genesis 3:8). On the other hand, the person who fears God has nothing to hide; in fact, he or she is scared to be away from God!

Therefore, the first definition of the fear of the Lord is simply *to be terrified of being away from God*. To fear God is to venerate Him. We overwhelmingly respect, honor, esteem, and reverence Him beyond anything or anyone else.

Holy fear gives God the place of glory He deserves; we quake and tremble before Him in profound awe. We firmly embrace His heart by esteeming His desires above those of any other, including ourselves. We love what He loves and hate what He hates. What is important to Him becomes important to us. This is why we are told, "All who fear the LORD will hate evil" (Proverbs 8:13 NLT).

Exodus 20:20 states that godly fear keeps us from sin. Along the same lines, we are told, "By fearing the LORD, people avoid evil" (Proverbs 16:6 NLT). Paul also writes that it's the force that motivates us to walk away from sin (see 2 Corinthians 7:1).

These scriptures became real when I visited a famous televangelist in prison. He was the most well-known minister on the planet in the 1980s. He'd committed crimes against our national government along with committing adultery.

The man had been in the penitentiary for almost five years, but in the early part of his sentence, he'd had an encounter with Jesus in his cell that turned his life around. One of my books had touched him deeply, and he'd requested that I visit him.

I will never forget that man walking into the visiting room of the penitentiary. He embraced me, in tears, for over a minute. He then grabbed my shoulders and passionately asked, "Did you write the book or was it written by a ghostwriter?"

"No, sir, it was me. I wrote every word."

He said excitedly, "We have so much to discuss and only ninety minutes to do it." He immediately sat down and shared his story.

One of his first statements was, "John, it was not the judgment of God that put me in this prison. It was His mercy, because if I had kept living the way I was, I would have ended up in hell forever." His statement stunned me. I was overwhelmed by his candor and humility.

After twenty or so minutes of listening to him, I asked a nagging question. I knew he loved Jesus greatly at the beginning of his ministry and had been on fire for God. I wanted to know how he had lost his passion.

Finally, I simply asked, "When did you fall out of love with Jesus? At what point?" I was seeking the signs of losing our love for Him, especially as a minister.

"I didn't," he answered firmly.

I was shocked and slightly appalled by his answer. How could he say that?

I shot back, "What do you mean? You committed adultery. You committed fraud—you were sent to prison. How can you say you didn't fall out of love with Jesus?"

Again, he looked me straight in the eye and without hesitation said, "John, I loved Jesus all the way through it."

I was silent, and I'm sure my face registered enormous confusion. He then said, "John, I loved Jesus, but I didn't fear Him."

There was silence for several moments. He let his words sink in. I was reeling with emotion. He broke the silence by soberly stating, "John, there are millions of Americans who are just like me. They love Jesus but don't fear God."

A Fictitious Jesus

That was a life-defining moment for me because this encounter aroused my hunger to get more answers. How can a man who loves God fall into habitual and even gross sin? How can millions who love God live unholy lives? They worship, are active in their local churches, and are passionate about the things of God; yet they are promiscuous, are bound to pornography, lie repeatedly, drink excessively, divorce for no scriptural reason—and that's the short list. They love Jesus, as did this man, so why aren't they keeping His words? Jesus said that if we loved Him we would have the strength to obey Him. What is missing?

Could the answer be that they profess love for someone they really don't know? Could this televangelist and the masses he spoke of have created an image of Jesus that, in reality, is not the real Jesus? Could this fictitious Jesus be the one who actually gives their fleshly nature what they crave?

Consider this: there are many in our nation taken with athletes and Hollywood celebrities. Their names are common in our homes, and the media has laid bare their personal lives through numerous television interviews and newspaper and magazine articles. I hear admirers talk as though these celebrities are close friends. I've seen people get emotionally caught up in their marriage problems and even grieve as if they were a part of the family when tragedies hit.

Yet if these fans ever met their celebrity "friend" on the street, they would not even receive a nod of acknowledgment. If they were bold enough to stop their friend, they might find the real person to be quite different from their image of him or her. Bottom line, it's a fictitious relationship.

Israel did this after their exodus from Egypt. Once Moses went to the mountain, away from the people, for forty days and nights, God became quiet—not to Moses but to the people. In this time of silence, Aaron and the leaders who were distant from God's presence began to create a "God" that would freely accommodate their cravings and carnal desires.

I missed something significant in this story for years from not reading Hebrew. Aaron named the calf he formed *Yhwh* or *Jehovah*, which is the proper name of God (see Exodus 32:5). Other than this incident, *Yhwh* is not used for a false god or idol anywhere in the Bible. The name is so sacred that the Hebrew writers wouldn't write the vowels. (We would write and pronounce it *Yahweh*.)

It wasn't just Aaron. The people acknowledged this calf by declaring, "This is *elohiym* who delivered us from Egypt" (see Exodus 32:4, 8). This Hebrew word is used thirty-two times in Genesis 1 alone. The first verse of the Bible says, "In the beginning *Elohiym* created the heavens and the earth."

Unlike *Yahweh,* roughly 90 percent of the time, this word is used for God Almighty. The other 10 percent of the time, it's used to describe a false god. Since Aaron identified the calf as *Yahweh,* we can safely assume the people were speaking along the same lines.

So here is the gist: The entire nation acknowledged that Yahweh had saved them, delivered them from bondage, and provided for them. However, they'd created a fictitious Yahweh, one quite different than the real One on the mountain with Moses.

We are told, "The fear of the Lord is the beginning of knowledge" (Proverbs 1:7). A good question to ask is, what knowledge? It can't be scriptural knowledge, because the Pharisees and lawyers were experts in Scripture, but they were away from the presence of God and were displeasing to Him. So what knowledge are we to have? Our answer is found in Proverbs 2:5: "Fear...the Lord, and find the *knowledge of God.*"

Allow me to say it like this. Through the right kind of fear you will come to know God intimately. You will know the true God—the true Jesus, not a fictitious one. Paul reprimands the Corinthians by saying, "You happily put up with whatever anyone tells you, even if they preach a *different Jesus* than the one we preach" (2 Corinthians 11:4 NLT).

This famous televangelist, along with the multitudes of others he referred to, don't love the unequivocal Jesus at the right hand of God. Instead, they love a fictitious Jesus, one who ignores and even permits the lifestyle they crave. They've either never truly known Him or have drifted in their relationship. In the latter case, it's no different than two friends who've drifted apart by going separate ways, only to find out years later they are quite different than before. Loving a fictitious Jesus doesn't give us the power to keep the words spoken by the real Jesus Christ. In essence, it's hard to truly love someone you don't really know.

Without the holy fear of the Lord, we cannot truly know God. Moses knew Him intimately. God's voice and ways were clear to him. Israel only knew God by His acts—the way He answered their prayers. To Israel, God's voice was thunder. Moses was permitted to be close to His presence. Israel was told to go back to their tents and play church (see Deuteronomy 5:29–30).

How Do We Get Holy Fear?

Our most important question then becomes, how do we receive the holy fear of God? We simply ask—but it must be done sincerely.

· Jesus states, "If you then, being evil, know how to give good gifts to your children, how much more will your heavenly Father give the Holy Spirit to those who ask Him!" (Luke 11:13) You may ask, "Isn't Jesus speaking of the Holy Spirit, not the fear of the Lord?" Hear what Isaiah states about Jesus and the Holy Spirit:

> There shall come forth a Rod from the stem of Jesse, and a Branch shall grow out of his roots. The Spirit of the Lord shall rest upon Him, the Spirit of wisdom and understanding, the Spirit of counsel and might, the Spirit of knowledge and of the *fear of the Lord*. His delight is in the fear of the Lord... (Isaiah 11:1–3)

The final characteristic of the Spirit of God listed here is "the Spirit of...the fear of the Lord." I personally believe it is the most important aspect we should ask for. There are two reasons I believe this. First, we are told the fear of the Lord is the beginning of wisdom, counsel, understanding, and knowledge (see Psalm 111:10; Proverbs 1:7; Proverbs 8 and 9). Second—and most convincing—the fear of the Lord is Jesus's delight. Shouldn't His delight be our delight? In fact, we are told Jesus was heard *because* of His godly fear (see Hebrews 5:7). It's one thing to *pray*, but it's another thing to be *heard*.

Both the fear of the Lord and the love of God are byproducts of being filled with His Spirit, for Paul writes, "The love of God has been poured in our hearts by the Holy Spirit" (Romans 5:5). I urge you to sincerely ask to be filled with the spirit of holy fear and the burning hot love of God.

Dirty Containers

This brings us to a widespread existing crisis. We have a serious shortage in the twenty-first century church. The lack isn't of containers, but rather of *clean* containers, for God to pour His Spirit into. Let's return to the final words Paul wrote on earth. He boldly states:

But the solid foundation that God has laid cannot be shaken; and on it are written these words: "The Lord knows those who are his" and "Those who say that they belong to the Lord must turn away from wrongdoing." (2 Timothy 2:19 TEV)

Paul discusses what makes us, both as a church and as individuals, unshakeable. There are two statements written on the foundation he identifies. The New King James Version says these words are "sealed" on the foundation; *The Message* says they are "engraved" on it.

First, the Lord knows who belongs to Him. These are comforting words. Once we've given ourselves completely to Him, He doesn't forget us. We become the apple of His eye.

The second engraving on the foundation is, "Those who say that they belong to the Lord must turn away from wrongdoing." Again we see the word *must*, not *should*. This is very strong language to communicate the importance of turning away from ungodly living. Why? The answer is in the next two verses:

In a large house some dishes are made of gold or silver, while others are made of wood or clay. Some of these are special, and others are not. That's also how it is with people. The ones who stop doing evil and make themselves pure will become special. Their lives will be holy and pleasing to their Master, and they will be able to do all kinds of good deeds. (2 Timothy 2:20–21 CEV)

The Greek word for *dishes* means simply "vessels" or "containers." If we as the container are clean, then we are fit for the Master's work. We are fit to be filled with His powerful presence.

Every morning I eat the same breakfast, no matter where I am in the world. I start out with a glass of warm lemon water followed by a cup of jasmine white tea. Fifteen minutes later is a bowl of oats, chia seeds, ground flax, and hemp hearts mixed with almond milk and pure maple syrup. For this breakfast I need containers—a tea mug, a drinking glass, and a bowl. Here is a fact: I've never used a dirty mug, glass, or bowl for my breakfast. I always search for clean containers. I love the taste of my breakfast, so I don't want it contaminated. The fact is that if there's dirt in a container—whether it's a bowl, plate, mug, or glass—the dirt will pollute any good substance put in the container. Why would God want to pour out His Spirit into a dirty container?

According to Paul's words, we have the responsibility of cleaning ourselves up. He didn't say, "The blood of Jesus cleanses us from all sin past, present, or future, so don't worry about the habitual sin you live in because you're covered." No, he stated, "So whoever cleanses himself [from what is ignoble *and* unclean, who separates himself from contact with contaminating and corrupting influences] will [then himself] be a vessel set apart *and* useful" (verse 21 AMP).

We must cleanse ourselves. Period. Paul was not discussing our positional relationship with Christ due to His work. He was addressing our behavior. Hear his words again: "The ones who stop doing evil and make themselves pure will become special."

Once again we see that God's presence—His Spirit—will not be poured into a dirty vessel but rather into a clean vessel.

The Consequence

We are informed that lawlessness (disobedience to God) is a mystery, and it's at work in society. But the good news is that there's a restraining force:

> The mystery of lawlessness is already at work; only He who now restrains will do so until He is taken out of the way. (2 Thessalonians 2:7)

Our question should be, who is He that restrains lawlessness? It could only be one of two options: the Holy Spirit or the body of Christ. The translators obviously believed it to be the Holy Spirit, hence the capitalization of *He*. Let's assume they are correct.

I'm more than fifty years old as I write this, and in my lifetime, I've never witnessed such a rate of increasing lawlessness in our nation. I've never seen such determination by government, media, and society to label lawless behavior as good. There is a reason. The restraining force—the Holy Spirit—is not as prevalent today. God's presence is rapidly diminishing in the West in the first part of the twenty-first century.

Why is this? If we proclaim a gospel that doesn't emphasize transformation, we end up with a deficit of clean containers, which consequently creates a shortage of God's manifest presence on the earth. Remember, once Jesus died on the cross, the veil in the temple was rent from top to bottom. God's presence immediately moved out of a man-made container and was about to be poured out on vessels not made with hands—the hearts of reborn men and women.

The Spirit of God didn't move out of the temple into a sunset, tree, beautiful landscape, song, video, or any other medium. He moved into vessels of flesh and blood. If the vessels are dirty, the presence of God in society diminishes and, consequently, lawlessness is less restrained.

We can change this rapid decline not by voting good candidates into office, lobbying against our government, firing existing media personnel, protesting at abortion clinics, or many other actions. The only way to really battle lawlessness is for us to yield to the empowerment of God's grace and live a godly life. In this way we give stronger voice and influence to the Holy Spirit in our society.

The lack of preaching about true holiness has cost us dearly on personal, corporate, and national levels. We can change this! Pastors, leaders, and all people of God—let's stand firm together in proclaiming the whole counsel of God from Scripture. Let's build a strong foundation and framework in the lives of those we influence. Let's see lawlessness held in check in our society by the restraining force of the Holy Spirit, which will result in a harvest of souls for the kingdom of God.

14

OUR PARAMETERS

"To those who use well what they are
given, even more will be given,
and they will have an abundance."
—Matthew 25:29 NLT

It is not my ability, but my response
to God's ability, that counts.
—Corrie ten Boom

L et's return to our illustration of building a house.
We first discussed lordship as our foundation. Next we considered the framework or structure, which is a sanctified lifestyle. Now let's move on to the final stage of the construction process. This phase defines the uniqueness of what we do. It involves our fruitfulness, dreams, plans, strategies, and life decisions. Paul writes:

We are God's masterpiece. He has created us anew in Christ Jesus,
so we can do the good things he planned for us long ago. (Ephesians
2:10 NLT)

We were created in Christ Jesus not only to be children of God, but equally to be productive kingdom citizens.

In the actual homebuilding process, it's the installation of the woodwork, cabinets, carpeting, tile, marble countertops, paint, and eventually the lighting that finishes the house. But this aspect will look good and last only if the first two building stages are strong.

We frequently face choices in life that appear good; however, quite often they are not God's best for us. Often we feel our choices are limited. Abram and Sarai concluded the only way for them to birth a son was for Abram to marry Sarai's servant, Hagar. From this decision Ishmael was born. Yet the Word of God is clear that "the son of the bondwoman shall not be heir with the son of the freewoman" (Galatians 4:30). In this situation God redeemed Abram and Sarai's choice; however, this is not always the case. Frequently these wrong choices and paths will rob us of our maximum potential.

One of many examples from the Old Testament is Saul, under pressure, making the decision to offer a sacrifice prior to Samuel's arrival. In this case, the choice wasn't redeemed; Saul lost the kingdom (see 1 Samuel 13).

Consider facing important decisions this way. If you're hiking and see a path that is most traveled, you'll naturally gravitate toward it. However, if you are with an experienced guide, he may know of another path that is more scenic and will get you to where you are going faster. The guide will help you make a better choice.

We are told, "Your word is a lamp to guide my feet and a light for my path" (Psalm 119:105 NLT). Being well grounded in the Word of God illuminates our path, which is crucial to making wise life decisions.

In Abram and Sarai's situation, they both limited God, which frequently occurs when we choose to go our own way. So let's examine God's Word to guide us in making choices.

"Not Available for Your Home"

In our first few years of marriage, Lisa and I lived in two cities, Dallas and Orlando. We could barely afford our first two houses. Initially we'd lived in apartments for several years because we didn't have enough money for our own place. We kept visiting model homes—but only to dream.

Once we were able to buy a house, the prevailing factor was the price. We couldn't afford most houses, as my salary was merely $18,000 per year in Dallas and $27,000 per year in Orlando. Remaining in an apartment wasn't an option because by now we had two kids and wanted a yard where they could play. In both cities we shopped for weeks, looking in the most affordable neighborhoods that were a reasonable driving distance from our church and work. In both cases we found that the most economical option was a low-end tract home development. Both builders had approximately a half dozen floor plans to choose from, and each time we chose one of the least expensive.

With one house, we were so excited when the day came to pick out our interior finishes. Our salesperson brought us into a general showroom where many beautiful materials were displayed. There were all sorts of marble and travertine tiles, a variety of wood floor finishes, beautiful cabinets, and a host of lush carpets. We saw exquisite crown moldings and unique fireplace stone.

Then our salesperson pointed us to a section of the showroom where we could pick out our materials. In this area there were no marble or travertine options; in fact, there was no tile of any sort. Maple, oak, and pine cabinets also didn't exist. There was no crown molding, fireplace stone, or wood flooring to select from. Our only choices were low-grade carpet, linoleum flooring, and cheap compressed wood cabinets.

We kept asking for better materials but continually heard one of two responses: "It's not available for your home" or "That will be an upgrade charge." When we asked the amount of the upgrade charge, a huge figure was quoted, which of course we couldn't afford. Lisa and I left the showroom trying to encourage each other, but in truth, we felt deflated.

Able to Do

We live in a world that is reflective of this experience at the builder's showroom. People are often told, "You can't." "Don't get your hopes up." "That's too lofty of an idea." "Fit in and be normal." Or, "That's out of your league."

The list of these restrictive comments is endless. Often the logic seems reasonable and of good counsel, but what's the truth?

> Now to Him who is *able* to do exceedingly abundantly above all that we
> ask or think, according to the power that works in us. (Ephesians 3:20)

This scripture communicates quite a different message than our experience in the showroom did. God does not give us limiting parameters. His borders are beyond what we can see, dream, imagine, hope, or ask for.

The key word in this verse is *able*. Let me illustrate with a scenario.

A multibillionaire approaches three young entrepreneurs and makes them an offer: "I want to fund your dream business. I expect no payback whatsoever; I just want to see you succeed. I'm *able* to give you as much capital as you need to begin."

First is a young woman who decides to build a bakery. She needs a storefront, a couple of ovens, baking pans, utensils, a cash register, ingredients, and a few other items. She brings her plans to the billionaire and asks for $100,000. Without hesitation he transfers the money into her account.

Next is a young man. He decides to build some houses. He needs to buy a few lots, raw materials, tools, and a pickup truck and rent a small office space. He comes up with his business plan and requests $250,000. Once again, the billionaire immediately transfers the money into his account.

The third entrepreneur is a young lady who wants to build a business complex with an adjoining mall and theme park. She finds one thousand acres of land for sale inside the city limits. It is prime real estate and has been on the market for quite some time because few could afford the property. She puts an offer on it that is accepted.

She acquires a team of architects to draw up her dream. She describes two unique, adjacent twelve-story office buildings with a courtyard. In another section she plans a beautiful outdoor mall filled with high-end retail shops and quality restaurants. Above the retail stores are luxurious condominiums. She requests a five-star luxury hotel to be right in the middle of the project. She saves the final section of land for her classy theme park. She lines all the streets with lush trees, inserts bike trails, and tops it all off with a stunning tree and flower park next to the mall.

Her vision is to attract successful businesses, residents, and hotel guests to her park. She will offer high-end shopping, peaceful surroundings, a unique experience at the theme park, and excellent restaurants. The hotel will offer fabulous accommodations for her business owners' guests. She also desires her complex to be a destination spot. It's her hope to attract people from all over the country to fly in and rest, shop, enjoy the theme park, and be pampered in her exquisite hotel.

She massages the plan with the architects until it's flawless, truly a work of art. She then approaches the billionaire, shows him her plans, and requests $245 million. As with the other two entrepreneurs, he immediately transfers the money into her account.

Three years later the billionaire calls the three young people together for a meeting. He would like a presentation on their progress. One by one they report. The bakery is netting an income of a couple thousand dollars per month. The homebuilder has built four homes and netted just over two hundred thousand dollars in the three-year span.

The third young entrepreneur gets up and gives a report on her complex. She presently has a 90 percent occupancy rate in her hotel and 87 percent occupancy in her high-rise office space. Her condominiums are sold out. Her mall is 98 percent filled with high-end stores and restaurants. Her net profit is in the millions of dollars per month. She reports that the city has set a date to recognize her complex with a civic award because it has benefitted the community in several ways: aesthetics, jobs, tourist spending, and tax revenue. She's also taken a percentage of the profits to open up and fund soup kitchens in the poor sections of the city.

But it doesn't stop there. She reports that a large percentage of the multiple millions of dollars in profit are being allocated for similar complexes in three other cities, which will open up six months apart over the next year and a half. She's trained three management teams that will oversee these new complexes. She expects profits over the next five years to create investment capital for five more complexes in other key locations.

After hearing her presentation, the other two entrepreneurs become quiet and their countenances fall. The billionaire, recognizing this, asks why they are downcast.

The young lady who owns the bakery speaks up first. "Well, sir, of course she's doing better than we are, because she asked you for more money than we did. She's capable of doing more because you gave her more."

The billionaire looks at the young homebuilder. "Do you agree with her?"

The young man says, "Honestly, sir, I do. She had more to work with."

The billionaire has his personal assistant get the records from their first meeting. A few minutes later she comes in with the transcripts.

The benefactor says to his assistant, "Please read the statement I made to each of these entrepreneurs three years ago."

The assistant reads: "I want to fund your dream businesses. I'm *able* to give you as much capital as you need to begin."

The billionaire looks at the two whose countenances have fallen and questions, "Why do you envy what she's received? Why do you believe she has an advantage over you? I told each of you I was *able* to give you as much capital as you needed to fulfill your vision. I put no limits on what I'd give and indeed gave you exactly what you requested. Why didn't you dream and plan bigger?"

The billionaire then turns to the young lady with the bakery and inquires, "Why didn't you plan a larger bakery? I would have given you the capital. Why didn't you request funding for more effective marketing? People love your goods; you would have succeeded. However, my biggest question is, why didn't you plan more bakeries throughout the city, and eventually plan franchises throughout the nation to grow your business?"

He then turns to the young man and asks similar questions. "Why didn't you train a few foremen and hire several subcontractors to build twenty houses per year, instead of just averaging a little over one per year? You could have created so many more jobs. Why didn't you buy more land? Why didn't you organize branch offices throughout the state so you could fill several cities with beautiful houses? I would have funded your vision because you were helping the families of this city and eventually the state. Your reach was limited because your capital was limited, because your vision was limited."

Abundance

As Christians we often subconsciously think we aren't supposed to have too much. Yet does such thinking align with what the Word of God teaches? Jesus declares:

> "To those who use well what they are given, even more will be given, and they will have an *abundance*." (Matthew 25:29 NLT)

God has no problem with abundance. What He is against is abundance possessing us. What's the difference? The person possessed by abundance is one who seeks blessing, possessions, finances, ability, or power just for the sake of appeasing his cravings. Or he hoards resources out of fear.

Many who heard the prosperity teaching in the late twentieth century lusted in this way. Their greed caused many leaders and believers to back off from speaking God's truth about abundance. Many came to disdain the word *prosperity*. But the truth is, we need abundance to do larger and more effective work in building lives for the kingdom. Could this be why God stated, "Beloved, I wish above all things that thou mayest prosper and be in health, even as thy soul prospereth"? (3 John 2 KJV)

In our illustration, the multibillionaire didn't give each entrepreneur $245 million, as he did the last young lady. He gave to each according to their vision. If you examine the parable containing Jesus's statement about abundance, each of the servants didn't start out with the same amount of money. They were given different amounts: "He gave five bags of silver to one, two bags of silver to another, and one bag of silver to the last—dividing it in proportion to their abilities" (Matthew 25:15 NLT). Their abilities were in accordance with what they could foresee.

In my example the first girl could only foresee a small bakery. The young man could only foresee a few houses per year. The third young lady's ability—what she could foresee—required much more.

To use empowerment well is to use it to build lives, to build the kingdom. If we look closely at this parable, we find an interesting fact. Two servants were faithful to their master. They multiplied what was given to them. (In our story of the three young entrepreneurs, only one multiplied.) The master in Jesus's parable called their multiplication *good* (see Matthew 25:21, 23).

The servant who maintained what was entrusted to him was identified as lazy. The master took his one bag of silver away and gave it to the man who possessed abundance. The master made this man's ten bags of silver into eleven. This is far from a *socialistic* response; in all honesty, it's actually *capitalistic* in nature.

We think a good Christian will "hold the fort," so to speak. In other words, they are content with having just enough to get by, when in reality that is being *lazy*. God's first commandment to humankind was to "be fruitful and multiply" (Genesis 1:22). He wasn't just talking about babies. He was declaring, "Anything I give to you, I expect you to multiply it and present it back to Me."

God's entrusted to me the ability to teach. By His grace (the power that is at work within our team, our partners, my wife, and me), that gift has been multiplied and presented back to Him through teaching all over the world, writing books, putting messages on the web, giving millions of resources to pastors and leaders globally, blogging, developing other teachers—and this isn't the full list. So far He's done far beyond what I could ever have dreamed of as a young man. However, I have two responses to all this.

First, my concern is, have I limited Him in some way? Second, my delight is, wow, look what His ability has done! These two thoughts keep me humble and passionate at the same time.

Our Container

There is so much more He could do through each of us. Whether we realize it or not, we all set constraints. According to Ephesians 3:20, these restrictions are determined by what we can "ask or think," in regard to helping others. God's clear message to us is, "My grace in you can go far beyond the border you set up." Jesus says it like this: "All things are possible to him who believes" (Mark 9:23).

Our boundaries—what we can contain—decide how much we will partake of the unlimited supply. In my story about the billionaire and the entrepreneurs, the first person's container was a vision needing $100,000, the second needed $250,000, and the third required $245 million.

Frankly speaking, it's the size of our container that limits God. Could it be God is asking us, "Why are you thinking only of what it takes to get by? Why are you merely thinking of you and your family? Why aren't you tapping into the potential I've placed within you? In My sight that mentality is not *good*. It's *lazy*."

This is why Paul passionately prays that we might know and understand:

…what is the *immeasurable* and *unlimited* and *surpassing greatness*
of His power in and for us who believe… (Ephesians 1:19 AMP)

Look carefully at the words I have emphasized in this verse. Stop and ponder each. *Immeasurable*. You cannot measure it. *Unlimited*. There is no limit to it. *Surpassing greatness*. There is no power greater in the universe.

Notice all of the power is *in* us. It's not power we might periodically get from the throne room. It's His power that is in us already.

It's also *for* us. It enables us to multiply. It aids us in being fruitful. It makes us effective in helping others. By it we shine as bright lights.

This power is nothing other than the grace of God!

Rule in Life[24]

The grace of God is overwhelming. It's an undeserved gift of salvation, forgiveness, a new nature, and empowerment to live a godly life. It also enables us to multiply, be fruitful, and reign in life. Grace is really amazing! Listen carefully to Paul's words:

> All who receive God's abundant grace and are freely put right with him will *rule in life* through Christ. (Romans 5:17 TEV)

The magnitude of this statement seems almost too far-fetched to be realistic because its implications are astounding. Perhaps this is why many have overlooked it. By God's grace we are to govern in life. We are empowered to overcome any obstacle this world would try to throw against us. Life on this earth is not to get the best of us; we are to rule over it. We are ordained to make a significant mark in our spheres of influence. This is our mandate.

How does this look in practice? We are to break out of the status quo, to surpass the norm. We are called to influence—to be the head and not the tail, above and not beneath (see Deuteronomy 28:13). Not only are we to rise above the adverse circumstances of life, but we're also to outshine those who don't have a covenant with God. We are to be leaders in the midst of an unenlightened world. The head sets the direction, course, and trends, whereas the tail follows. We should be leaders in all aspects of our society, not followers. Is this a reality? Or are we falling short of what God calls good?

Allow me to spell it out clearly. If your profession is in the medical field, by God's grace, you have the ability to discover new and innovative ways of treating sickness and disease. Your potential is immeasurable and unlimited. Your fellow workers should marvel at your discoveries, and your work should inspire them. Your innovation and wisdom will cause them to scratch their heads and say, "Where is he (or she) getting these ideas from?" Not only can you shine, but you will also multiply your effectiveness in your field. Others will aspire to follow in your steps and seek to know the source of your ability.

If you're a web designer, your creations should be fresh and innovative, so much so that others emulate your work. You and other believers in your field should set the prevailing trends that society follows. You are sought out for your work and are known for your innovation. You're so ahead of the curve that others in your field scratch their heads and say to one another, "Where does he (or she) get this creativity from?" You multiply by imparting your knowledge into others and growing your industry and by giving into the kingdom.

If you're a public schoolteacher, by the empowering grace within you, develop fresh, creative, and innovative ways of communicating knowledge, understanding, and wisdom to your students that none of the other educators in your school system have considered. You can set the bar and inspire students in such a way that others marvel. Your fellow educators will discuss among themselves, "Where is he (or she) getting these ideas?" You will multiply by reproducing your abilities in your students and by developing other educators.

As a businessman or woman, you can come up with inventive products and sales techniques that outclass others. You'll engage keen marketing strategies that are ahead of the curve. You deftly perceive what's profitable and what's not. You know when to buy and when to sell, when to get in and when to get out. Other business people will scratch their heads trying to figure out why you're so successful. You will multiply by developing young entrepreneurs and by generous giving to build the kingdom.

The same principle applies if you're a musician, researcher, athlete, scientist, policeman, flight attendant, stay-at-home mom, or if you're in the media, the military, or any other arena of life. All of these examples, lofty or not, model our mandate.

Each of us is called to different sectors of society. Wherever we're located, we should manifest headship and leadership. Our businesses should thrive even when others struggle. Our communities should be safe, more delightful, and prosperous. Our places of employment should boom. Our music should be fresh and original, emulated by secular musicians. The same should be true of our graphics, videos, and architectural designs. Our creativity should inspire and be sought after on every level.

Our performances, whether in athletics, entertainment, the arts, media, or any other field, should stand out. When the righteous govern, our cities, states, and nations should flourish. Our schools should excel when we teach and lead. When believers are involved, there should be an abundance of creativity, innovation, productivity, tranquility, sensitivity, and integrity. We disciples of Jesus are to be light in a dark world. So in essence, through God's grace we should *distinguish ourselves* in the midst of a dark society.

Beyond the Norm

Read this testimony about Daniel:

> Daniel so *distinguished himself* among the administrators and the satraps by his exceptional qualities that the king planned to set him over the whole kingdom. (Daniel 6:3 NIV)

This is astounding. First, notice that Daniel *distinguished himself.* It doesn't say "God distinguished Daniel." Every major Bible translation says that it was Daniel who "distinguished himself." *The Message* Bible states that he "completely outclassed the other" leaders.

How did Daniel do it? He had exceptional qualities because he was a man who was connected with God. It should be no different for anyone who has the Spirit of God living on the inside of them.

The New American Standard Bible says, "Daniel began distinguishing himself…because he possessed an *extraordinary* spirit." The word *extraordi-*

nary means "to go beyond the norm, to break out of the status quo, to exceed the common measure." Sometimes we can better comprehend a word by examining what it's not—its antonyms, which for *extraordinary* are *common*, *ordinary*, or *normal*. So living a normal life would manifest the opposite lifestyle of that of one possessing an extraordinary spirit.

Daniel's spirit was extraordinary. If our spirit is extraordinary, our minds and bodies should follow suit. If our spirit leads us, creativity, ingenuity, wisdom, knowledge, and all other aspects of life are shaped differently than if we merely live by our own strength. If we really understand the grace *in* and *for* us, we know there are no restrictions.

Let's not forget the words descriptive of God's power within us: *immeasurable*, *unlimited*, and *surpassing greatness*. Daniel tapped into what was available in his relationship with God. He knew his covenant with the Almighty—that he was to be the head and not the tail. And we have a more powerful covenant with God than Daniel did.

Let's examine Daniel's situation more thoroughly. He and his three friends were brought captive out of the tiny nation of Israel and escorted into the most powerful nation in the world. If you're American and you think our nation has been great in the past century, the fact is that our country's not nearly as powerful as Babylon was, relatively speaking. The Babylonians ruled the world—all of it! They were number one economically, politically, militarily, socially, scientifically, educationally, and artistically.

The Babylonian people were the most sophisticated on the planet in practically all fields. Yet we find that in regard to Daniel and his friends, "No matter what question the king asked or what problem he raised, these four knew *ten times more*" than the other leaders of the kingdom (Daniel 1:20 TEV). Other translations say they were ten times better, ten times wiser, and understood ten times more. They implemented ideas the wise men of this leading nation had never thought of, and their ideas worked. In essence, their creativity, innovation, and insight were ten times more powerful than that of the other leaders who didn't possess God's Spirit.

Greater Than Daniel

With this in mind, read Jesus's words: "John is greater than anyone who has ever lived" (Luke 7:28 TEV). This means John the Baptist was greater than Daniel. Don't try to compare the two by what they did. John was in ministry; Daniel served in civil government. However, Jesus clearly reveals that John was superior. But He then goes on to say:

> "But the one who is least in the Kingdom of God is greater than John." (Luke 7:28 TEV)

Why is the one who is least in the kingdom of God greater than John? Jesus hadn't yet gone to the cross to liberate humankind, so John didn't have a reborn spirit. It could not be said of John, "As Jesus is, so is John the Baptist in this world" (see 1 John 4:17). Yet this is said about us! John was not raised up and made to sit together with Christ in heavenly places (see Ephesians 2:6). Yet this is true about us! This is why the least in the kingdom now is greater than John. *Are we getting this?*

Some scholars believe there have been approximately two billion Christians on this earth from the time of Jesus's resurrection until this day. The chances are very slim, but if it so happens that you're the least of those two billion believers, you're still greater than John the Baptist—which means *you're greater than Daniel.*

The questions that now arise are, do you really know who you are? And are you distinguishing yourself? Are you ten times smarter, better, wiser, more creative, and more innovative than those you work with who are not in covenant relationship with God through Jesus Christ? If not, why? Could it be we do not believe for a greater measure of God's grace?

Let's think this through a little further. Jesus declared that we are "the light of the world" (see Matthew 5:14). Our being referenced as light in the midst of darkness is not a one-time occurrence in the New Testament. (See Matthew 5:14–16; John 8:12; Acts 13:47; Romans 13:12; Ephesians 5:8,

14; Colossians 1:12; Philippians 2:15; 1 Thessalonians 5:5 and 1 John 1:7; 2:9–10.) This truth should be an overwhelming theme of our lives in Christ.

What does it mean to be the light of the world? Most see it applying only to our behavior—being sweet, kind, and nice—along with the fact that we can quote John 3:16. What if Daniel had seen being a light this way? What if his goal each day as he entered the government offices was to treat people in a nice manner and say to his fellow workers, "Hey, Babylonians leaders, Psalm 23 says, 'The Lord is my Shepherd, I shall not want…'"

What would the administrators and governors have said to each other when Daniel left the office to pray at lunchtime? (He did this every day). I'm sure it would have been something like, "We're so glad the fanatic is out of the office. Hope he prays all afternoon. He's so *weird*!"

Why did they make it a law that Daniel couldn't pray? (See Daniel 6:6–8) Could it be because he was ten times smarter, wiser, more innovative, and more creative than any of them? Since he was getting promoted over each of them until he was head of all the leaders, maybe they were a little jealous.

These leaders were baffled and probably consulted each other, saying, "We just don't get it! We were trained by the most knowledgeable, most gifted, and wisest teachers, scientists, and leaders in the entire world. He's from this insignificant little country, so where is he getting these ideas? How is he so much better than us? It must be the praying that he does three times a day. Let's make a law against his praying so he doesn't continue to outshine us." (Of course, this did serve their purpose of getting him arrested as well.)

Daniel was a bright light due to the fact that he was an astonishing individual. His exceptional qualities caused him to shine intensely in the eyes of his contemporaries. They didn't like it because they were envious. However, I can only imagine that many others, including the king, saw evidence of the living God in Daniel's abilities, and it was attractive to them and caused them to honor Daniel's God.

It wasn't Daniel's knowledge of Scripture or that he was nice and prayed three times a day that caused others to take notice. It was the fact that he both was much better in his field of work and possessed godly character. His personal foundation, structure, and finishing materials were all outstanding.

The Evidence in My Life

I've personally witnessed the power of God's grace on my life. One of my worst subjects in high school was English and creative writing. I struggled anytime I was assigned a three-page paper. It would take many hours for me to write, but not before going through half a notebook pad. I'd rip up and throw away page after page of awful writing. I scored 370 out of 800 points on the English portion of the SAT. To give you an idea of how bad that is, in all my travels I've only met one person who scored lower!

When God showed me in prayer in 1991 that He wanted me to write a book, I thought He had me mixed up with someone else. Kind of like Sarah in the Old Testament, I had a good laugh. How could I write a chapter, let alone a book? What I didn't originally factor in was the immeasurable, unlimited, and surpassing greatness of the grace of God in me.

Within ten months of receiving my "write a book" directive from God, two women from different states approached me two weeks apart and spoke these words: "John, God wants you to write. In fact, if you don't, He'll give the messages to someone else." After this I wrote a contract with God and acknowledged my complete dependence upon His grace. I'll tell the rest of this story in the next chapter, but I'll just report here that now there are nineteen books written, and millions of copies have been distributed worldwide in over ninety languages.

Grace enabled not just my writing but also my speaking. The first time Lisa heard me speak publicly after we married, she fell asleep in the front row. I was that bad. One of her best friends sat beside her and fell into such a deep sleep that I saw saliva drool down her face from her wide-open mouth. That was encouraging! Now people don't go to sleep when I speak publicly. Before I did it in my strength; now I've learned to believe for, depend on, and yield to His grace.

I was a failure in these two areas in my own ability. However, it is through them both that God has given me the privilege of ministering to millions of people.

A Truly Good Life

Let's summarize our parameters for living the good life. If you can believe, nothing is impossible for you. For He is able to do through you exceedingly, abundantly above all you can ask or think. The available inward power by which He will accomplish your life's work is immeasurable, unlimited, and surpasses all others. Your life should not be like what Lisa and I experienced in that showroom while picking out finishing items for our new home. You have no limitations because who you are and what you do are by the grace of God! So allow the Holy Spirit to expand your vision. Dream big, believe, and move forward with corresponding actions.

There is a factor that is crucial to the fulfillment of what's been spoken of in this chapter. Without an understanding of this trait, chances are good we will be frustrated and even misled in our quest to be effective and multiply. In our next chapter, we'll discuss this attribute called *discernment*.

15

DISCERNMENT

Solid food belongs to those who are of full age,
that is, those who by reason of use have their
senses exercised to discern both good and evil.
—HEBREWS 5:14

Holiness is not the luxury of the few;
it is a simple duty, for you and for me.
—MOTHER TERESA

Those who are of full age are the ones who are mature, not physically but spiritually. Physically we are born as babies and grow into adulthood. In the same way, we are born spiritually as babies and are expected to grow into maturity, to the measure of Christ.

There's a significant difference between the two. Physical maturity is bound to time. Have you heard of a two-year-old being six feet tall? It takes fifteen to twenty years to hit that mark. However, spiritual growth is not bound to time. Have you encountered believers who are only one year old in Christ but are more mature than those who've been saved for twenty years?

According to Hebrews 5:14, an indication of maturity is when our inward senses accurately discern between what's truly good and evil.

It's important to note that your heart has five senses, just like your body does. This fact is evident throughout Scripture. "*Taste* and *see* that the LORD is good" (Psalm 34:8 NLT). Two senses are covered in just that verse.

Jesus once announced to the multitudes, "Anyone with ears to *hear* should listen and understand" (Matthew 11:15 NLT)! Most everyone in attendance could hear physically; He was speaking of their inward ears.

Paul quoted God's statement to Israel: "Don't *touch* their filthy things, and I will welcome you" (2 Corinthians 6:17 NLT). The same apostle also wrote that God "through us diffuses the *fragrance* of His knowledge in every place" (2 Corinthians 2:14).

All five senses are covered in these four verses alone!

Discernment

How do we keep from mixing up good and evil, especially in a day when deception is rampant? How do we not fall into the same trap Eve fell into when she believed evil to be good, pleasant, and wise? The answer is, by *discernment*. So how do we develop it? Through authentic, godly fear.

The prophet Malachi foretold that in the latter times there would be two groups of believers—those who fear God and those who don't. In the midst of hard times, those lacking godly fear complain, compare, and murmur. They dislike that they must serve God yet suffer opposition, affliction, and hardship, while those who are wicked and possess no relationship with God are prospering.

Those who fear God go through the same hardships but do something different. They speak of the goodness of God. They fight through adversity by believing what He says about their difficult circumstances. They are more concerned with God's desires, plans, and kingdom than with their temporary discomfort. They know and are established in His faithfulness. Their attitude is this:

> Though the cherry trees don't blossom and the strawberries don't
> ripen, though the apples are worm-eaten and the wheat fields stunted,
> though the sheep pens are sheepless and the cattle barns empty, I'm
> singing joyful praise to God. I'm turning cartwheels of joy to my

Savior God. Counting on God's Rule to prevail, I take heart and gain strength. I run like a deer. I feel like I'm king of the mountain! (Habakkuk 3:17–19 The Message)

God stated through the prophet Malachi that He will make them His special treasures. (Recall how Paul referred to "special vessels" in 2 Timothy 2:21 CEV.) Malachi predicted that one of the delightful benefits to those who fear God would be, "You shall again *discern* between the righteous and the wicked" (Malachi 3:18). In other words, these believers won't confuse what isn't good for *good*.

In the previous chapter we identified the parameters of God's goodness: abundance beyond what we can even ask or think. To one person, abundance may be his downfall, yet to another it's great opportunity. If abundance is your goal, you will surely fall into the same trap as Eve, Cain, Balaam, Korah, Saul, Gehazi, Judas, Alexander, the Laodicean church, and countless others. However, if pleasing God is your primary objective, you'll have the ability to discern what is good and evil—the capacity to properly handle your abundance.

The key is found in discernment, and the degree of our ability to discern is proportional to our fear of God. Allow me to reiterate: the more we fear God, the more we are able to wisely discern. In the beginning of his reign, Solomon cried out, "Give to Your servant an understanding heart…that I may *discern* between good and evil" (1 Kings 3:9).

The wisdom by which Solomon ruled was astonishing. In his years when he was following the Lord, he wrote, "If you cry out for *discernment*… if you seek her as silver, and search for her as for hidden treasures; then you will understand the fear of the Lord" (Proverbs 2:3–5).

However, once Solomon lost his fear of God, he was confused and couldn't tell the difference between good and evil. To him everything had become "vanity" and "grasping for the wind." The entire book of Ecclesiastes is a picture of a bewildered and perplexed man who's lost his fear of God and, consequently, his discernment. He was in a sad state of mind. Through the years, my heart's been broken for the many leaders and believers I've witnessed similarly losing the fear of Lord and succumbing to deception due to a loss of discernment.

As stated earlier, godly fear motivates us to cooperate with God's grace to cleanse ourselves from impurity. Interestingly, our discernment hinges on living a godly life. So yet again, we see holiness as the structure supporting our life decisions, whether they involve our career, relationships, finances, social opportunities, or any other aspect of life.

Our passion first and foremost should be to fear God. If this is our top priority, then abundance will not deceive us. We are told, "He who trusts in his riches will fall" (Proverbs 11:28). Yet in the same book we read, "I am understanding... Riches and honor are with me" (Proverbs 8:14, 16). And again, "By humility and the fear of the Lord are riches" (Proverbs 22:4). True riches are the resources that enable you to fulfill what God has placed you on this earth to do, and this always entails impacting others, which is building the kingdom.

A question you should honestly ask yourself each morning is, am I motivated today by the fear of the Lord or by obtaining abundance? If your target is godly fear, it will protect you from the deception of engaging in evil to obtain what is good.

Allow me to clarify: resources, riches, wealth, and abundance are *good*. But if those are your target, you'll lack the discernment to recognize if the means to acquire them are *evil*. A biblical story will help explain how this works.

Is This the Time to Receive?

In Israel it was customary to bring an offering or gift to a prophet. As a young man, the future King Saul and his servant were searching for his father's lost donkeys. After an exasperating hunt, the servant recommended they travel to a nearby city to see if a prophet named Samuel who lived there could help them locate the donkeys. Saul's immediate response was, "If we go, what do we have to give him? There's no more bread in our sacks. We've nothing to bring as a gift to the holy man. Do we have anything else?" (1 Samuel 9:7 The Message) This was the typical attitude when approaching a prophet.

Let's go to a different time period in Israel. A Syrian army officer named Naaman came to the prophet Elisha's house. He was given instructions that, when finally obeyed, brought him complete healing from leprosy. He returned to Elisha to give thanks and a gift. The prophet replied, "As the Lord lives before whom I stand, I will receive nothing" (2 Kings 5:16). Naaman urged him to take the gift, but Elisha again refused.

Elisha's personal assistant, Gehazi, witnessed the entire interaction. He watched in shock as Naaman left without giving the customary gift. Once Elisha left his presence, Gehazi chased after Naaman's party. Naaman saw him and brought his caravan to a halt, asking Gehazi if anything was wrong.

Gehazi assured him all was well but then lied to Naaman, stating that Elisha now had a sudden need. His words were, "Two young prophets from the hill country of Ephraim have just arrived. He would like 75 pounds of silver and two sets of clothing to give to them" (2 Kings 5:22 NLT).

Naaman responded by giving twice as much as was "needed." They parted company, and Gehazi returned and secretly stored the gifts among his own belongings.

Gehazi returned to Elisha and stood before him. Elisha asked where he had been. He lied by insisting he hadn't gone anywhere. Elisha then pronounced:

> "Don't you realize that I was there in spirit when Naaman stepped
> down from his chariot to meet you? Is this the time to receive money
> and clothing, olive groves and vineyards, sheep and cattle, and male and
> female servants? Because you have done this, you and your descendants
> will suffer from Naaman's leprosy forever." (2 Kings 5:26–27 NLT)

Gehazi's lack of godly fear (and hence, of discernment) positioned him to be deceived. He thought it was time to receive when it wasn't time. He believed the gift was deserved, perhaps thinking that he should receive it since his boss had refused. After all, like Elisha, he too had made sacrifices and given his life in God's work. Wasn't God's will for them to prosper? And now here was this wealthy heathen who worshipped foreign gods. Were not the riches of the sinner stored up for the just? He concluded that to not receive rightful payment for the ministry was unwise on Elisha's part.

Gehazi's rationalization justified the means he used to obtain what he thought was justly due. He lacked discernment, identifying evil as good. And he paid a terrible price for his disobedience.

The End Justifies the Means

There are so many stories I could share to illustrate how pursuing earthly riches over fearing the Lord has tripped up leaders and believers. I've witnessed many paying dearly in the long run. Up front the opportunity for gain looked inviting, sensible, and good. In the early stages, it appeared their efforts were blessed and success was just around the corner. Then things changed for the worse, and the long-term consequences were costly. I've witnessed marriages broken, ministries lost, businesses failed, financial ruin, health complications, relationships destroyed—all accompanied by the loss of personal integrity and the trust of loved ones.

Businessmen and women have shared numerous unpleasant experiences in dealing with other Christians in the marketplace. They've experienced selfishness, lying, stealing, envy, fraud, and embezzlement. Why does this happen? The simple explanation: the end that appears *good* justifies the compromising means to get there. The thought is, *It's God's will for me to succeed, have resources, and enjoy influence.* But they don't use God's Word as a filter in scrutinizing the journey. Often the compromise appears to be the only path to take. *Our ship will sail if we don't act. We're going to miss out on a great opportunity or blessing.* It takes mature character to wait for God's provision.

Satan presented Jesus with a compromise early in His ministry. He tempted Jesus by offering Him a painless shortcut to recovering the kingdoms of this world—what Jesus had come to accomplish—if He'd just worship him. To Jesus's human side, this probably sounded like an attractive offer. If He accepted Satan's proposal, He would be able to propel His ministry quickly and avoid a tremendous amount of hardship and suffering. All He had to do was worship Satan.

How often does Satan offer to fulfill what God has placed in our hearts, but to get it, we must compromise integrity, character, and obedience? Worship isn't defined by a slow song with edifying lyrics. Worship is expressed by whom we obey. We might sing slow songs in church while our lifestyle—which speaks so much louder than our songs—is actually worshiping darkness.

Earlier I shared that most authors showcase the primary meaning of an unfamiliar word in its first appearance in a book. If you look at the first time the word *worship* appears in the Bible, you'll get a true understanding of its meaning. It was used initially when God told Abraham to offer up the most important person or thing in his life and He didn't give a reason why.

After Abraham journeyed for three days with his son, Isaac, to the foot of Mount Moriah, he said to his servants, "Stay here with the donkey; the lad and I will go yonder and worship" (Genesis 22:5). He was not going up the mountain to sing a slow, melodic song to God. Abraham was going up, in obedience to God, to put his most prized "possession" to death. His worship was defined by his obedience.

Could this be why God once said to His people, "Away with your noisy hymns of praise! I will not listen to the music of your harps. Instead, I want to see a mighty flood of justice, an *endless river of righteous living*"? (Amos 5:23–24 NLT) I love the term "endless river of righteous living." That's what I call *unswerving obedience*.

The lifestyles of the people in Amos's day were not consistent with God's Word, but they were still writing, gathering, and singing new songs of worship. *True worship is revealed by who we obey, not who we sing to.*

Choosing Good Over God

Allow me to share how I once fell into an enticing trap that compromised my obedience. Our ministry was in its infant stage, less than two years old. It consisted solely of my traveling to small churches with an attendance of one hundred people or less. Often our means of transportation was our Honda Civic, with two babies in the back seat. We had just enough room for luggage and two boxes of cassette tapes to make available at our meetings.

As I mentioned earlier, God spoke to my heart one morning to write. I delayed obeying for two reasons. First, as I said earlier, creative writing was one of my worst subjects in high school; and second, who would want to publish a book by an unknown author? Finally, though, I obeyed and began to write.

The book took a year to complete, with many hours of hard work. I then approached two publishing houses and submitted to them the manuscript, which was entitled *Victory in the Wilderness*. One said it was "too preachy." The other didn't respond at all. I was discouraged. Lisa and I settled on our only option: self-publishing. We raised the money to print a few thousand copies and sold them in the small churches we visited. The people who read the book loved it, so I wrote a second book the following year. Again, we had no option other than to self-publish.

A few months after the second book was printed, an acquisitions editor at a national publisher called our office. After introducing himself, he eagerly shared the reason for his call. "John, someone put in our hands your book *Victory in the Wilderness*. Our publishing house believes in its message, and we want to help you get it out to the multitudes." We spoke for several minutes. He described the various ways they would sell the book and boasted about their marketing and publicity team. It seemed too good to be true; finally the book would be available nationwide.

However, after hanging up from the call with the editor, I felt uneasy. The conversation didn't sit right in my spirit. I prayed the next morning and strongly sensed that God was saying, "Don't accept their offer."

I spoke to Lisa about it. After discussing it, she agreed with me that even though the offer seemed good, she also had a hesitation.

Later that day, Lisa said, "Honey, I don't have a good feeling about this when I pray." At this point I was convinced I should not accept.

The following day the acquisitions editor called again. Even though I now knew God's will on the matter, I still wanted to hear what the editor had to say. Though I didn't recognize it at the time, my desire to prolong this discussion was an indication of a problem. Why wasn't simple obedience enough for me? Why did I listen to more of his reasons to publish with them? Could it be that it was feeding a wrong desire in my heart? Was my ego being stroked?

The editor passionately shared his company's excitement to get my message out. He insisted my message was needed and it was a word from God for our nation. Their company worked with all the top distributors and could most likely get our book in every Christian bookstore, and many secular bookstores, nationwide. He cited stories of other unknown authors who'd published with them and how their messages had now spread across America. They had become popular conference speakers. He claimed it was all due to his company's influence.

This man continued to call me every other day for the next few weeks because I didn't say no. The longer I listened, the more it seemed to make sense to publish with them. It came to the point where there was no longer any caution in my heart. The inward witness of the Holy Spirit had been silenced. I had allowed flattery and human reasoning to quiet God's directive on the matter. Simply put, my discernment was silenced.

Exodus 23:8 states, "A bribe blinds the discerning." Flattery is a form of bribery, and it blinded me. I was choosing opportunity and abundance over the fear of the Lord.

Even though my wife strongly warned against it, we signed the contract, and immediately all kinds of trouble broke out.

At the time Lisa and I had been married eleven years. Periodically she would make comments to me like, "You seem to never get sick!" It was true;

I rarely caught any bug, and if I did it was over within twenty-four hours. But from the day we signed that contract, I fought sickness and couldn't shake it.

It began with the flu, when I threw up for only the second time in my adult life. Once the flu was over I caught a virus. Lisa and I had gone out of town to celebrate our anniversary, and I fought a high temperature the entire time. The fever continued into the next week. I was speaking at a church, and right after each service I had to rush back to my hotel room, where I shivered under the covers.

The fever went into the third week, and we couldn't believe it. I had never fought sickness like this. A strong antibiotic finally wiped it out, but a week after finishing the medicine, I caught a severe cold. I was miserable, with a sore throat, stuffed-up head, and all the other annoying symptoms. The sickness dragged on and on.

Less than two weeks after recovering from the cold, I injured my knee. The injury was so severe I wore a brace and hobbled on crutches for several weeks. As if this wasn't enough, right after this I got hit with another virus. This cycle of sickness and injury lasted over three months. Lisa remained totally healthy the entire time.

While all this was going on, we were having huge struggles with the publisher. It seemed we couldn't agree on anything. The relationship was under severe duress, and there was absolutely no flow in the project.

If all this wasn't enough, we encountered all kinds of other problems that seemed impossible to resolve. Life was extremely difficult in those three months. Could this be why David wrote, "Before I was afflicted I went astray, but now I keep Your word"? (Psalm 119:67)

God was quite merciful in this situation, and He allowed me to see my folly. I'd put ministry success before obedience to Him. I admitted my error to God and my wife. I was forgiven and cleansed. His mercy is so amazing!

However, I was still trapped. We needed a miracle to get out of the contract with this publisher. Lisa and I joined hands and pleaded for God's intervention.

Within a couple weeks, the publisher wrote and said they were canceling the contract. I was relieved, but it came with a price: the ordeal had cost us over $4,000. That was an enormous sum of money for a young ministry—in fact, it equaled just about half of one month's budget.

The God Opportunity

A few months later a friend named Scott asked me to lunch. "John, I want you to meet a friend of mine." I agreed.

At the restaurant Scott introduced me to his friend, who was also named John. It turned out he was the leader of a well-known publishing house. After the normal conversation of getting to know each other, in the midst of lunch, John asked what I was currently speaking on. I don't think I ate another bite after his question.

I began to share with him on the subject of offense. I spoke to Scott and John with great passion for approximately fifteen minutes.

At one point John interrupted me by stating, "I just want you to know we can't publish this message because we only publish roughly twenty-four books a year. These titles are with well-known authors or pastors."

"I'm not asking you to publish this message," I replied. "I'm just answering your question about what I've been speaking on lately."

"Of course," he said. "Please continue."

I continued to share for another five or ten minutes about the trap of being offended.

After I finished, John asked, "Can you get me a manuscript?"

Taken aback, I countered, "I thought you said you couldn't publish this?"

"This message must get out, and I want to submit it to our owner."

The publishing company accepted this message, and the book was titled *The Bait of Satan*. In time it became an international best seller. At the time of this writing, it has sold well over a million copies and has been translated in over sixty languages.

I will never forget the day the second publisher called me and said they definitely wanted the manuscript and would get me a contract right away. I hung up, went to prayer, and heard God clearly say to my heart, "The other publishing house was your idea. This publishing house is My idea."

This experience clearly illustrated to me the difference between good and God. As it so often happens, the opportunity for good came first. Then God's opportunity came later. The same happened with Abram and Sarai: Ishmael came first, Isaac came later.

The Proof of Godly Fear

What positioned me to make a bad decision with the first publisher? The honest answer is that my focus was on abundance—getting the message to the masses—rather than on the fear of the Lord. This opened the door for logic and apparent success to override and silence what God was making clear to my heart.

Obedience is the outward evidence of the true fear of the Lord. When we fear God, we will…

- Obey Him instantly
- Obey Him even if it doesn't make sense
- Obey Him even if it hurts
- Obey Him even if we don't see the benefit
- Obey Him to completion

An examination of Abraham's actions reveals that he fulfilled each of these criteria. Let's relive his great test.

One night God instructs him to sacrifice his son, Isaac. Is he hearing correctly? Is this a bad dream? *No way,* he thinks. *How can this be! I love my son. I can't put Isaac to death. Kings and nations are promised to come through him. How can this promise be fulfilled if I kill him?*

Abraham cries out, "What! How can You tell me to do this? You promised me that nations would come through him!" There is no divine response, only silence.

Abraham runs the gamut of emotions. I'm sure it wasn't a great night of sleep. How many of us would take a few weeks, months, or even years to ponder the command, and eventually convince ourselves it wasn't reasonable?

But Abraham is different. We read, "Early the next morning Abraham got up and saddled his donkey" (Genesis 22:3 NIV). He obeys *instantly*.

Have you ever been around someone who lightheartedly comments, "God's been dealing with me about this for several months," and laughs it off? It's tragic when you think about it, for they are bragging about their lack of godly fear.

God instructs Abraham to sacrifice the greatest promise of his life— what he had waited on for twenty-five years—and doesn't give an explanation for the request. It *doesn't make sense* for Abraham to give Isaac up, yet he still obeys.

The thought of sacrificing his young son *hurts* deeply. The inward pain continues to nag Abraham through the three days of travel. It was a little easier up front, after hearing the voice of God, but with each passing day of divine silence the pain intensifies. The struggle hits its highpoint as Abraham and his beloved son build the altar. Yet Abraham still obeys.

The Almighty doesn't tell Abraham that if he obeys, another sacrifice will be provided in place of his son. Unlike you and I, Abraham doesn't have the book of Genesis to read, so he doesn't know the outcome. He sees *no benefit* in this command, yet he still obeys.

How different it is today. So many need to see the benefit in obeying God before they actually obey. As teachers, so often we gear our messages to show the personal benefit in obeying God. As authors, if we don't include a personal advantage to the reader in the title or subtitle, the book won't sell.

Finally, Abraham goes the distance: climbs the mountain, builds the altar, ties Isaac up, and is ready to thrust the knife into his beloved son's heart. He obeys to *completion*.

While the knife looms over Isaac, an angel suddenly appears and cries out, "Do not lay your hand on the lad, or do anything to him; for *now I know that you fear God*" (Genesis 22:12).

How does the angel know Abraham fears God? Because he obeyed instantly, when it didn't make sense, when it was painful, and with no promised benefit, and he went the distance. He is a man of great wealth, with his most valued possession being his son. But wealth isn't the focus for Abraham. His priority is obedience to God.

Godly fear equips us to handle abundance, resources, and wealth in a healthy manner. This is what Scripture means when it states, "The blessing of the Lord makes one rich, and He adds no sorrow with it" (Proverbs 10:22).

A Foolish Approach

If we compare Jesus's disciple Judas to Abraham, we see a huge difference. Judas conveniently ignored truth if it benefitted his cause. He embezzled funds from the ministry's treasury, was deceptive, betrayed his Leader, didn't care for the poor, and was a hypocrite (see Matthew 26:25, 49 and John 12:6; 13:2). His judgment was clouded. Because he lacked godly fear, he couldn't discern between right and wrong, good and evil.

On a particular day a wealthy woman poured an entire bottle of expensive perfume on Jesus. Judas was indignant and outspoken about her "foolish" behavior. "That perfume was worth a year's wages. It should have been sold and the money given to the poor," he said (John 12:5 NLT). His comment was logical and persuasive, and it influenced the other disciples. They too chimed in, condemning her actions.

Jesus corrected Judas's influence by stating, "Leave her alone. Why criticize her for doing such a *good* thing to me? ...This woman's deed will be remembered and discussed" (Mark 14:6, 9 NLT). Jesus identified her action as *good* and *lasting*; Judas judged her behavior as *bad* and *fleeting*. His discernment was warped. He was out of sync with God's heart.

Look at the very next verse:

Then Judas Iscariot, one of the twelve disciples, went to the leading
priests to arrange to betray Jesus to them. (Mark 14:10 NLT)

This was the straw that broke the camel's back. Judas had had it; he
was fed up with Jesus's leadership strategy. He had followed the Man from
Galilee, expecting Him to reestablish the throne of David. According to
the prophet Isaiah, ruling forever is what the Messiah is supposed to do.
After three years, what was Jesus waiting for? If Jesus would just set up the
kingdom, then Judas—as one of His chief leaders and His treasurer—could
come into a place of honor, possessing wealth and authority.

Judas thought, *I'll speed up the process. I'm not waiting any longer. I want
my place of power, influence, and riches. I've had enough of being a target of ridi-
cule and persecution by the leaders. I don't want to be viewed as the companion of
a lunatic any longer. If I turn Him over to the leaders, He'll finally show off His
power and set up His kingdom, and I'll have my place of prominence.*

You may question my interpretation of Judas's motives; however, I think
it's sound. Judas consistently saw the power of Jesus in healing the sick, calm-
ing the storm, raising the dead, cursing the fig tree, opening up blind eyes
and deaf ears, and numerous other miracles. Judas heard Jesus frequently
speak of the kingdom. He heard Peter and others confess—even hail—Jesus
as the Messiah. Jesus's greatness was before him daily.

However, once Jesus was condemned to die, Judas realized he was wrong
in his thinking, regretted his actions, and hung himself. His plan of action
hadn't accomplished what he lusted for.

These two men, Abraham and Judas, clearly illustrate the difference between one who fears God and one who doesn't. One had discernment; the
other was living in deception. Their individual choices only mirrored what
was in their hearts. The outcomes of these men were vastly different. They
are both remembered, but for different reasons.

We will all be remembered; there's no doubt of that, for we are eternal
beings. The question we should ask ourselves is, how do we want to be remembered? Your fear of God will determine the answer.

That's the Whole Story

We need a pure heart so our judgment will be sound, not clouded. Then, when it comes to determining whether an endeavor is inspired or simply carries the appearance of fleeting good, we won't be misled. We'll make wise choices in regard to our spouses, people we associate with, our closest friends, careers, opportunities, investments, the way we raise our children, the churches we serve in, the educations we embrace, and the endless other decisions we face in our lives.

When Solomon came to the end of his life, after experiencing great glory and even greater folly, he cried out, "That's the whole story. Here now is my final conclusion: Fear God and obey his commands, for this is everyone's duty. God will judge us for everything we do, including every secret thing, whether good or bad" (Ecclesiastes 12:13–14 NLT).

Solomon had become a madman, had lost his discernment, and could no longer distinguish what was truly good and what wasn't. God gives us a glimpse into his madness through the book of Ecclesiastes. But the great news is that we get a peek into Solomon's coming back to sound judgment. He realized there was nothing more important in life than maintaining godly fear. In his words, "That's the whole story."

So, my friend, if you desire to see things the way God sees them, to perceive and know wisdom in its highest order, then choose the fear of the Lord. You'll never regret your decision.

16

THE BIG PICTURE

"As You sent Me into the world, I also
have sent them into the world."
—John 17:18

The destined end of man is not happiness,
nor health, but holiness.
—Oswald Chambers

L et's step back and look at the overall picture.

God loves you deeply and dearly. He only wants the best for you. Everything from God is good, but not everything good is from God. Hence, there is a *good* that can displace us from receiving what's *best*. We all desire the best, but the pathway that leads to it is not always obvious; it takes discernment to identify it.

In our journey on earth, there is someone besides God we must deal with—our adversary, Satan. He desires to hurt us, with the primary intention of breaking the heart of the One who loves us. Scripture states that our enemy "disguises himself as an angel of light." Then we read, "His servants also disguise themselves as servants of righteousness" (2 Corinthians 11:14–15 NLT).

Finally, there are numerous choices and ways that seem good, but their final outcome is sorrow, misery, loss, and death (see Proverbs 14:12). Think of it: our enemy, his servants, and his ways—all of which ultimately seek our demise—are all disguised as *good*. Scripture doesn't say they *can be* disguised, but rather that they *are* disguised. So do not miss this: usually, what is most dangerous to you will not appear as blatant evil. Rather, it will mask itself as good.

In the early years of Christianity, our adversary set out to destroy the church. Believers were persecuted, tortured, and put to death. But the more our enemy attempted to destroy God's people, the stronger the church became. Because Satan is not stupid, but is in fact quite clever, he concluded that the way to destroy God's people would be to offer them a good life outside of God's wisdom. This was essentially the same strategy he had employed in the Garden of Eden.

Now, after many centuries of subtle tactical maneuvers, perhaps we better understand Satan's effectiveness, for we find ourselves in a place where we've embraced *variations* of truth—ones that seem good and convenient—in place of *actual* truth. We shout out the goodness of Jesus and His role as Savior (which are categorically true) but belittle the value, power, and extent of His lordship and its impact in our lives. We've embraced the sovereignty of God and our positional right standing with Him but have overlooked our responsibility to believe and obey His commands in our pursuit of holiness. Due to the "good" doctrines we've created, the purity of our conduct and lifestyle has become nearly irrelevant.

In their Christian walk, many believers have bought into maintaining rather than multiplying—just barely getting by instead of experiencing abundance. In essence, we've formulated a theology based on our own reasoning and backed by isolated portions of Scripture, instead of embracing the full counsel of God's Word as the final authority on what heaven intends for us.

This trend can and must be broken. It's time for us once again to dig into Scripture and honestly ask the Holy Spirit for His guidance in order to know truth. We must no longer read into Scripture what we already believe but instead come honestly with an open mind and heart and believe what we read, asking God's Spirit to reveal and remove preconceived assumptions.

Church leader. I urge you to teach the whole counsel of God. Make sure your chief motive is feeding the sheep truth and genuinely reaching the lost with the full biblical message of salvation rather than building a big following. If your primary goal is to get those who attend to come back to next week's service, ask the Holy Spirit to forgive you and refocus your principal strategy on shepherding the flock of God with truth. Stay relevant, fresh, and innovative in *method* but timeless in *message*.

Believer. Wherever your influence lies—whether in the classroom, the lab, the office, the field, the home, or the marketplace—with a love-filled heart, live and speak the truth in all your dealings with others. Let them be in awe and declare that in seeing you they see Jesus. Let them experience His presence upon your life. If you pursue true holiness, you will exude His majesty.

If we don't live according to Christ's commandments, we miss out on His presence and He isn't made known to the world through His church. To put it frankly, we suffer. And even more than we do, those in our communities suffer. First, the revelation of Jesus is withheld, so the lost are denied contact with the presence of the only One who can fulfill them. Second, our fellow believers are exposed to a contagious disease called compromise, which has the potential to lead them away from God's heart and presence.

Jesus said it like this: "For their sakes I sanctify Myself" (John 17:19). It was for the sake of those in His community that He set Himself apart to obey the Father. His primary motive for doing so is revealed in the rest of His statement: "…that they also may be sanctified by truth."

Until His return, you and I are the only Jesus the world will ever behold. Let's show them the true Jesus, not a fictitious, powerless Jesus. Let's not settle for anything less than the best. Let's embrace the truth and see truly good fruit result from our unswerving, loving obedience.

———

Live long, pursue holiness, and succeed in your endeavors. In so doing you'll make a difference in the lives of others.

> Now to Him who is *able* to keep you from stumbling,
> And to present you faultless
> Before the presence of His glory with exceeding joy,
> To God our Savior,
> Who alone is wise,
> Be glory and majesty,
> Dominion and power,
> Both now and forever.
> Amen. (Jude 24–25)

Dear friend,

Good or God? is more than just a book. It's a message that can inspire people to join the movement of holiness. You now know how abundant life can be under the lordship of Jesus and living by His grace. I want to equip you to carry this revelation into your world of influence.

You can engage with this movement by connecting your friends, family, and community with what you've learned. It took one man, Paul, teaching a handful of people in a small school to eventually reach all who dwelled in Asia in just two years! They became carriers of the presence of God. (See Acts 19:1–10) What might God do through us if we unite in shared passion for Him?

Opportunities to share this message exist within your daily life. You can use it for:

- A small group study
- A church-wide study
- An office book club
- A school of ministry class
- And more!

Whether you use one of these ideas or one of your own, my team is committed to supporting you. We'll create a custom solution for you with discounted resources, free materials, and more. In addition to this book, we've created a six-session *Good or God?* curriculum with audio and video sessions—all to equip you to get this message into the hearts and lives of the people around you. Please contact us, and we'll work with you to determine the resources and approach that best fit your needs.

Thank you for partnering with us to share God's Word with people everywhere!

Sincerely,

John Bevere

For support and resources, call 1-800-648-1477
or write to GoodOrGod@MessengerInternational.org.

DEVOTIONS
AND
DISCUSSION
QUESTIONS

WEEK 1

Read chapters 1–3

This week corresponds with video session 1

DISCUSSION QUESTIONS

1. Eve decided to eat fruit from the forbidden tree because it seemed *good*, *pleasant*, and *desirable*. Explain these attributes. What does it mean for something to seem good? To seem pleasant? To seem desirable? In what distinct ways can each of these three things draw us away from obedience to God?

2. The entire Eden story hinges on the one thing God's authority had forbidden. What does this tell us about trust and human nature? How can we counteract the tendency to pursue what God calls off limits?

3. Books, podcasts, blogs, and other tools that teach us about God are valuable resources. But does understanding the distinction between revealed and communicated knowledge change your perspective on them in any way? If so, how?

4. From the story of the rich young ruler, we learn there is a difference between knowing that God is *associated* with good and acknowledging Him as the *source* of good. How can we be sure God is the source of our concept of goodness?

5. What do you believe about the accuracy and authority of the Bible? Read 2 Timothy 3:16 again. Are there any gaps between what this verse teaches and what you believe? Discuss them in light of what you learned this week.

DEVOTION

The LORD is good to everyone.
—PSALM 145:9 NLT

The story of Satan's scheme to deceive Eve in Eden is sobering. When Eve was tricked into believing God had withheld something good from her, she wasn't getting over a disappointment. She wasn't grieving a loss or recovering from mistreatment. She was living in a perfect environment where she enjoyed complete provision and daily communion with God.

Accepting God as the source of what is good starts with possessing an unwavering conviction that God Himself is good. This was challenging enough in Eden. Today, we face many more factors that can challenge our faith in God's goodness.

Unlike Eve, you have surely faced disappointment, loss, mistreatment, confusion, lack, or pain. The influence of these things may go undetected as long as there is no conflict between what we want and what God directs us to do. But when temptation comes, any unaddressed causes for doubt begin to whisper in our minds. We wonder if God is holding something back from us, and we start to suspect that there isn't any benefit to doing things His way. But remember Proverbs 14:12: "There is a way that seems right to a man, but its end is the way of death." Nothing outside of God's will for us will lead to lasting life, joy, fulfillment, or blessing—no matter how good it may appear.

Over the next week, I encourage you to honestly assess your faith in God's goodness. Ask the Holy Spirit if you are holding onto any memory or mindset that might cause you to distrust or disobey God. Then, find and declare scriptures that reveal God's truth for your specific situation. Humbly invite God's Spirit to renew your mind by His Word. His truth will bring you into freedom!

Reflect

Give thanks to the LORD, for he is good! His faithful love endures forever. (Psalm 107:1 NLT)

Apply

When Joshua and the people of Israel entered the Promised Land, they had to cross the Jordan River. It was harvest season, and the swollen river was overflowing its banks. But God intervened and cut off the flow of the water so all of Israel could cross on dry land. Afterward, God told Joshua to have the people build a memorial of stones nearby so they would always remember what He had done for them.

It is often easier to remember things that go wrong than to recall the good things God has done. So this week, start making memorials to God's goodness in your life. Buy a journal, start a note on your phone, make voice memos, or find another way to capture moments (big or small) when you see God's faithfulness. These memories will become testimonies that encourage your heart and stir your faith when difficulty or doubt attempt to dismantle your conviction that God is good.

WEEK 2

Read chapters 4–5

This week corresponds with video session 2

DISCUSSION QUESTIONS

1. Discuss the distinction between Jesus's position as Lord and His work as Savior. How does this compare with what you've heard or believed? Does anything in your thinking or behavior need to change to align with the Bible's teaching about lordship?

2. If we were all to move to a new country today, our entrance into that new land would require an agreement to abide by its laws and standards. Is this the way you've viewed your relationship with God? Why or why not?

3. Imagine that you're talking to someone who wants to become a Christian. Based on what we learned this week, what would you say to them?

4. Read Mark 8:34–35. As we've discovered, desiring to deny yourself isn't the same as actually denying yourself. Explain what might cause a person to settle at the level of desire instead of acting on Jesus's words.

5. Let's revisit Matthew 7:21. Jesus identifies four good traits that even some people who don't truly follow Him will possess: belief in His teachings, emotional investment, engagement in sharing the gospel, and participation in ministry. We know God doesn't call us to operate out of condemnation or fear. So what do you think is the proper response to this revelation?

DEVOTION

> But we are citizens of heaven,
> where the Lord Jesus Christ lives.
> —Philippians 3:20 NLT

From the New Testament perspective, the declaration "Jesus is Lord" is essentially a summary of Christianity 101. According to Romans 10:9, recognizing Jesus's lordship is where the Christian life starts. But for many of us, "Jesus is Lord" doesn't hold much meaning. It might be a phrase that we say, sing, or pray; but we tend to be disconnected from the fact that calling Jesus *Lord* means recognizing Him as the utmost authority in our lives.

Before we entered the life of faith, we were citizens of the world. We had no reason to know or seek God's will for us. But we aren't citizens of the world any longer. We're citizens of God's kingdom—the kingdom of heaven. Everything about our lives should meet the standards of this kingdom and reflect the nature of its sovereign: the Lord Jesus Christ.

What is His nature? To find out, study the story of Jesus in Gethsemane, found in Mark 14:32–42. This story takes place right before Jesus is betrayed and handed over to the Romans to be crucified. Pay special attention to the end of verse 36, where Jesus tells His Father, "Yet I want your will to be done, not mine" (NLT).

Going to a cross is a significant act of submission, but the truth is that there are no small issues of obedience. When we honor Jesus as Lord, we submit to His will even when compromise seems minor and when obedience is inconvenient or unpopular. We say, "I want Your will," in everything.

Have you accepted Jesus on these terms? Or is there still something in your life—maybe a habitual sin or a selfish ambition—that you regularly prioritize over what God directs you to do? You don't need to feel condemned or ashamed. But now is the time to seek a new way of living. Go to God in prayer and ask the Holy Spirit to help you truly honor Jesus as your Lord. As you spend time in His presence and His Word, He will teach you how to live like a citizen of heaven.

Reflect

Throw yourselves wholeheartedly and full-time...into God's way of doing things. (Romans 6:13 The Message)

Apply

Later in this study, we'll discuss the way God empowers us to live in obedience without falling into legalism or shame. But this week, I encourage you to allow yourself to really ask, *Have I submitted myself fully to the lordship of Jesus?*

All of us have areas of oversight. So here's what I suggest you do: Find someone you love and trust—a spouse, close friend, or leader who believes in you and wants the best for you. Share what you learned this week about the principle of lordship, and ask your friend for their perspective. Do they see any unaddressed areas of compromise in your life?

If they have something to share, listen with open ears and an open heart. Then take the feedback to God in prayer. Ask Him to reveal the truth in what was spoken. Humility is a powerful weapon against deception; this simple exercise may lead to extraordinary transformation!

WEEK 3

Read chapters 6–7

This week corresponds with video session 3

DISCUSSION QUESTIONS

1. Any good goal becomes dangerous when it displaces our desire to know and honor God. Discuss the following goals. In what ways are they good? By contrast, how might they lead us off course if we make them our primary aim?
   - Financial security
   - Popularity
   - Influence
   - Generosity
   - Humanitarian achievement
   - Effective ministry

2. Imagine that you were with Moses when God offered to send Israel into the Promised Land without His presence. In that moment, what would you think about to help you make the decision Moses made?

3. What are some signs that a person's relationship with God has become more about what He can give them than about who He is? If your relationship with God started to show these signs, how could you correct your course?

4. Share your perspective on what it means to be effective in reaching the world without becoming a friend of the world.

5. Legalism is nothing more than another form of worldliness. So how do you think we can guard our friendship with God without falling into a religious mindset?

DEVOTION

> ...In your presence there is
> fullness of joy...
> —PSALM 16:11 ESV

One of the greatest tests of faith is something that seems pretty tame: the shortcut.

Moses faced a shortcut during his time in the desert. He'd traveled from Egypt to Mount Sinai with a complaining and rebellious people, and the prospect of entering the Promised Land must have been attractive. But would Moses say yes to the promise at the expense of God's presence?

Thousands of years later, Jesus also encountered a shortcut in a desert. When Jesus was about to start His public ministry, Satan gave Him an opportunity to bypass the hardship ahead and skip straight to claiming authority over the nations. All Jesus had to do was worship him. Would Jesus compromise to get with ease what God would deliver through suffering?

The fact that Satan tried this tactic on the Son of God says a lot about how effective he knows it can be. We'll look at this story again later in our study; the important point now is Jesus wasn't the only one who successfully withstood Satan's ploy. Moses weighed the options of staying in the desert with God or entering the land without Him, and he chose the desert. Why? He knew what he'd be missing.

I want you to be able to answer a wholehearted *yes* to the question, "Is God's presence your ultimate goal?" But for your response to be more than an intellectual exercise, you must first be able to answer another question: do you know what it means to be in God's presence?

My friend, I want you to fall in love with the presence of God like Moses did. I want you to possess such longing for intimacy with Him that no shortcut seems worth taking. That kind of passion only comes from experiencing the presence of God firsthand.

James tells us, "Draw near to God, and he will draw near to you" (verse 4:8 ESV). Drawing near means we make time to pray, worship, and read God's Word, not as tasks to be completed but as a way of pursuing relationship with a Person. Seeking God now will position you to make the right choice at any crossroads still to come.

Reflect

If you look for me wholeheartedly, you will find me. (Jeremiah 29:13 NLT)

Apply

In every relationship, the two parties have something to offer each other—things like encouragement, advice, and practical support. But healthy relationships are not about what we get from people; they're about the people. Sometimes we forget this in our relationships with God. Because God is the source of everything we need, we can get so focused on asking Him for things that we forget to actually get to know Him.

God wants us to bring Him our requests! But if you're serious about making His presence your ultimate goal, try focusing your time with God this week on Him. Meditate on His character. Learn about what brings Him joy. Select a story from Scripture and reflect on what it reveals about who He is. I pray that during this time, you'll discover things that make you fall more deeply in love with your Creator.

WEEK 4

Read chapters 8–9

This week corresponds with video session 4

DISCUSSION QUESTIONS

1. It wouldn't be unusual for someone to think their mind was set on knowing God only to find they'd been distracted by something else. How could a person begin to discern what their mind is truly set upon?

2. In many modern cultures, people engage in extreme behavior to look like, act like, or get close to celebrities or well-known people they may never know. By contrast, God promised that those who seek Him will find Him. Why do you think people often resist the lifestyle changes that would help them know God when they're willing to make drastic changes to know another human being?

3. Can you think of any ways to ensure you're seeking God's presence and not merely pursuing a good atmosphere? Suggest ideas for both individual and corporate settings.

4. It's important to discuss holiness in terms of relationship because holiness is ultimately about knowing God. As an exercise in this principle, try looking at the familiar Ten Commandments found in Exodus 20:1–17 from a relational point of view. What does each of these commands tell us about God?

5. Here's an impossible challenge: try to think about holiness from God's perspective. (Impossible, yes, but do your best!) Knowing what you do about who God is and what He desires for us, why would it be important for His people to be holy in both position and behavior?

DEVOTION

> ...Now you do those things that
> lead to holiness...
> —ROMANS 6:22 NLT

I have waited until this point in our study to examine the topic of holiness because I want to be sure you understand that it is not about control, guilt, or adherence to a man-made standard. It's about relationship.

Suppose you had a family member you loved dearly but who was constantly disrespectful, destructive, and untrustworthy. Though you love this person, my guess is you would find it hard to enjoy their company. If they were unwilling to change, you'd have to set some healthy boundaries in the relationship. This would probably include the decision not to be around them on a daily basis.

As we discussed last week, God is a Person whose presence we seek. But God is also completely holy. It may be difficult or unhealthy for us to be around bad behavior, but it is actually impossible for someone to dwell in God's presence without being holy. That's why holy living is a big deal!

Read Hebrews 12:14 again: "Pursue...holiness, without which no one will see the Lord." The word translated *pursue* means "to do something with intense effort and with definite purpose or goal."[25] Notice the two elements of pursuit: intense effort and a definite goal. Our goal, as we've established, is to be in God's presence. So now let's turn our attention to the effort of pursuing a holy life.

Holiness has nothing to do with legalism and lifeless religious rules. The pursuit of holiness, therefore, will require each of us to be two things:

1. **A student of God's Word.** There are many things human reasoning or society would call good that God does not. Likewise, some restrictions that sound spiritual are not found in the Bible and are

merely imposed by culture or tradition. Scripture is our standard. We must immerse ourselves in it to understand God's definition of a holy life.

2. **Attentive to God's Spirit.** God will never direct you to do anything contrary to His Word. But He knows you better than anyone else does. He knows the areas in which you are especially vulnerable to temptation, so He may give you specific directions about things He does or doesn't want you to do.

The guidelines you receive from these two sources will keep you on course!

Reflect

...Let us strip off every weight that slows us down, especially the sin that so easily trips us up. And let us run with endurance the race God has set before us. (Hebrews 12:1 NLT)

Apply

Paul told the Corinthian church, "Follow my example, as I follow the example of Christ" (1 Corinthians 11:1 NIV). Is there someone in your life who obviously knows God's Word and listens to His Spirit? Invite them to sit down with you for a conversation sometime this week. Ask about their relationship with God and how they have grown in understanding the Bible and recognizing God's voice. Their insights were likely gained over many years, so listen well!

WEEK 5

Read chapters 10–12

This week corresponds with video session 5

DISCUSSION QUESTIONS

1. According to the Bible, the central characteristic of both God and His church is holiness. Until now, what would you have said is the defining attribute of God? Of the church? Does what you've learned this week challenge any of your assumptions or inspire any new insights?

2. A partial version of the grace message reduces grace to something that merely covers our mistakes. According to the New Testament, grace both forgives our sins and empowers us to walk in holiness. To some, the first message may sound easier. Explain why the New Testament's message about grace is better news.

3. Read Proverbs 27:6. Discuss this verse in relation to the idea that it's better for us to not preach or teach anything that sounds negative.

4. Just because a message is beneficial does not mean it's desirable. In fact, encounters with truth often initially cause pain or discomfort, but they bring lasting freedom and transformation. Give an example of an experience that is beneficial but not desirable. What does your illustration illuminate about the way we should engage with God's Word?

5. When people talk about changing the world, they often think of things like legislation or social movements. What makes personal holiness a powerful force for inspiring change in society?

DEVOTION

...Be strong through the grace that
God gives you in Christ Jesus.
—2 TIMOTHY 2:1 NLT

There's a clear distinction between the two prevailing messages we hear about grace today. It can be summarized with a simple question: do you want to feel good or do you want to be good? (And by *be good* I mean *be God's*.)

It's not that accepting the New Testament's message of grace means we choose to be miserable. On the contrary, Jesus described His mission among humankind this way: "My purpose is to give them a rich and satisfying life" (John 10:10 NLT). Lasting joy will always be found in Christ. Rather, this is a matter of aligning our priorities with heaven's. God will never elevate our comfort over our good. But will we?

The fact is, we can decide which message of grace we want to believe. We can read Scripture and decide to heed only the things that line up with our way of thinking. We can turn away from difficult messages and listen only to people who tell us what we want to hear. Like our man with his two doctors, we can choose to live by the diagnosis we find most pleasant.

If we choose this path, we'll feel good! But let's heed Jesus's familiar words: "And what do you benefit if you gain the whole world but lose your own soul?" (Mark 8:36 NLT) So to return to our question, do you want to feel good or do you want to be good?

I hope you're beginning to realize that the message of grace as empowerment is astoundingly wonderful news. When we believe grace merely covers up our mistakes, we're stuck stumbling through life, crippled by habitual sin and plagued by fear and lies. But when we receive empowering grace, we're able to live more like Jesus did: free, confident, compassionate, powerful, and blessed. God's grace isn't a weight that holds us down. As the apostle John says:

Loving God means keeping his commandments, and *his command-ments are not burdensome*. For every child of God defeats this evil world, and *we achieve this victory through our faith*. (1 John 5:3–4 NLT)

If God really is good, and if He really wants the best for us, we don't have to wonder—what He commands is our best path! And thanks to the power of His grace at work within us, we find that His commands are no burden. That's amazing!

Reflect

"My grace is all you need. My power works best in weakness." (2 Corinthians 12:9 NLT)

Apply

Are you ready to forsake what may seem easier or more comfortable in order to enjoy life God's way? If so, express it to God in prayer:

Father, thank You for Your empowering grace. I want to receive it not only as forgiveness of my sins but also as Your power that enables me to do things I could never do by my own strength. I believe that You are good. Therefore I know whatever You command is in my best interest. I want to bring You glory, God! Transform me to be more and more like You. In Jesus's name, amen.

WEEK 6

Read chapters 13–16

This week corresponds with video session 6

DISCUSSION QUESTIONS

1. What causes people to expect less from God than He is able to do? If you've encountered any of these factors, how did you overcome them?

2. Reflect on the illustration of the billionaire and the three business owners. What do you think would cause the third entrepreneur's vision to be so much bigger than the visions of her counterparts? Imagine her attitude about the past and the future. Picture the way she prepared for the meeting with the investor. What would she have done that you can also do to raise your expectations about God's plan for your life?

3. Based on what you have learned from this study, explain how someone with an earthly mindset will approach discernment differently than a mature child of God will. What unique tools and frameworks help a Christian discern well?

4. How does the fear of God change the way we experience difficulties? What do people who fear the Lord do and say when the pressure is on? What kind of behavior don't they engage in?

5. As we come to the end of this study, identify your takeaways both individually and as a group. What practices, principles, and values will you implement in your daily life from now on? What will this look like? Make your action steps practical and concrete so you can move forward with strength!

DEVOTION

The payoff for meekness and Fear-of-God is
plenty and honor and a satisfying life.
—PROVERBS 22:4 THE MESSAGE

Over the course of this study, we've examined some weighty subjects: lord-ship, holiness, and the true nature of grace, to name a few. You've answered challenging questions about your perspective and the life you've been living. Now I want to shift your attention forward to the life you can live.

Look at Ephesians 3:20 from *The Message* Bible:

God can do anything, you know—far more than you could ever imag-ine or guess or request in your wildest dreams! He does it not by push-ing us around but by working within us, his Spirit deeply and gently within us.

God spared no expense in making us His. He purchased us at the high-est possible price when He paid our ransom with the life of His Son. There's no reason to think He's suddenly going to get stingy now.

God has given us everything we need to enjoy His best for us: the truth of His Word, the guidance of His Spirit, and the power of His grace. Yet as our Ephesians verse says, God doesn't strong-arm us into partnering with His purpose. He invites us to use faith, discernment, and humility to dis-cover a life beyond our wildest dreams.

So what's holding you back? What's limiting your imagination? What makes you ask for small sums when unlimited resources are available to you?

It's time for you to dream with God. Where are you expecting too little and believing too small? What promises are you afraid to embrace? Why? Let God's goodness inspire you. Begin to ask for things you can hardly believe might come true. He's promised to deliver even better!

Reflect

No one's ever seen or heard anything like this, never so much as imagined anything quite like it—what God has arranged for those who love him. (1 Corinthians 2:9 The Message)

Apply

We've talked about dreams and limitations; now let's get specific. Dedicate some time this week to dreaming in depth. To start, grab some paper or its digital equivalent and list the main areas of your life. Your list will probably include:

- Relationship with God
- Other relationships
- Marriage and family (current or future)
- Finances
- Career
- Local church and ministry
- Specific gifts or passions

Under each heading, write your expectations for that area. This should be a record of the way you think about your life in the privacy of your heart and mind. What do you really expect out of your relationship with God? What is the best future you foresee for your finances? Your family?

Now, prayerfully go back through the list. Ask the Holy Spirit to reveal His perspective and promises. Where is fear restricting your outlook? How have past hurts or disappointments limited your imagination? What do you think doesn't matter to God, and what does He have to say about it? Remember, your vision determines your capacity. God has taken the limits off your life. It's time for you to do the same!

NOTES

1. Lawrence O. Richards, *New International Encyclopedia of Bible Words* (Grand Rapids, MI: Zondervan, 1991), 315–316.

2. Peter Stoner, *Science Speaks: Scientific Proof of the Accuracy of Prophecy and the Bible* (Chicago: Moody Press; online edition, 2005), Foreword, http://sciencespeaks.dstoner.net.

3. Ibid., chapter 3.

4. Ibid.

5. Ibid.

6. Ibid.

7. Spiros Zodhiates Th.D., ed., *The Complete Word Study Dictionary: New Testament* (Chattanooga, TN: AMG Publishers, 1992), s.v. "polus."

8. Timothy Keller, *The Timothy Keller Sermon Archive* (New York City: Redeemer Presbyterian Church, 2013). Accessed via Logos Bible Software.

9. *The Complete Word Study Dictionary: New Testament*, s.v. "kosmos."

10. Daily Mail Reporter, "Living together before marriage no longer increases chances of divorce," *Daily Mail.com*, March 22, 2012, accessed February 26, 2015, http://www.dailymail.co.uk/news/article-2118719/Living-marriage-longer-increases-chances-divorce.html.

11. Jason Koebler, "More People Than Ever Living Together Before Marriage," *U.S. News & World Report*, April 4, 2013, accessed February 26, 2015, http://www.usnews.com/news/articles/2013/04/04/more-people-than-ever-living-together-before-marriage.

12. Lawrence O. Richards, *New International Encyclopedia of Bible Words* (Grand Rapids, MI: Zondervan, 1991), 639.

13. Charles Spurgeon, "Holiness Demanded" (sermon, Metropolitan Tabernacle, London; published September 22, 1904). Accessed via Logos Bible Software.

14. Survey conducted by Messenger International. See: John Bevere, *Relentless: The Power You Need to Never Give Up* (Colorado Springs, CO: WaterBrook Press, 2011), 26–27.

15. "The Stats on Internet Pornography," Daily Infographic, accessed January 24, 2014, http://dailyinfographic.com/the-stats-on-internet-pornography -infographic.

16. "How Many Women are Addicted to Porn? 10 Stats that May Shock You," Covenant Eyes, accessed March 27, 2014, http://www.covenanteyes.com /2013/08/30/ women-addicted-to-porn-stats.

17. The previous three paragraphs are adapted from: John and Lisa Bevere, *The Story of Marriage* (Palmer Lake, CO: Messenger International, 2014), 181–182.

18. Covenant Eyes, *Pornography Statistics: 2014 Edition*, 20.

19. Jason Rovou, "'Porn & Pancakes' fights X-rated addictions," CNN, April 6, 2007, accessed February 9, 2015, http://edition.cnn.com/2007/US/04 /04/porn.addiction/index.html.

20. "Alcohol Facts and Statistics," National Institute on Alcohol Abuse and Alcoholism, accessed February 9, 2015, http://www.niaaa.nih.gov /alcohol-health/overview-alcohol-consumption/alcohol-facts-and-statistics.

21. Steven Reinberg, "Third of Americans Have Alcohol Problems at Some Point," *The Washington Post*, July 2, 2007, accessed February 9, 2015, http://www.washingtonpost.com/wp-dyn/content/article/2007/07/02 /AR2007070201237.html.

22. "Alcohol Facts and Statistics."

23. Ibid.

24. A version of the material about grace that follows was included in my book *Relentless: The Power You Need to Never Give Up* (WaterBrook Press, 2011). This is based on a message I have shared frequently in my preaching ministry, and I have rephrased the essence of the teaching here.

25. Johannes P. Louw and Eugene Albert Nida, *Greek-English Lexicon of the New Testament: Based on Semantic Domains* (New York: United Bible Societies, 1996), 662.

GOOD
OR
GOD?

GOOD *OR* GOD?

If it's good, it must be God. Right?

Learn to discern the difference between what seems good and what God calls good. This six-session curriculum is perfect for groups and individuals who want to engage with *Good or God?* at a deeper level.

Included:

- 6 sessions on 2 DVDs and 3 CDs (30 minutes each)
- *Good or God?* hardcover book
- Promotional materials

Churches & Pastors:

Local churches are the passion and heart of this ministry. It is our joy and honor to encourage leaders, pray for churches, provide life-transforming resources, and build authentic relationships. We'd love to connect with you!

Pastors and leaders, connect with our Church Relations team to receive a special resource discount!

Call: 1-800-648-1477 Online: MessengerInternational.org

"I'm passionate to see
God's people excited
about His Word,

and Logos Bible Software
is one of the best tools I have
discovered for better Bible study.
Logos will help you dig deeper
than you ever imagined. I can't
recommend it more highly."

—John Bevere

UNDER COVER
CURRICULUM

Under the shadow of the Almighty, there is liberty, provision, and protection. Unfortunately, many don't understand how to find this secret place. In this curriculum you will learn how biblical submission differs from obedience. You will also learn the distinction between direct and delegated authority and how to respond to and overcome unfair treatment.

HONOR'S REWARD
CURRICULUM

This curriculum will unveil the power and truth of an often overlooked principle: honor. If you understand the vital role of this virtue, you will attract blessing both now and for eternity. This insightful message teaches you how to extend honor to your Creator, family members, authorities, and those who surround your world.

RELENTLESS
CURRICULUM

This 12-session curriculum is designed to instill perseverance and build your faith. Whether you use this study as an individual or in a group, it will help you uncover life-changing truths about tribulation, resistance, and the fulfillment of God's destiny for your life.

EXTRAORDINARY
CURRICULUM

The *Extraordinary* curriculum is an extensive journey with 12 video and audio sessions, a thought-provoking devotional workbook, and a hardcover book. Through this study, you will be positioned to step into the unknown and embrace divine empowerment.

BREAKING INTIMIDATION
CURRICULUM

Everyone has been intimidated at some point in life. Do you really know why it happened or how to keep it from happening again? In this curriculum, John exposes the root of intimidation, challenges you to break its fearful grip, and teaches you to release God's gifts and establish His dominion in your life.

Messenger International exists to help individuals, families, churches, and nations realize and experience the transforming power of God's Word. This realization will result in lives empowered, communities transformed, and a dynamic response to the injustices plaguing our world.

teach reach rescue

Messenger
International®

CLOUD
LIBRARY

Cloud Library is an online platform that allows pastors and leaders around the world to access free digital resources in their own languages. We'll use this platform to share *Good or God?* with believers in restricted or hard-to-reach areas worldwide.

BOOKS BY JOHN

A Heart Ablaze*
The Bait of Satan*
Breaking Intimidation*
Drawing Near*
Driven by Eternity*
Enemy Access Denied
Extraordinary*
The Fear of the Lord*
Good or God?*
The Holy Spirit: An Introduction*

Honor's Reward*
How to Respond When You Feel Mistreated
Relentless*
Rescued
The Story of Marriage*
Thus Saith the Lord
Under Cover*
Victory in the Wilderness
The Voice of One Crying

*Available in curriculum format

Messenger International.
teach reach rescue

A Ministry of John & Lisa Bevere

Messenger International was founded by John and Lisa Bevere in 1990. In over two decades of ministry, Messenger International's God-entrusted messages have transformed millions of lives worldwide. Today, our mission to teach, reach, and rescue encompasses a wide variety of efforts to disciple the nations.

Call: **1-800-648-1477**

Email: **Mail@MessengerInternational.org**

Visit us online at: **MessengerInternational.org**

Connect with John Bevere:

JohnBevere.com

NOTES